"We are a family of performers. Give us cameras, lights, and a national election and we look like we all get along...But if you leave the lights on too long, something will start to show..."

THE BOOK THAT SHOCKED AMERICA

THE WAY I SEE IT

An Autobiography by
PATTI DAVIS

THE WAY I SEE IT

An Autobiography by

Patti Davis

JOVE BOOKS, NEW YORK

Stanza from T. S. Eliot poem. Excerpted with permission of Harcourt Brace Jovanovich, Inc., from *Four Quartets* by T. S. Eliot, © 1943 by T. S. Eliot, © 1971 by Esme Valerie Eliot.

This Jove Book contains the complete text of the original hardcover edition. It has been completely reset in a typeface designed for easy reading and was printed from new film.

THE WAY I SEE IT

A Jove Book/published by arrangement with the author

PRINTING HISTORY
G.P. Putnam's Sons edition published May 1992
Jove edition/March 1993

ISBN: 0-515-11089-2

Jove Books are published by The Berkley Publishing Group, 200 Madison Avenue, New York, New York 10016. The name "JOVE" and the "J" logo are trademarks belonging to Jove Publications, Inc.

PRINTED IN THE UNITED STATES OF AMERICA

10 9 8 7 6 5 4 3 2

ACKNOWLEDGMENTS

I WOULD LIKE to thank my editor, Andrea Chambers, for seeing the essence of this story, probably before I did, and for keeping it on course. Phyllis Grann for being a guiding hand, an overseer whose insight I always felt in the background. Marilyn Ducksworth for her kindness and enthusiasm. Dolores McMullan for working so hard, for her laughter, and for caring. Special thanks to Savina Teubel, Paul Sand, Dian Roberts, and Molly White for letting me read passages to them, and for always responding with honesty. Thank you to the friends who have stuck by me through thick, thin, and everything in between: Bernie Leadon, Paul Grilley, Gloria Steinem, Elizabeth Stone, Donna Burton, Nancy Neuman, Susan Magrino, Kristi Zea, Sue and Dino Barbis, Shad Meshad, Bob Franco, Lanetta, and Michael. To the people who—not accidentally—reappeared in my life during the writing of this book: Peter Strauss, Don Henley, Anne DeSalvo, Nick Weschler, Richard and Pam Powell, Wendy Worth, and Peter Asher, thank you—long absences or short, the returns have been magical and much appreciated. To the people who have recently entered my life, with wisdom and humor: Gloria Allred, Thom Waner, Carla and Lou Ferrigno, Fran Carpentier, Robert Marshall, and Bill Broyles—I hope I can return the gifts you've given me. Thanks to Mirabee Nowell, Bob Schiller, Naomi Shiell, Rosellan, and Cory Allen for sharing their memories. And to Michael Grecco for a painless photo session—

thanks for making it fun, and I still don't know if I have a good side. Thank you to Sarah Rozen for ferreting through the photographic evidence of my past, and for doing such a great job.

This book is dedicated to Gloria Steinem who,
by example and through friendship,
has taught me that strength is
incomplete without compassion.

And the end of all our exploring
will be to arrive where we started
And know the place for the first time.

—T. S. ELIOT
Four Quartets

PROLOGUE
. . . .

IN 1985, WHEN my husband Paul Grilley and I were moving out of a tiny, one-bedroom apartment and into our first house, I opened a cardboard box and found two scrapbooks—my childhood from infancy through age fifteen. I lifted them out and tentatively opened them, dreading the idea of handling the fragile remnants of my past.

The photographs confirmed what I had long known, but had tried to shunt aside. I saw, in some pictures, the fear and anger in my own eyes; in others, my mother's tight, determined smile that always hid too much, and my father's vacant eyes that looked right through me. And there was my brother, a stranger to me, a little boy who always seemed able to laugh everything off.

I wasn't ready to accept those pictures, for that would mean going back and revisiting my family, my history. I had been taught to keep secrets, to keep our image intact for the world. My father was president, the world was watching. Under our family's definition of "loyalty," the public should never see that under a carefully preserved surface was a group of people who knew how to inflict wounds, and then convincingly say those wounds never existed.

That night, when I closed the scrapbooks, I took the whole box out to the trash dumpster and threw it away.

"I just threw away my childhood," I told my husband when I came back inside.

But we can never just throw away our childhoods.

1

Ultimately, we have to go back if we are ever to go forward. Unless you can return to a damaged childhood with a different perspective—with understanding and forgiveness—you will remain a child.

A little later, my mother gave me another scrapbook, and I didn't throw that one away. I studied the pictures, tried to go back in time and look at my family with different eyes.

There is a picture taken at the 1980 Republican Convention of my parents, Ron, Michael (holding up his son Cameron), Maureen, and me. Everyone is smiling. What you can't see is the enmity, that hours before, my mother drove Doria, Ron's girlfriend and future wife, out of the hotel room with the ice of her eyes. I had turned furiously to my mother and said, "What are you trying to do—lose your son?" Nor does the photo show that Michael and Maureen's presence there was not welcomed by the Reagan camp, because they were children of a former marriage and that brought up the specter of divorce. The camera captured a family, smiling on cue, with balloons dropping behind them.

A print of that picture sits behind my father's desk in his Century City office—silver-framed, part of a group of photographs in which we have all posed on command. It was the one he pointed to when I went to visit him not long ago. "Look," he said. "We were a happy family."

Sometime around the age of forty, you realize that if you're lucky, you have half your life ahead of you, and how you're going to live it has a lot to do with the half that's already gone.

When I was a child, there was a crazy man living at the end of our street. I crept around his house, looking for him, spying on him. I felt as if I understood him, because I thought we were the crazy people at the other end of the street. I never wanted to ask friends back to my house. There was something unpredictable about my home; opening the front door was a gamble. I was

never sure what I would be walking into, and that un-
predictability was a frightening feeling.

Often, what I feared most was the silence. There were
two children in our house, but it didn't resonate with
the clamor of their voices or the chaos of laughter and
tiny stampeding feet. My brother and I were cautious,
tentative about the perfectly vacuumed floors and the
fragile objects of irreplaceable value that seemed to be
everywhere. Things rarely got broken in our house;
Kool-Aid wasn't spilled on couches, chocolate wasn't
smeared on draperies. Fabergé eggs and antique china
vases were safe from us. Visitors, when they came,
seemed to speak quietly in deference to the glass atmosphere of our home.

Yet, all too often, the sound of a raised voice would
crash through the rooms. My father was not part of the
noise. I don't remember him ever yelling or even speaking loudly. But he was part of the emptiness.

When I visited the White House, I realized that my
parents had brought with them the same hushed atmosphere that always waited beyond the front door of our
home. People walked softly, closed doors gently behind
them. My mother's footsteps were louder than my father's, more determined, just as they had been in California. I still had to stop and listen carefully to hear his.
I don't know what the White House feels like when
other people live there, but I suppose every family
brings along the sound of their own history.

There have been volumes written about my family,
some things are true, others aren't. Many of the stories
are harsh, leaving no room for compassion, particularly
the stories about my mother.

But I, too, have indicted my parents over the years—
for crimes of my childhood. For so long I didn't see that
there were no crimes; just insecurities and flaws, some
of them very deep. When I began to consider this, my
childhood and my family took on a different perspective. No one looked like a criminal anymore. I have
gradually stopped thinking in terms of parents and chil-

dren, and begun to examine the Reagans as just people, with problems that go back generations.

In the story of a mother and daughter locked in battle is the story of people who had nowhere to turn, because such things weren't discussed in the Fifties and Sixties. In the story of a father whose presence felt like absence is the trauma of a child who hurt inside, even though she now understands the reason for the distance.

I've spent too many years being angry at my parents. Mostly I was angry at my mother, whose violence made me fear her, and fear that she may have passed along that rage to me in the mysterious linkage of chromosomes. But now I understand better what drove her, and how she, too, was pained inside. It's usually the most wounded among us who inflict pain on others.

I've felt anger toward my father as well—for his distance, his abandonment, his question to my brother: "Do you think a child can be born evil?" He was talking about me. My brother told me about it years later, but age didn't make it hurt any less. Now I can look past my father to the boy he once was, the boy who had to detach himself from his home life in order to survive.

Anger is still part of this story, however. So is abuse and addiction. To present a story truthfully, everything has to be told. But families are complicated. In the midst of battle, there are gestures of love; there are loyalties that contradict the betrayals.

My mother was always more gentle in her task of raising a son. There were times, though, when my mother and I forgot our wars and reached out with nothing except love. Now I see those moments as the ones that count.

After I peeled away enough layers, pieced together enough ends, I was left with a story that needed to be told—for myself, and for others who might be motivated to turn inward to their *own* stories. After all the volumes, after all the misperceptions, it makes sense to me to set the record straight.

• • •

My father tells an anecdote that when I was around four, I climbed onto his lap and asked him to marry me. He says that he didn't know what to do and my mother, from across the room, nodded and mouthed, "Say yes." There is something delicate and achingly pure about a little girl's love for her father. That child's love may grow more complicated, more cautious, over the years. My father tells the story in soft tones, his memory caught in another time. But something tightens in my throat when I hear it. Because I wonder if that moment was my Waterloo. I wonder if a part of my mother's heart darkened, if behind her smile and her admonition to "say yes," a judgment had been handed down. My parents' love for each other was territory circled by fences and border patrols, and at that moment I may suddenly have appeared as a trespasser. It's taken a long time for me to stop resenting my parents for the exclusion of their love, and just be happy for them that they *found* this love.

I was thirteen when I discovered the refuge of writing. It became my lifeline, my sanctuary. For years, I have buried truths in my writing, but you had to look hard to find them. Writers put stories on shelves for a while, but eventually, we get to everything. I probably should have known that, in time, I'd get to this one.

I know that my parents are not happy about this book, and my attempts to explain to them that it's simply time to tell the truth have made little difference. But making the attempt mattered to me, even if my explanation wasn't understood.

There is a child's voice in this story, because part of it is her story and she deserves to be heard. But I waited this long because now there is an adult's voice as well. I had to wait until I had gained more understanding, and until anger wasn't guiding my hand. I had to look back at our battlefield and see that no one emerged from the war unwounded.

And I had to wait until I could feel grateful to my parents for turning me into a writer, even though they didn't realize that's what they were doing and may not be accepting of the results. But my intention has never been to cause pain or unhappiness. There is much good in this story. In stepping back, I can appreciate not only the privileges of my childhood, but also my unique moment in history as the daughter of a president.

For a long time, my perceptions of my family were clouded by deep political disagreements. Those disagreements remain, but I have to look at the rest of our story as something that stands apart, on its own. I have had little contact with my parents in the last few years, but I feel as though estrangement was *always* part of our history. My family has long stood on fractured ground, and I don't know if that will ever be changed.

For me, at least, what *has* changed is a realization that though we could have all done things better, we did the best we could. I don't have a child, but I still hope that someday I may. I would like to know that I have broken the cycle of anger in my family, and telling this story is part of that effort. It's also a way, hopefully, to replace judgment with understanding.

CHAPTER 1

. . . .

INSIDE THE ARMY *transport plane carrying us to Washington, Michael, Maureen, and I sat in silence, all wondering if our father would be alive when we got there. We knew no more than the rest of the country, no more than what had gone out over news broadcasts. My brother Ron was flying in separately from Nebraska where he was performing with the Joffrey Ballet.*

It was late when we got to the White House—well after midnight. I stood outside my mother's door, listening to the quiet all around me. There is always something that seems hushed about the upper floors of the White House, but at night it's as though sound just ceases to exist. I stood there, debating whether or not I should knock, and finally turned away, even though I was certain she wasn't asleep.

When I went into my mother's room the next morning, she was sitting up in bed, eating breakfast from a tray. I sat down on the edge of the bed after kissing her cheek and waited for her to tell me how my father was.

"He almost died—several times," she said. "They gave him so much blood. An inch from his heart—that's how close the bullet was. And then when they put the tube down his throat—so scared—he was so scared."

Her sentences were choppy, her voice dull and tired. "When I got back here last night," she continued, "I went in and got one of his shirts and slept with it. I just needed to have something of his next to me. The bed seemed so empty."

7

*Something happened to me as I sat there listening to
my mother, and imagining her clutching my father's shirt
in her sleep. Suddenly, she wasn't my mother. She was a
woman who had been called to the hospital because her
husband had a bullet in him, and who went through the
day not knowing if he would live. And if he didn't live, she
didn't know how she could live—that's how intertwined
they are. For a few moments that morning, I walked away
from the child who feared her mother's anger, her
mother's hand, and I looked at a woman who had fallen
in love so fiercely that there wasn't room for anyone else
in her world. It was the first time I discovered what forgiveness would feel like; it wouldn't last, at least not right
then, but it had tapped me on the shoulder.*

To understand your parents, you need to understand
theirs. You need to know what shaped them, how they
became the people they are, what legacies they carried
with them into adulthood.

I will probably never fully understand my mother's
rage, because she edits her own history and reinvents it
constantly. It is always a work in progress. The only
consistencies in her stories are the things that contradict
the person she is today. But there are pieces which, if
fitted together carefully, start to form a picture.

My mother talks very little about her father except to
say that he walked out on her and her mother. The
name of Kenneth Robbins was not spoken in our home;
I can't even remember how I found out his name, but
I knew enough to keep it to myself. That abandonment
was followed by another. My grandmother, Edith
Luckett, was a working actress on the road for long
periods of time, and her daughter, then Anne Francis
Robbins, was sent to live with her cousins in Bethesda,
Maryland. Because the house was small and they were
not well off financially, my mother never had her own
room. I think of this when I remember how Michael,
my father's son from his first marriage, never had a
room in our house even though he was living with us.

I'm sure that this childhood was often difficult for my mother, and that she always harbored a need to be noticed. I suspect that she grew up clamoring for control, because the world was unpredictable, because people left her and hurt her. It must have been hard for my mother to come up against her own child's defiance— against a daughter who wanted some control too, because she had the same mistrust of the world around her. I think, finally, I understand this.

My grandmother remarried Loyal Davis, a neurosurgeon from Chicago, when my mother was seven, and she became Edith Davis. But my mother's last name remained Robbins. She wanted her stepfather to legally adopt her. She wanted his love. But it would be ten years before he would agree to adopt her.

"He wanted me to earn his love," she once told me, emphatically, as if she were trying to convince herself that this was normal. "He wanted to be sure that I was serious about it. So I did everything he wanted. I never disobeyed him. And I used to go watch him perform surgery. Sometimes I'd even stand in the operating room."

"Didn't it make you sick?" I asked.

"I didn't let it. I wanted to be near him, watch him work. I was so proud of him."

I think now of the rage building up in a child who is expected to "earn" love. I think of a child swallowing the nausea, fighting back the dizziness, the cold sweats that we've all felt when someone is bleeding in front of us. And I can now sympathize with how much she wanted her stepfather to adopt her and give her his name.

My mother used to tell me how overweight she was as a young teenager and on into college at Smith. Her recollections of Girls' Latin School in Chicago were of her discomfort with her weight. When she recounted her weight problems, she laughed, as some of us do when we recall our years of bad skin, stringy hair, or overeating. We laugh because, underneath, we still

blush; we still hurt. With age, we may transform ourselves, become thin, fashionable, perfectly groomed.
But there is still that uncomfortable adolescent inside,
waiting in the corner for someone to ask her to dance.

It makes perfect sense to me that given her upbringing, my mother wanted to become an actress. Acting is
an escape; you can be someone else for a while, change
reality. It's a sweet relief from whatever you don't want
to look at in your own life.

But I don't think my mother got the validation she
needed in her career, either. It was another fight for
recognition, and she didn't emerge victorious in the way
Lana Turner or Ava Gardner or some of the major
female stars of the Forties did. Whatever insecurities
festered in her childhood and in college were very probably reinforced in Hollywood, which has never been
famous for its nurturing, supportive atmosphere. By the
time I came along, my mother had adopted a veneer of
total confidence, total control, perhaps to hide what
was within.

My father and his brother Neal (whose nickname became Moon) grew up poor in Dixon, Illinois, the sons
of a shoe salesman who was frequently unemployed,
probably because he was an alcoholic.

Jack Reagan was a hard-drinking Irish Catholic,
married to a Protestant woman whose mission in life
was to spread the word of God, both through the Bible
and charity work. Nelle read the Bible to inmates in
prison and later to patients in California hospitals. I
only knew her when I was very young, so my memory
of her is sketchy; but I have an impression that she was
always carrying a Bible. I don't know if she ever acknowledged her husband's alcoholism; my suspicion is
that she didn't, that she made excuses. That's what was
done in those days, and it might explain my father's
ability to tune out any reality he doesn't like. What I
want to know are the things that no one will ever tell

me: Was Jack a violent drunk? Did he drink every day? Did anyone ever talk about it?

In my father's first autobiography, published in 1965, he wrote about Jack in a mild, affectionate way, but I had to keep reminding myself that he was writing about a child dealing with an alcoholic parent. He identified the alcoholism, but not his own pain, his own struggle to deal with it:

"I bent over him, smelling the sharp odor of whiskey from the speakeasy. I got a fistful of his overcoat. Opening the door, I managed to drag him inside and get him to bed. In a few days, he was the bluff, hearty man I knew and loved and will always remember.

"Jack (we called him by his nickname) was a handsome man—tall, swarthy and muscular, filled with contradictions of character. A sentimental Democrat, who believed fervently in the rights of the working man."

My sense is that my father escaped his own father's alcoholism by adhering more to his mother, to her strict puritanism and her denial. The story about dragging his father inside has always been told as an isolated incident; I'm sure it was probably one of many. He never tells about his feelings, his pain; he never lets the listener visit the child he once was. It's as if the story happened to someone else and he is just reciting it. I've thought a lot about that boy who, over time, must have learned how to block out the pain of living with an alcoholic. I need to understand that child because, if I do, I might understand what made my father block out his own children.

My father once told me that Jack died while he was in college; he said he was nineteen. The story was that he'd come home to visit and as he was leaving, something made him turn back and hug his father.

"It was the only time since I was a kid that I'd hugged him," he said. "And it was the last time I saw him alive. Maybe something in me knew . . ."

I don't discount the premonition part of the story—I believe in such things. But my father was really thirty-

five when Jack died; he bought his parents a house in
Hollywood where they lived until Jack's death. After
that, Nelle became forgetful and had a nurse live in with
her. My father has written about all of this, and talked
about it, but he chose to tell me a different account that
day, and I may never know why.

My last memory of Nelle is of visiting her in a nursing
home. I can see the room—a dingy linoleum floor, bare
beige walls, and across from the bed, a single window.
The image of my grandmother sitting in the narrow bed
is tarnished and faint; I think I was around seven.

No one told me when Nelle died; they waited for me
to ask. It was the strategy my parents used on a number
of things—our dog's death, the existence of two siblings
from my father's first marriage. Information wasn't offered, but provided upon request. I vaguely remember
asking when I could go see Nelle again, at which point
my parents told me that she was no longer there, she
had died.

As reticent as my father was about his own father's
drinking, he was more forthcoming about how the family's poverty had spurred him to seek success and pros-
perity. He washed dishes to put himself through college,
and he was a lifeguard during the summers; he was
determined to make something of himself. In his determination, I think he was not only distancing himself
from the poverty of his upbringing, but from his father's alcoholism, too. After all, the two things were
connected. There were no Christmas presents one year
because Jack drank away the money.

Alcoholism makes a jumpy passage through generations. One person might inherit the alcoholism and another won't. But everyone is affected. In looking at my
own drug addiction, I've had to face the fact that I come
from an addictive family. Jack's alcoholism wasn't
passed down to my father; I've never seen him abuse
liquor. But it's there, in our history—in the cycles that
are sometimes hard to understand.

What Ronald Reagan inherited from his childhood is

an astounding ability to turn away from any reality which is too harsh and paint one that is softer, gentler to the eyes. It's the secret behind his smile which is always right there, either blazing across his face or tugging at the corners of his mouth. And the wink that says, "Don't take anything too seriously. Everything's fine." Long ago, a child tuned out the sight, sound, and smell of a drunk father by telling himself that everything was fine.

By the time I was born, a pattern had emerged: My father, and my mother, too, had learned how easy it was to paint pictures as they wanted them to appear. The story of my birth has been sketched and highlighted over time.

According to my parents, on the evening of October 20, 1952, they were at a horse show. When my mother felt a contraction, she told my father, but said she was sure it wasn't a labor pain because she wasn't due for two more months. They drove back home to Pacific Palisades and an hour later her contractions were so close together it was obvious that she was in labor. They got back in the car and drove to what is now Cedars-Sinai, but was then called Cedars of Lebanon.

The story starts to get strange at this point. After eighteen hours of what my parents have described as excruciating labor, the doctor decided to do a cesarian section. It was about two-thirty in the afternoon of October 21. My mother says that, because of the drugs they gave her, she was introducing the doctor to the anesthesiologist as they were wheeling her through the corridors to the operating room, apparently under the impression that she was at a cocktail party.

What they lifted out of her, according to this version, was a baby who had performed the superhuman task of hooking its fingers onto her ribs. This extraordinary baby came out with scabs on its tiny fingers and was then put into an incubator for two months—not as punishment for its aggressive display of temperament, but because this little girl was supposed to be born eight weeks later. The difficult birth and athletic prowess of the child prompted the doctor to warn my mother against having any more children.

I was first told this story at a young age, and I studied my fingers under the lights, looking for telltale scars.

There is another version, and that is simply that, since my mother was two months pregnant when she married my father, those first contractions were hardly a surprise. And after long hours in labor, a C-section was done because that's the usual practice. My mother is small and I was large—seven pounds, three ounces. That sort of shoots down the incubator theory.

But this was the Fifties. Good girls weren't supposed to have sex before marriage. If they did, they were supposed to be ashamed of it and hide it. So, if you had a baby seven months after you got married, pretending prematurity was one option.

My parents have never gone for simple, state-of-the-art lies. They weave bizarre, incredulous tales and stick by them with fierce determination. When I was in my twenties, my mother was still repeating the story about my fingers hooking onto her ribs.

My father once told me, around the time I started college, that promiscuity was a very detrimental thing.

"Your mother and I waited, no matter how difficult it was sometimes," he said. "Sometimes it was I who wanted to give in, and she would make us stop. And sometimes it was the other way around. But we knew it was important to be married first."

I could have said something, but I didn't because he looked so sincere; I suspected he'd convinced himself that this was true.

Despite the fact that I was innocent of the crime of punching my way through my mother's uterus, shoving a few organs out of the way, and grasping onto her ribs, I was guilty of something else. I was a girl and my mother, by her own admission, had wanted a boy.

CHAPTER 2

· · · · · · · · · · · · · ·

UNTIL I WAS five, we lived on Amalfi Drive in Pacific Palisades, in a one-story white house with a wood shingle roof and geraniums in the flowerbeds out front. I had an English nanny named Penny, whose room was next to mine. A tiny bathroom joined the two rooms and often, when I was supposed to be napping, I would sneak into her room and sit in her lap. She never revealed these clandestine meetings, and I wasn't about to. Penny wore white uniforms and her body was thick and comforting; in my earliest recollections, hers are the arms I remember.

While we were living on Amalfi, a new house was being built for us on San Onofre Drive, about five minutes away. My parents would keep that house until 1980, when my father was elected president. Because my father worked for General Electric, hosting the weekly television show called "General Electric Theater," and traveled around the country as their spokesman, much of the house was being built at their expense. It was called a "Gold Medallion" home; everything was electric, with the G.E. logo on it.

Frequently, my parents took me with them when they went up to check on the progress of the construction, and I would climb over piles of lumber, trying to make sense of a house that had no walls yet. It was on a hill, with a swimming pool, a wide deck, and a view over the rooftops to the ocean. In the center of the deck was an oak tree that offered a canopy of shade on summer

days. When it was finished, there would be large picture
windows and sliding glass doors, but at first there were
just open walls and a stone fireplace in the middle of
nothing.

One day, shortly before it was completed, my mother
got angry at one of the workmen and demanded to
know what the holes were in the ceiling.

"They're for the lights," he said.

"But they're just holes! There are holes in my ceiling!"

"That's because the lights aren't installed yet," he
explained.

My mother walked away from the workman; I followed, and my father lagged behind, checking on things
as he passed through the house. I don't even know if he
noticed the discussion—my guess is that he didn't. We
were passing behind the house, and at a spot where the
earth had been dug away, probably for pipes, my
mother tripped and almost fell into the hole. I was
closest to her, but my arms didn't reach out to help her.
I stood frozen while my father ran over and helped her
up.

I was a student at the Brentwood Town and Country
School then. The property has since been subdivided,
but at that time it was one large lot with a house at one
end, used for classrooms, and a long, green field bordered by trees at the other. It was the school of choice
for many Hollywood families. Tony Curtis's children
went to Brentwood, as did Dick Powell and June Allyson's, Jimmy Stewart's, Kirk Douglas's, and Angela
Lansbury's daughter Deirdre, whom I used to play with
after school. For a while, Lorna Luft was my classmate.
One year Judy Garland came for Parents' Day, which
impressed me because I'd seen *The Wizard of Oz* several
times.

The Powells' children, Richard and Pam, were also
friends outside of school. There were long weekend
days spent at the ranch they owned in Mandeville Canyon. Pam had a blue-eyed horse named Bright Eyes,

and there was a lake on their ranch. Robert and Ursula Taylor, close friends of my parents, also had a ranch in Mandeville Canyon, although not quite as large as the Powells'.

So many children at the school had famous parents that it seemed normal to us, and I fit right in. Every Sunday night, my father appeared on television, hosting "General Electric Theater" and occasionally acting in some of the segments. It was an elite atmosphere, but it didn't seem so to us. We just accepted celebrity as a part of life.

Shortly after we moved, I and most of my classmates transferred to the John Thomas Dye School in Bel Air, which was run by the same people. Brentwood was for the early years; the John Thomas Dye School continued until eighth grade.

More famous offspring were added to our circle. Pat Boone's children, Ernie Kovacs's daughter. The school was high above Los Angeles; from a wide green field, this privileged group of children in navy blue uniforms and white blouses could look down on the city.

Penny had left us by the time we moved into our glass house on the hill. And Julia, the black woman who had cooked for us, also left. I was never told why. One day, she just wasn't there.

These departures became regular occurrences, as did maid interviews. Women would come, sit in the den with my mother, and she would read questions that she'd written down. I wasn't allowed to come into the room, but their voices would travel through the house. Then, a few days later, one of them would return with a suitcase or two and move into the maid's room just off the kitchen. But then, almost as quickly she'd be gone, suitcases packed up again, uniform returned to my mother. What happened between arrival and departure was yelling. I remember sitting in my bedroom with my hands over my ears because I could hear my mother's voice in the kitchen, yelling at the maid about dishes in the wrong cupboards or something not being prepared right. I would sing to myself to block out the sound.

There was a lull in this when my mother was pregnant. I wasn't as frightened of her then because she seemed to be happier, more content. She had to stay in bed for almost three months; I was told this was because I had been such a difficult birth that this new baby might fall out before it was supposed to.

On May 20, 1958, my brother was born. Ronald Prescott Reagan was tiny and splotchy when he came home—not at all what I thought a baby should look like. As much as I wanted to participate in this new adventure of having a baby in the house, I was usually ushered out of my brother's room. I didn't know it then, but Ron's and my relationship was being defined at that point. There were nights when I snuck into his room and stared at him sleeping, smelled his baby smells, listened to his breathing. I had to be very quiet because there were intercoms in both his room and mine. I knew I was taking a risk, but it was worth it.

I used to ask my mother if I could hold Ron, but the answer was always the same. "No. You might drop him." Eventually, I stopped asking.

Ron was barely a year old and I was seven when I learned that my family was actually larger than I'd been led to believe.

Michael arrived at the house, a fourteen-year-old boy with black-framed glasses and an eager smile, and was introduced to me as my "half-brother." The "half" part of the label tugged him away from me, told me he wasn't supposed to matter as much as the baby my mother held in her arms, who suckled her chin, mistaking it for a breast. I was told that Michael had a different mother, but he was my father's son. He was going to start living with us on the weekends; during the week, he would be away at a boarding school. His bed would be the living-room couch.

Then I learned the identity of the blond girl who sometimes came to talk to my mother. I knew her name was Maureen, and that she was eighteen, which seemed quite old to me then, but I knew nothing else about her.

According to Maureen, I rushed up to her excitedly and told her that I had two brothers, not just one. Michael was my older brother.

"Yes, and do you know what that makes me?" she said. "I'm your sister."

I burst into tears and went running into my room. I don't remember the tears, although Maureen does, but I do remember feeling confused. How many more brothers and sisters were going to arrive at the house and be introduced to me?

Maureen says that when she confronted our father with the fact that he had said nothing to me about who she was, he answered, "Well, we just haven't gotten around to that yet."

There was something transitory about many people in my parents' lives. Friends were discussed as though they had a place in our lives, but they were rarely present. Mary Martin came for dinner once and autographed my Peter Pan book. My mother frequently mentioned her, but I only met her that one time. My godmother was Colleen Moore, the silent film star. She existed for me mostly as a name on Christmas and birthday presents, and in photographs. I didn't get to know her until I was an adult and made a point of getting in touch with her and going to see her.

I heard many names in my childhood, but never met the people who were talked about as friends. Charlton Heston, Katharine Hepburn, Nat King Cole, Raymond Massey—it seemed to me that by keeping them alive in conversation, my parents believed these people were in their lives. But what I saw was, for the most part, a rather isolated existence in which the two of them were there for each other. The closest friendship they seemed to have was with Robert Taylor and his wife, Ursula. My father's relationship with Robert was the only time I observed my father being close friends with another man.

Others who managed to touch my parents' lives were A. C. Lyles, a producer who had been a friend since the early Fifties, and his wife Martha. They spent time on other occasions besides Christmas. The same was true for Armand and Harriet Deutsch, who years later would join Alfred and Betsy Bloomingdale as part of "The Kitchen Cabinet."

In my mother's dressing room, there was a picture of William Holden and his wife. They were standing with my parents on their wedding day, my mother in a gray suit, my father with his boyish grin as they cut the cake.

"He's your godfather," my mother told me.

But I met him only once during my childhood. He came over one night with a different woman because he was no longer with his wife. I watched him, listened to him, tried to memorize him. I wanted him to come back, but after he left, when my mother complained about the "show girl" he brought with him, I knew he wouldn't. I wasn't sure what a show girl was, but my mother's tone of voice said it was bad.

In 1981, we saw each other in a restaurant and met in the middle of the floor. "I've missed you," I told him. "I've missed you in my life." I saw tears in his eyes and felt them in my own; I took his phone number, promising to call. But I waited too long. He died before I made the call, and I have wondered since if growing up as my parents did, with a sense that no one is really rooted in your life, makes you too casual about relationships.

CHAPTER 3

· · · · · · · · · · · · · ·

As UNCOMFORTABLE AS it is to talk about, and write about, abuse is part of this story. I first remember my mother hitting me when I was eight. It escalated as I got older and became a weekly, sometimes daily, event. The last time it happened was when I was in my second year of college. This is something I never thought I'd disclose, partly because I didn't want to revisit it, but partly because abuse is never as simple as it initially appears.

Like most children who were hit, I thought I must have done something to deserve it; the blame must, at least in part, be mine. But the truth is that no child deserves to be hit.

And then I came to understand something else. There is a fine line between blame and participation. As I got older, I became intimately familiar with what would set my mother off, and I would push those buttons, even though I knew it would end up with her hand aimed at my face. But any kind of contact is preferable to absence. I couldn't find my father—he was there but not there—and that kind of absence made me desperate for interaction. So I preferred my mother's anger to my father's absence. It was tangible, it was non-negotiable, it left a handprint on my face, but at least I could look in the mirror and say, "Oh, there I am. Someone knows I exist."

This is how our long siege began, at least this is my first memory. By the age of eight, I was already afraid

of my mother. I think that the rage that led her to hit
me had been there for many years before and grew as
I grew. My mother loves tiny things—babies, puppies,
kittens. I think my smallness gave her pleasure once.
But things changed when I was no longer tiny.

So, I will describe the beginning as I remember it,
with dialogue that may be, in part, actual recollection
and in part a lifetime of familiarity with my mother's
voice. That voice—the cadence, the phrasing, the repe-
titions—was the rhythm track of my childhood.

I'm about nine years old, round, with wide dark eyes
that always seem to be asking something. My mother
and I are in the Brentwood Country Market, where she
shops frequently, almost daily it seems, and where
many mothers bring their children. The market has a
bakery with a low window and a bench below it for
children to stand on and watch. White-hatted bakers
come out with trays and pass them to small out-
stretched hands. It keeps the children busy, quietly
munching while mothers stand across the aisle in the
produce section, talking and smiling.

I'm not supposed to stand at the window with the
other children; my mother has told me I'm overweight
and can't have cookies. But she is talking to someone by
the oranges and isn't paying attention. There is a sweet,
thick smell drifting from the bakery and I wander over
to the window, step up on the bench, and stare in. A
man with a white hat waves at me, picks up a tray of
newly baked cookies, and comes out. As he leans toward me with the tray, my mother enters my field of
vision, walking quickly, purposefully. She grabs my
arm and pulls me off the bench.

"I told you, didn't I? I told you, you can't have
cookies." I don't answer. People across the aisle stop
their carts, stop their conversations, and stare.

"You just can't do what you're told, can you?"

I look at the patterns on the linoleum floor.

"Can you?" she repeats in a louder voice.

"No," I answer in a small voice.

With her hand clamped on my arm, we go down other aisles; as she throws groceries into the cart, everything seems to land with a thud, punctuating my mother's anger.

We walk fast out to the car. A man follows us with the shopping cart filled with bags. I'm trying to keep up with my mother's stride.

On the way home, my mother drives too fast, her hands gripping the wheel.

"Why can't you just do what I say?" she asks.

"I don't know," I mumble.

"What?"

"I don't know."

"I cannot keep going through this with you!" She pauses, takes a deep breath, and starts counting. Apparently, counting to ten is supposed to make her less angry, but it doesn't work that way. By the time she gets to five, she is screaming, driving even faster, and her face is red. I lean against the car door and stare out the window.

Suddenly she pulls over. There is a policeman behind us. My first thought is, maybe he'll arrest my mother for yelling while driving, for screeching around corners. His dark blue shape fills the window on the driver's side; when he leans down, his face is calm, nice.

"Driving a little fast, aren't you, ma'am?"

"Yes, I was," my mother answers, her voice and her expression softening like warm butter. "My daughter is being so impossible, I'm just at my wits' end. She deliberately disobeys me; she just pushes and pushes. It just gets too much sometimes and, well, I'm sure you understand that someone can only take so much . . ." It goes on like this, with the policeman looking across at me. I start to wonder if he's going to arrest me.

"Well, all right," he says. "I understand how kids can be—got a couple of my own. Just try to be more careful, and take it slow."

When he leaves, my mother doesn't start the car right away. She faces me instead.

"I could have gotten a speeding ticket."

I say nothing, turn away. I'm always turning away.

"Don't you ignore me, young lady," she says, hand on my arm, other hand drawing back, and as my head turns toward her, her open palm crashes into my cheek. The numbness starts at the corner of my mouth and travels up to my eye.

When we get home, I run into my room, shut the door, and pull the arms and legs off one of my dolls.

An old friend, who grew up in my neighborhood, asked me recently to meet her for coffee at the Brentwood Country Market.

"Can we go someplace else?" I asked.

"Sure." Her tone asked me why.

"Memories," I told her. "There are too many of them there."

I have another early memory, too. Maybe I'm ten now. I'm not exactly sure. We pull into the parking lot, and my mother is already angry because I have stared out the window on my side during the ride. I never did figure out where I was supposed to look while riding in the passenger seat, but out the window was definitely wrong. She takes the ignition key, gets out of the car, and I start to climb out my side.

"You get back in that car, young lady!" she screams. She is standing at the front end of the car and people are stopping, watching. "I did not tell you that you could get out. You just sit in there until you learn to behave yourself!"

I slide back in the seat and close the door. It's hot in the car—summer, probably—and it feels hotter because people are staring, making my face flush. My mother is still screaming, oblivious to the attention she is attracting. More people come out of the market to see what the noise is all about. They watch, then drift away. When she stops screaming, they all drift away; a child sitting alone in a car is not that interesting.

•   •   •

Our more private warfare usually took place in specific areas of the house: standing in front of the window, in my room, in my parents' bedroom if my father wasn't there, or in the bathroom.

In my house there were very few doors that locked. My parents' bedroom door did, but all of the other bedrooms had doors that anyone could open at any time, including the maid's room. The bathroom doors locked, but I got in trouble if I exercised that option. Privacy was something to be squashed, the assumption being, I suppose, that if you were alone, you had to be planning some sort of mutiny.

I have a memory of when I was nine. It's my bedtime, and I go into the bathroom to get ready. As I start to close the door, my mother pushes it open and comes in. She is wearing a long, white quilted robe and slippers with some sort of feather on the top. I wait for her to say something, but she just waits.

"What?" I say, defenses rushing into position.

"Get ready for bed."

I start to put toothpaste on my toothbrush, but she takes it from my hand.

"Go to the bathroom first."

"I don't have to."

"Patti, do you have to argue about everything? Everything becomes a federal case, doesn't it?" Her hand grabs my arm; it's a gesture she learned from her father. I know this because he's done it to me.

"I don't have to," I repeat, standing firm.

"Well, we'll just stay here until you do."

Moments pass. I don't move. Finally, my mother takes her hand off my arm, draws it back and slaps my face.

Night after night we repeat this; night after night I don't go. But I do, later, after midnight, when the house is quiet and I can slide my bedroom door open carefully, so the intercom won't pick up the sound and alert my mother.

As this nightly ritual went on, month after month,

my grandfather, who was visiting for Christmas, told
me that I was going to weaken my bladder; I'd have to
wear diapers when I grew up or I'd "dribble" walking
down the aisle to get married. "If anyone would even
want to marry you," he added.

I don't remember how this particular battle ended—I
only know it did. It was replaced by arguments about
my hair. I wanted long hair more than anything, but as
soon as mine grazed my jaw it was cut.

I have an image of my mother, reflected in the mirror,
standing behind me at the dressing table in my room.
She is tugging at my hair, which is tangled. The brush
is scraping my scalp.

"Ow!" I complain. "That hurts."

"Patti, stop being so dramatic." The brush continues
to make me wince. "We have to get your hair cut."

I start crying. "No, please—it's so short right now."

A few days later, my mother and I come back from
the beauty parlor with my hair barely covering my ears.
I run into my room, sobbing, and shut the door hard
behind me. Later, my father comes in—soft footsteps,
a soft knock, an uneasy presence in my room. I know
he doesn't know what to do with children, especially a
daughter.

"Why do you do this to your mother, Patti? All she
wants is to have a nice time with you, and every time
you go out . . ." His voice trails off, he shakes his head.

"But look at my hair." My voice is thin, pleading; I
hate the sound of it.

"It looks very nice. You've just made up your mind
to be difficult."

"Why is she mean to me?"

"She never is."

"Well, why does she hit me?"

"Patti, that never happened."

I stop because I'm confused, because there are no
witnesses, because maybe they're right and I'm crazy,
and I'm just inventing things that never happened. I

stop because I hear anger stirring in my father's voice and I can't take anger from him.

One day, though, there was a witness. Holmes Tuttle, who became best known as one of my father's financial backers, and who encouraged him to enter politics, was at our house. My father wasn't there; my mother and I were. I don't remember what provoked it but my mother started hitting me—not one slap as usual, but blows raining down on my head and my ears. Holmes Tuttle jumped up and pulled her off me.

"Don't ever do that in front of me again," I recall him saying to her. Even at the time, this struck me as a strange thing to say. If Holmes wasn't around, then it was okay?

I don't think he ever said anything to my father about that incident; if he did, my father never mentioned it, which wouldn't have been unusual either.

My mother still did some acting when I was younger; I remember her coming home wearing her stage makeup. I don't know if this was because my parents needed extra money or because creatively she still needed to work, but she was always in a brighter mood on these occasions. Intuitively, I think I knew that we were all supposed to be actors. If photographers came to the house, we behaved differently. When they shot the whole family in a Crest commercial at our home, we smiled and touched and talked about toothpaste. I used to look forward to dinner parties at our house, because then it was show time; we all rose to the occasion, became a happy family for the audience of guests.

But once the audience departed, the sad private show continued. It was always my mother and I who were the players.

My mother's rage was never directed at my father, nor did it find its way to my brother except on rare instances in his teenage years when some rebellion provoked it. The only other people who felt the brunt of her anger in those years were maids. This may be part of the reason I liked spending time with them—playing cards or watching television. I felt as if we had something in common. I tried, though, not to get too attached to them, because I knew from experience that their days were numbered.

One woman was thin, with steel-gray hair and glasses. My mother would squint at the food as she served it, and I knew her cooking skills were not passing the test, although the food tasted fine to me. In less than two weeks, she was fired because my mother said she had at one time been under psychiatric care. Another heavyset black woman had the courage to argue when my mother would storm into the kitchen and accuse her of doing something wrong. She was gone in a flash. Another was fired because my mother said she threatened her with a knife.

Gardeners were very confusing to me because they changed so fast. As soon as I learned the name of one, he was gone and there was someone else in his place. Once I ran out to the backyard, came up behind the gardener, tugged on his shirt, and said, "Hi, Tom."

A stranger turned around and told me his name wasn't Tom. Tom was gone.

On another occasion, I watched from the playroom, which bordered the backyard, as a gardener knocked on the back door and asked my mother for a glass of water. He said he didn't feel well. My mother started screaming at him because he had taken a step into the house and had gotten mud on the floor. I shut the sliding glass door, put my hands over my ears, and started singing to myself. But I saw her slam the back door in his face. Years later, I learned that this story had traveled like wildfire around the neighborhood because the man went to a neighbor's house, so ill that she had to call an ambulance for him. It turned out he was having a heart attack.

One afternoon, when I was in my twenties, I was at my parents' house and for some reason which I can't even remember, I got into an argument with the maid who had managed the impressive task of staying with my family for years. Suddenly, I yelled at her; my voice took on the shrillness that used to make me cringe when I heard it from my mother. And I felt the firestorm that it created inside me. After I apologized to her, I went off by myself and thought, "What a horrible feeling—what a horrible way to live." And I thought of how long my mother had lived that way, and how many firestorms had raged through her.

CHAPTER 4

. . . .

I WAS NEVER sure why my father was an actor; for as
long as I can remember, I've been aware that his passion was politics. It was as if acting was just a day job,
something to pay the bills until he could do what he
really wanted. He has said on a number of occasions
that I have different views from his because I haven't
listened to his side. But he's wrong. I've been listening
to it all my life.

Part of the reason I paid attention was because I
wanted him to notice me. Ron already had everyone's
attention because he was the baby in the house. Michael
clamored for our father's attention by getting into trouble at school. I tried to share in my father's interests—
horseback riding, swimming, and politics, which was
the subject of dinner-table conversations. And my
mother listened the same way she does now, in a mild
state of rapture, clearly impressed with his opinions and
viewpoints.

When we did a Crest commercial, my father showed
me the check and said, "Look how much the government has taken out of this."

"For what?" I asked.

"Taxes. They're just taxing us to death."

And when my father and grandfather were together,
there were heated discussions about Medicare. According to both of them, Medicare was socialized medicine
and would destroy America. Communists were also discussed at length—infiltrating Hollywood, lurking out in

the ocean. Socialism—never a good sign—first step to Communism.

I also heard these topics discussed whenever we got together with the Taylors; Robert Taylor and my father thought alike on these matters. So did A. C. Lyles. I remember being at the Lyles' house and hearing the two men commiserate on the sad state of Hollywood, with Communists poised to take it over.

There was something that kept nagging at me through all of this, but I never told anyone about it. The only way I can explain it is to call it a premonition. When I was around six or seven, the thought came into my head that my father would one day be president.

I was at school, and my front teeth hadn't come in yet. I had started to think they never would, because I was always inclined toward dramatics. In case tooth-lessness was to be my fate, a lot of my school hours were spent folding tiny pieces of notebook paper into the shape of teeth and wedging them into the gap in my mouth.

We were learning about Abraham Lincoln one day, and I was half-listening, busy folding up teeth. When the teacher started describing his assassination, my hands stopped and I imagined the theater. I thought about a bullet whistling through the crowd and ending a life. I shut my eyes and tried to see Lincoln, but all I could see was my father.

I thought about this every time politics was discussed in our house, which was a lot. I wondered about it, tried to ignore it, and swore I would never tell anyone. I just kept trying to listen to my father, although I was never as quiet and attentive as my mother. I asked questions, which usually didn't endear me to anyone. But it kept me in my father's world, which was what I wanted.

There is a perception that my mother is the political force in my family; this is not the way I've seen it. She is aggressively supportive of my father's interests; his interests become hers. My observation is that she takes

on responsibility for making sure all my father's dreams
come true and all his goals are realized.

Politics is my father's arterial flow, his lifeblood. It
strengthens him, runs through his veins, and makes him
get up in the morning. My father appears to be simple,
but you would have to spend time with him, years
perhaps, to understand that this is only an appearance.
It's his greatest illusion. His complexity can show itself
without warning. Just when you thought you were in
the company of someone remote, suddenly he's there,
leaning over you, spouting rhetoric and opinions.

My uncle on my mother's side, Richard Davis, once
said to me, "It must have been hard growing up with
your father. You'd have to be Mother Teresa just to get
his attention."

"I don't know if that would have done it," I told him.
"Unless Mother Teresa is a Republican."

One evening when I was watching "Sea Hunt," one
of my favorite shows, my father said, "They wouldn't
let Lloyd Bridges work for a long time because he's a
Communist."

"He is?" I said, glancing at the television.

"Uh-huh. He was exposed when the Communists
were infiltrating Hollywood. Card-carrying Communists. They were trying to take over the movie industry."

"What did they want to do with it?" I asked. "The
movie industry, I mean."

"Spread propaganda," my father said.

"Spread what?"

He left the room and returned with a map highlighted
with a large mass of red.

"This is all Communist," he told me, pointing to the
red land mass. "That's what they wanted to do."

"They wanted to paint Hollywood red?" I couldn't
understand any of this.

"Actually," my father continued, "the cities in Communist countries are all gray and dingy. You wouldn't
like to live like that, would you?"

"If the cities are gray, why do they paint the map red?" I asked.

"We'll talk about this when you're older," my father said, exasperated by my questions.

And we did—endlessly—which is how I remember this conversation so clearly. Versions of it were repeated frequently.

In 1960, Richard Nixon was running against John Kennedy. My parents were voting for Nixon.

What I picked up from the conversation around our house was that Kennedy's politics were so dangerous, no one in their right mind would vote for him.

"Is Kennedy a Communist?" I asked my father one night. I remember he was watching television, but if you asked my father about Communists, you had his attention immediately.

"Well, Patti, his views are very socialist and, you know, that's the first step to Communism."

Sounded like a yes to me. So I was understandably confused when I heard my classmates in school talking about how their parents were voting for Kennedy.

"Isn't he a Communist?" I asked self-consciously, regretting it as soon as I'd said it.

All I remember is a wall of eyes staring at me. "Okay," I thought, "maybe I should question what I hear around the dinner table."

I started to listen more carefully. It was definite that my parents thought Kennedy was a bad person. I, on the other hand, thought he had a much kinder face than Nixon's. I wanted him to win and I suppose this was the beginning of my political disagreements with my parents. Over the years, they would get far worse.

Shortly after Nixon lost the election to John Kennedy, he came to our house for dinner. I was informed, before I left for school that morning, that he would be there when I got home.

"Mr. Nixon will be using your room to change, Patti," my mother said as I was running out the front door, the school bus honking for me at the foot of the driveway.

That afternoon, I came home to find Richard Nixon sitting in the den with my parents.

"Come in and say hello," my mother told me, leading me over to him.

I shook his hand and tried to think of something to say. "I'm sorry you lost the election."

"Well, thank you," Nixon answered. "But if I'd won I guess I wouldn't be here now, getting to meet you." I smiled, said thank you, and headed for my room.

The clothes Nixon had changed out of were on one of the twin beds—a dark suit and white shirt, just like the one he had on. I lifted up the jacket, the pants, the shirt, wondering why there were no socks or underwear there. When I heard my mother's footsteps, I ran over to the other bed, sat down, and tried to look innocent, which I probably didn't since I was just sitting there, looking at the wall.

"What are you doing, Patti?" she asked, giving me a puzzled look.

"Nothing."

"Well, why don't you go into the kitchen and get some juice. Your brother is taking a nap, so I don't want you making any noise."

I found Ron's nanny, Lela, in the kitchen drinking coffee while the cook was preparing dinner. Lela was strict and rarely smiled. I got a glass of juice and sat down at the table beside her.

"Mr. Nixon changed clothes in my room," I told her.

"Yes, I know."

"But I don't think he changed his underwear. Or his socks either."

"What?"

"I looked at his clothes and I didn't find any underwear or socks."

"Patti," Lela said, "you shouldn't be going through someone else's things. It's not polite."

"But my mother goes through my things all the time."

Lela didn't answer me; she just looked away.

Even though I tried to listen to my father's lectures on politics, I was often confused. I didn't understand why, if the government was taking over half of my parents' money, which was what I was being told, we seemed to always be able to hire maids. And there was no lack of expensive antiques in our home. I was warned not to touch them. I didn't understand why it was wrong to help poor people. "They have to learn to help themselves" was the answer I got. And why was it wrong for the government to provide health care for those who couldn't afford it? I never got a satisfactory answer to that, but I kept asking questions because I knew that politics was the way to my father's heart.

Crisis was the way to get my mother's attention. I learned this early on during the period when my best friend was Bridget Duff, Ida Lupino and Howard Duff's daughter. She lived about ten minutes away in a house that seemed magical to me because of the people in it. Bridget's Irish nanny told us stories about leprechauns and haunted castles; she fixed us tea in the afternoons, and I remember rainy days in the warm, steamy kitchen listening to her stories. Ida Lupino called everyone "darling," smoked cigarettes in long holders, and wore flowing dressing gowns and high-heeled slippers. She was the most glamorous woman I'd ever seen, but she was full of magic too. One night, when I stayed over, she let Bridget and me sleep in the living room in sleeping bags. Before we dozed off, she came in and sprinkled gold glitter over us.

"There you go, darlings, you'll have beautiful dreams now."

One weekend, Bridget invited me to go to Malibu and stay with her and her nanny at a house which, I assume, had been lent to them. After my mother dropped me off, I was led into the living room and

immediately wished I hadn't come. There were animal
heads on every wall; a moose stared down at me from
above the fireplace, his brown glass eyes shiny and
dead.

The second day I was there, Bridget and I were playing "let's pick each other up." I never got my turn
because I slipped through her arms, fell onto the fireplace hearth, and cracked my head open. I lay on the
floor, staring up at the moose head, feeling warm blood
seep out of my scalp into my hair.

My mother was called and she said not to take me to
the Emergency Room in Malibu; she would come get
me and drive me to my own doctor in Beverly Hills.

By the time she arrived, I was already queasy and
dizzy, blood had soaked through one bath towel and I
was working on my second. On the way down the Coast
Highway, I threw up on my mother's lap, but she didn't
get angry; she didn't even seem to mind. She was calm
and concerned and, through my sickness and the throb-
bing in my head, I felt closer to her than I ever had.

For nearly a week, I stayed at home, with the back of
my head shaved and a white bandage covering my
wound. My mother was soft and nurturing and I
learned the value of being sick; it was the way to have
a mother. After I recovered, I would sometimes fake
being ill. I'd do it when I was desperate for my parents'
attention. My mother's hand would touch my forehead
and stroke my cheek, as though she were erasing all the
times her hand had struck me. I believed her love, I
wanted it to last, but I knew that our war had not been
left behind. It was always just around the corner.

My father would come in, sit on the edge of my bed,
and tell me stories; he has always been a willing story-
teller. I remember lying in bed with the covers pulled up
to my chin, feeling that my parents were close and
accessible.

I was learning some important lessons about the
inner workings of my family. Crises have always been
part of our repertoire. They allow my mother to assume

control, which she loves. My mother becomes calm in
a crisis; she takes charge, her temperament evens out,
her anger wanes. She can handle almost any crisis; it's
the little everyday things that set her off.

My father was never aware of how the atmosphere of
our home shifted from one extreme to another, depending on whether or not he was there.

Until I was ten, he worked for General Electric and
often took four- or five-day business trips. Gardeners
got yelled at during those times, maids ran for cover
and were frequently fired, and I always seemed to be
right in the middle of the warpath, unless Michael was
home for the weekend—he absorbed some of the anger
usually aimed at me. My mother grew to enormous
proportions during these times. When my father returned, she seemed less daunting to me, her voice was
softer.

My father adopted an attitude which seems to be
fairly prevalent among men. He believed that the
woman should take care of the home and not bother the
man with it. My parents had a very traditional relationship, and still do. The most important moment of my
mother's day was when my father came home, and
whatever had gone on in his absence was either shoved
under the carpet or used to support my mother's position on something.

My mother clearly never told my father she hit me. I
do believe, however, she told him about something else
that went on because I don't think she saw anything
wrong with it.

When I was around nine or ten, my mother and I
were in the car, and we had had an argument. She
reached into her purse, brought out a brown pill bottle,
and she shook a white tablet into her hand and swallowed it without water. Sometime after that, after I'd
seen these white tablets appear and disappear on other
occasions, it became important to me to find out what
they were. In part, this was because my father frequently told me that I was ruining my mother's health,

depriving her of sleep, causing her to lose weight. My mother never seemed sickly or frail to me; in fact, she always seemed very healthy. But there were these pills; pills were for illness, so I had to find out. I snuck into her bathroom one day, found the bottle, and read the name—Miltown. "For nerves," the label said.

After that, I started to find excuses to go into my parents' bathroom; I became the self-designated pill monitor, checking bottles in the medicine cabinet, looking for other labels that read "for nerves." I found one that read "for sleep"—pink capsules labeled Seconal. For years, every night, she would lay out two Seconals and one Miltown. These started to appear beside my mother's toothbrush at night.

"Your mother can't sleep at night," my father told me. "You upset her so much; her nerves are frayed. It's not healthy for her, this lack of sleep."

"But she takes pills to sleep," I answered cautiously.

"They don't help. Some people have the opposite reaction to sedatives. They actually wake them up instead of putting them to sleep."

"Then why does she take them?"

"Because you upset her so much."

When we visited my grandparents in Phoenix over Easter vacation, the pills went too—in a small leather case with loops to hold plastic prescription bottles. In my memory, the white tablets of Miltown look large, although I think this was probably not the case. They probably seemed larger the more I saw them, because what they suggested to me was that there really was something wrong with my mother and that it was my fault. I counted the pills, took note of their disappearance; I knew she was taking at least three or four a day. I'm sure now that I was keeping better track of this than her doctor.

"Why does my mother take pills?" I asked my grandfather.

"Her doctors know what's best."

"But why?" I persisted.

"They are doing what's best for her," he answered, in a tone that shut the door on the conversation.

After some of our frequent arguments, my mother would storm into her bathroom; I'd walk by her door and glance in discreetly. Often, I'd see her tossing a pill into her mouth. Because I kept track of how many pills were in the bottle, I also noticed when the empty bottle was placed by the phone, reminding her to get a refill. Once I said, "Why are you getting this refilled?" I wanted to add "already," but my voice wouldn't say it.

"Because it's empty," she answered.

Over the years, the name of the drug would change, but the behavior wouldn't. Certain drugs come in vogue and are then replaced by a new-drug-on-the-block. But that's just a name change; underneath, everything's the same. I have to look now at my history and particularly my long battle with my mother in the context of her pills. That way, I can explain things I didn't understand before. I now feel her unpredictable moods, her ability to alter facts at will, may be related to the pills she took over the years.

I later became a drug addict. Like my mother, I got pills from doctors. I chose different pills, but that was the only act of rebellion in an otherwise identical pattern. It also had to do with different personalities. It defies logic, but I have sometimes observed that depressed people tend to choose depressive drugs, while anxious, angry people often choose drugs that will rev them up more. What I think of now is the sadness that drew my mother to tranquilizers in the first place. The fact that these have been prescribed to her for decades has made me see her as a victim of a medical profession which, all too often, has relied heavily on pills.

My mother was part of what has been called "the Miltown generation." In the Fifties and early Sixties, Miltown was the tranquilizer of choice, and women often filled their prescriptions without asking a lot of questions.

In my parents' generation, people in general seemed to question their doctors less than they do now. If pills came from a doctor, how bad could they be? Addicts were people who bought drugs wrapped in tinfoil from a guy on a street corner, or from someone who made them in his garage. Addicts were *not* people who got prescriptions that had been phoned in by a doctor and delivered from Schwab's Drug Store. It was a mind-set, but it claimed a lot of victims.

I didn't know all of these things when I was young. But I knew that people took medicine when something was wrong. The more pills I saw my mother take, the more convinced I was that something was wrong. My father reinforced this feeling on one of our Saturday trips to the 365-acre ranch my parents owned in Agoura, inland from Malibu.

I usually rode alone with my father because my mother didn't like riding and Ron was still too young. Sometimes Michael went along, but he had friends who lived around the ranch and he went off with them.

On one of these Saturday rides, my father said, "Patti, your mother isn't well. She could actually die.

"It's nerves," he continued. "You cannot keep treating her this way. She can't sleep, she can't eat. She might have a nervous breakdown. And it could be fatal. Now, she doesn't know I'm telling you this, but I just can't sit back and let you destroy her health."

I rode the rest of the way in silence, wondering if it was true, feeling guilty even if it wasn't. But the story was not to end there. More people participated in it, adding even more drama.

CHAPTER 5

· · · · · · · · · · · · · ·

EVERY EASTER VACATION, we visited my grandparents in Arizona. In those days, a sleeper train ran between California and Phoenix. We would arrive in Phoenix at dawn, with the sky just starting to lighten, and my grandparents would be there to pick us up.

They lived in the Biltmore Estates along the edges of a golf course. The road leading to their house was lined with orange trees; sweet perfume filled the warm desert air. In the mornings, rabbits scampered by the windows.

My grandmother was salty and direct; Edith Davis had never succumbed to the theory that women were just there to serve tea. She might serve tea, but she'd also serve up dirty jokes and swear words. I give her partial responsibility for the fact that I often use language that would make sailors blush. She also fed me more candy than my parents allowed me to eat at home. She chose to marry a man who couldn't have been more opposite from her.

My grandfather was stern and precise—a brain surgeon who seemed to approach everything as if he had a scalpel in his hand and was perfecting his skill at dissection. I don't remember him ever hugging me, and his kisses were always awkward and quick, his lips pursed tightly as though he wasn't too sure how this kissing-thing was done. It didn't take long for my grandparents to adopt their roles in our latest family drama. My grandmother went first. Her fingers dug

41

into my arm and her face was so close to mine I could smell the chocolate she loved on her breath. "How are you going to feel when they're lowering your mother into the ground?" she asked. "She's my daughter and you're killing her. I'll never forgive you for that. I don't like you very much right now. I love you because you're my granddaughter, but I don't like you."

My grandfather was next. He called me into his office, a small room between the living room and the guest bedroom. He shut the sliding doors and sat down behind his desk. I sat on the couch facing him.

"Do you know what this is?" he said, holding up a manila envelope.

"No, sir." There was something about my grandfather's formality that invited people to call him "sir"— even me.

"This is a medical report on your mother. Her condition is very serious. Emotions can kill someone, you know. And if you don't start behaving, we could lose her." His jaw was set and his voice was stern and cold.

Lose her. I wasn't sure what he meant. I imagined turning around to discover that my mother had been lost, misplaced somewhere. I wondered if I would look for her.

"Why does she take pills?" I asked my grandfather.

"Because you upset her so much."

"But the labels say for nerves."

"That's right. Because you're destroying her nerves, and the medicine might not help."

A few days later, I was walking along the golf course, going to my friend's house. There were tall hedges between the houses that formed a border around the course, and at one end of the hedge, a large king snake was stretched out motionless on the grass. I knew enough about snakes to know that it wasn't poisonous, and I approached it with a child's fearless curiosity. But it didn't move. I touched its back and knew it was dead. I crouched down beside the snake, stroking it, studying its lifelessness—introducing myself to death.

Later that afternoon, on my way home, I went back to see the snake and found that some predator had torn apart its flesh. I screamed and ran crying back to my grandparents' house. Death suddenly seemed a terrible thing, and inside a voice reminded me that this was what people said I was doing to my mother.

I ran through the back door into the air-conditioned house and almost collided with my mother. She was in shorts and a bathing suit top and she smelled like Coppertone.

"What's the matter? Why are you crying?" she said.

"There—there was a snake—he's dead," I stammered.

"Where?"

"On the golf course—between the houses."

My mother grabbed my arm. "Patti, are you lying?"

"No. And something ate him," I said, my voice rising.

"Come on. Let's go back there. I want you to show me," my mother said, moving toward the door.

"No! I don't want to go back!"

But she pulled me toward the door, toward the death and decay I'd run away from moments before.

When we got there, the snake was gone. "First you're torn apart," I thought, "then you vanish." A lesson I hadn't wanted to learn yet.

"Why did you lie to me?" my mother said. The afternoon sun was still strong and hot; golfers were hitting balls in the distance, small figures on a blanket of green.

"I didn't—he was there," I said, starting to cry again.

We walked back to my grandparents' house in silence. I knew what was coming and my knees were weak with fear. When we got inside, my mother turned to me.

"Why do you always have to make things up? Why can't you tell the truth?"

"I *did* tell the truth. He was there."

She moved toward me, and I started running toward the hallway that led to my grandparents' bedroom. I felt her hand as she caught me and we both stumbled, the carpet scraping my knees. Her hand swung at my face as it usually did, but the impact was less because we were both on the floor and she couldn't swing very hard.

There was a moment when I looked at her after she had slapped me, when I realized how well I understood her. We were like two generals who had been at war so long that they knew each other's strategy. I realized on some intuitive level how intimate enemies can be. Underneath my faked illnesses, my missed school days, was insecurity. But my mother had gone further—she was pretending she was dying. What I remember about that hallway was not feeling angry at her. We both had to pretend we were sick to get attention, and I understood her as well as I understood myself.

Except for that particular vacation, Easter at my grandparents' house was a time I looked forward to. My parents were more social then, there were more people in our life—the Goldwaters, and other neighbors; one year Ray Bolger visited and did his *Wizard of Oz* scarecrow dance for me. Visitors came and went from my grandparents' house. At our home in California, people made appointments and they didn't stay long. Often, they came only as far as the entryway. But at my grandparents' house, visitors wandered into the kitchen, came to the back door, dropped by for iced tea, and lounged on the porch.

Our vacations there usually brought harmony to my family. We would go horseback riding and even my mother, who didn't usually ride, would go along. On a few occasions, there were horse shows in which I competed. My father would spend hours instructing me on riding techniques and how to make the horse understand what I wanted of him.

"Now remember," he said, "the horse doesn't know he's bigger than you. He only knows you're riding him, and you're the boss. So if you're hesitant, you'll only confuse him."

On Easter mornings, there would be eggs hidden in

the bushes along the golf course. When I was very young, my mother would hold my hand and lead me across the grass, telling me to look closely—the Easter bunny thought of good hiding places, so I had to pay attention. For years, I thought I knew what the Easter bunny looked like. Rabbits often scampered across the golf course and one year, early in the morning, one was right outside the living-room window.

"That's the Easter bunny," my father told me. "He probably just finished hiding the eggs."

Just then, another rabbit ran across the grass.

"Well then, who's that?" I asked.

"That's his wife," my father said, without cracking a smile.

I would swim at a neighbor's pool and I remember my mother drying me off, her hands on my back as she rubbed suntan lotion into my skin. I remember her face, tanned and relaxed, with no makeup and her hair pushed back with a scarf; I remember thinking how beautiful she was.

One evening, not too long after our vacation in Phoenix, I was in my room doing my homework, my head bent close to the paper because I didn't want to wear the glasses I was supposed to be wearing. I heard footsteps approaching my room. They were soft and slow; I knew they were my father's. He came into my room but didn't sit down. "Patti, could you come into the bedroom for a minute, please?" he said. His voice was casual and unassuming, but that didn't mean there wasn't danger.

As I got up to follow him, I ran the day's events through my mind, trying to determine if I'd done anything wrong. My mother was waiting for us in their bedroom.

"Sit down for a minute, Patti," my father said to me, pointing to one of the chairs by the fireplace. I glanced at my mother but couldn't read her face.

"Why?"

"We just want to talk to you," he answered. He was still standing, motioning me to the chair. He was never good at acting like these things were his idea; I noticed my mother's eyes following him, prodding him—instructing.

"Now you know your mother has been having trouble swallowing at night," my father began.

I'd been told sometime that week that her throat had started to close up at night, that stress was the reason . . . that *I* was the reason. I nodded, wondering where this could possibly be leading.

"I went to see your mother's doctor today," he continued, "and he felt it was important that we know how to give a tracheotomy."

"A what?" I asked, suspecting that this was probably something I didn't want to know about.

"A tracheotomy. In case your mother is choking and can't get air, her breathing passage would have to be opened."

He walked over to his desk and got a pen. Maybe he was going to draw a diagram for me? But he walked back without any paper.

"So, Patti," my father said to me, "why don't you lie down here on the floor?" He pointed to a spot between the bed and the television.

"Why?" I was getting more nervous by the minute.

"So he can show us how to do it," my mother answered.

I obeyed, lay down on the carpet, and stared up at my parents' shapes leaning over me. My father lowered the pen toward my throat until it grazed my skin.

"Now, right here in the hollow of the throat," he began, directing his words to my mother, "is where the trachea has to be opened to allow air in. If there isn't a knife or scissors around, anything sharp will do. Even a pen—you punch it through right here in that spot." He emphasized this by bouncing the pen lightly against the hollow of my throat.

I tuned out, stared at the ceiling. Why was he demonstrating on me, showing this procedure to my mother? Was she expected to run to the mirror and give herself a tracheotomy while fighting for breath? I wasn't frightened, lying there with my parents' faces looming over me—there wasn't a second when I thought my father would actually hurt me—but I was confused, off balance, overwhelmed.

I glanced toward the oil painting of my mother and me that hung above the fireplace. I think I was about three. Her face wore a half-smile and her eyes were warm, soft. I wondered if I had ever seen my mother look at me with the expression she wore in that painting. Something told me I had, that it was buried somewhere in our history together.

After my parents finished with me and I got up off the floor, I went back to my room, shut the door, and wished for the thousandth time that it had a lock. I'd lock everyone out and only come out after midnight.

It was only years later that I figured out what was going on in this simulated home-surgery procedure. My father was showing my mother what he would have to do to her if things got desperate and she really couldn't breathe. It never occurred to him that to simulate a tracheotomy on a young girl might scare the hell out of that child. I could have been a doll lying there. It was one more instance in which my father was in his own world, behaving in a way that seemed perfectly appropriate to him. The only visitor he allowed into his world was my mother. I was almost invisible at times, and so, for that matter, were his other three children.

Around this time, I started walking on the balls of my feet because it made me feel taller. I was already tall, but I felt tiny, particularly at home. This started one day when my mother and I had an argument and I saw her hand coming toward me. I suddenly wished I were a giant and she couldn't reach me, and I stretched myself up and stood on my toes. She hit me anyway, but the idea caught on. I began walking that way all the time, which produced leg cramps that got so bad after a while that I'd wake up screaming in the middle of the night. My parents would come into my room, get on either

side of me, and help me walk around the room, because
that was the only thing that un-cramped my calves. And
I had to go to a doctor who put my legs in a warm
whirlpool bath and made me stretch my heels down.
The curious thing is that no one asked why I was doing
this, but I probably would have lied anyway.

"Heels down" became the chorus that followed me at
home and school. My parents had asked my teachers to
tell me at every available opportunity to get off the balls
of my feet. My grandfather said to me, "What are you
trying to do, cripple yourself? You'll shorten your ten-
dons and then you won't be able to walk at all."

None of that worked. I finally just gave up trying to
feel taller than my mother. I could look in the mirror
and see that I was almost bigger than she and somehow
I felt better.

I observed that other people, too, felt diminished by
my mother, even if they towered over her. The maid
who finally fit in with our family was nearly six feet tall
and very hefty. Anne remained with my family until
after my father was re-elected in 1984, taking care of
cooking and cleaning at the ranch when they went up
there. I don't think it ever occurred to her that she
towered over my mother. In all those years, she never
stood up for herself when she was reprimanded; she
always shrank back. I would look at my mother standing in front of Anne, scolding her for putting flowers
she didn't like in the entryway, and I'd think, "Well, so
much for what mirrors tell us about our size."

CHAPTER 6

. . . .

I USED TO watch television programs like "The Donna Reed Show" and "Father Knows Best" and wonder what it would be like to be part of a family that was noisy, hectic, tumbling in and out of each other's rooms, borrowing each other's belongings.

In my home, I approached Ron's room on tiptoe because I was never supposed to be in there. Michael only came home on weekends, slept on the couch, and kept his duffel bag in the powder room. He never even unpacked. When he wasn't there, my mother complained that she had to take him to the dentist and we had to eat fish on Fridays because of him. Maureen lived somewhere else, with a mother we weren't supposed to talk about. Jane Wyman's name was forbidden in our house. I don't think Michael or Maureen ever came into my room or shared my belongings; we didn't have food fights or spats like I'd seen television families have. We just passed each other at a safe distance.

My mother's footsteps echoed throughout the house —hard, determined steps, marking territory. My father's were usually inaudible. He seemed to float in and out of rooms, coming from nowhere, disappearing into the distance.

When my parents started building an extra room onto the house, taking up part of the backyard, I thought Michael was finally going to get his own room. So did he. I found out the truth before he did and didn't tell him because I didn't want to be the one to hurt his feelings. The room was for Anne, the maid, and the room that she had been using would become an ironing room for the laundress who came once a week.

Sometime after he was told that he still didn't have a room in our house, Michael was moved to the daybed in the playroom, between Ron's room and mine. It might have made him feel better—I don't know—but I viewed it as moving him from one couch to another. The message was the same: You're not really part of this family.

In 1961, my mother was angry at Maureen for telling them in a sudden phone call that she was getting married to a Washington, D.C., policeman.

"How *should* she have done it?" I asked.

"Well, she could have told us that she was dating him," my mother answered. "Brought him home to meet us."

But Maureen, who was then twenty, lived in Washington, and she was hardly ever mentioned in our home. I didn't understand how my mother could expect any more than a phone call. My parents did go to Maureen's wedding, though, and I ended up meeting her first husband once—at Christmas, I think.

I kept God in my closet. I had constructed an altar there, out of a cardboard box, a piece of purple satin that Anne had given me, and two long strips of cardboard that I pasted together into a cross. My parents usually insisted that I go with them to the Bel Air Presbyterian Church on Sundays, but I always tried to get out of it. To me, church had nothing whatsoever to do with God—I preferred to keep Him in my closet where I could discuss things with Him in private.

The problem was, the intercom in my room was always turned on at night and whatever sound I made was piped into my parents' bedroom. So before I whispered my prayers at night, I'd take out another piece of cardboard and a roll of Scotch tape and block off the intercom. I wasn't sure how effective this was, so I still spoke very quietly. Then I'd leave the intercom taped up the rest of the night because sometimes the tears I refused to cry in front of my mother when she hit me would spill out in the dark.

One of my prayers, when I was around ten, was that my parents would get divorced and I'd get to live with my father.

While my father was away on one of his business trips, my mother was escorted to a dinner party by Cesar Romero. As soon as he arrived, I thought my prayers had been answered. My mother had a date with another man; she'd leave my father, and I could appear in court at the divorce hearing and tell the judge everything.

The next day, locksmiths came and changed the locks on the front and back doors. That confirmed my suspicions. I went to bed that night elated. My fantasy was coming true. My mother was locking my father out of the house and probably giving the new key to Cesar.

But the following morning, when I went into the kitchen, Anne was fixing two breakfast trays.

"Why are there two trays?" I asked her. Cesar?

"For your parents. Your father came back late last night. Why do you look so surprised? What's the matter with you?"

"Nothing," I said.

But inside, everything was wrong. My fantasy of telling some kindly old judge how my mother hit me was over. Nor would I get to go live with my father.

Later, I did ask my mother why the locks had been changed. Apparently, she went through her key drawer, counted the house keys, and noticed one missing. She assumed that some maid who had been fired had neglected to return one, so she changed the locks.

In 1962, my father was fired by General Electric. His business trips had been getting more and more frequent over the years and, from the reports he brought back, more successful. What I noticed, though, was that the speeches he talked about giving never had anything to do with General Electric. I thought he was supposed to be advertising their products, but after he returned from one of these trips he would sit at the dinner table and talk about the hundreds of people who had shown up to hear him speak about "Big Government."

From what I gleaned, this was a problem. General Electric wasn't happy with the political nature of his speeches and they started to get threats that millions of dollars' worth of contracts might be cancelled.

"Government contracts," my father said one night at dinner. "This is exactly what I've been out there speaking about. We're on our way to a controlled society. The government is trying to control everything. And Robert Kennedy is behind this attack on me."

"He is?" I piped up. "Why would he want you fired?"

"Because I'm speaking out against the Kennedy Administration and the road they're trying to lead us down."

"*Of course* Bobby Kennedy's behind it," my mother said. "It's obvious."

The fact that my father was now unemployed meant that he wouldn't go out of town on business trips; he'd be around more—at least that's what I thought. I was looking forward to a lull in the battles that erupted between my mother and me whenever he wasn't around. But he began going to the ranch almost every day, so I still found myself trying to avoid my mother's wrath, and often failing. Many of our fights still took place in front of the window in my bedroom. Now, however, my mother had found a new place to hit me.

I was developing very fast in those pre-teen years, growing out of my clothes, heading toward sexual maturity, and this necessitated shopping trips, to I. Magnin's and Saks Fifth Avenue in Beverly Hills. Today, I still avoid these stores, not because there's anything wrong with them, but because of the painful memories. En route to these stores, in the car or in the parking lot, my mother would often scream at me. As we headed into one store or another, she would roughly pull my arm. I would shuffle along beside her, a tall girl, uncomfortable in her body. I knew I would hate what my mother picked out for me and that, no matter how I felt, these clothes would end up in my closet.

Walking briskly up and down the aisles one day, my mother picked out a navy and white sailor dress, shapeless and boxy. I remember hating it. Then she picked out a maroon dress with little white polka dots, a little white collar, and a white bib down the front. I suppose she thought that dressing me up like a toddler might stop this horrible process of seeing me grow into a woman, tall and threatening.

"Do you like this?" my mother asked, holding up a dress, as though suddenly she remembered I was there.

"Not really."

She looped it over her arm. "Well, try it on."

"But I don't like it."

My mother wheeled around, brushed the rack, and hangers clattered. "Just stop it!" she shouted, as people around her stared.

I followed her into the dressing room and sulkily tried on the dresses she had chosen, hating every one of them and making that clear. I think it was the bib dress that really set things off.

"I am paying good money to buy these clothes for you," my mother said, her voice rising. "You are just too high and mighty to appreciate anything! You have a chip on your shoulder a mile high!"

I heard footsteps outside the dressing room—slowing down, eavesdropping—how could they not?

"But why do I have to wear things I don't like?"

"Because I said so!"

I wondered if the people passing heard the slap of my mother's hand on my cheek; I wondered if they knew what the sound was, or even if it carried. Maybe it was only loud to me. I know that probably, if I said I liked the dresses, my mother wouldn't buy them. But I was too defiant to practice reverse psychology. Our horns were locked in battle.

My mother took the dresses up to the counter; I followed.

"Cash or charge?" the salesgirl asked.

"Charge," my mother replied.

"Could I have your card?"

"I don't have it with me."

I knew this wasn't true. All my mother's charge cards were in her wallet, but this was a familiar scene.

"Oh, well . . . what's your name?" the salesgirl asked, trying to be helpful.

The answer was a long, chilly moment of silence, meant to indicate displeasure at being asked a name which everyone should know. I was familiar with this language of refrigerated pauses; to the salesgirl, it was obviously foreign.

"Mrs. Ronald Reagan," my mother finally said, after her silence had made its point. Her voice was a hammer hitting one more nail into the poor girl's coffin. I hoped it was not her first day on the job.

I wanted to ask the purpose of this game, the I-don't-have-my-card game. But I kept quiet, partly because I was frightened of my mother, but partly because I knew how to use silence as a weapon. We drove home not speaking.

Now I think I do understand the game; it had to do not only with establishing control, but with establishing identity. A person whose identity seems fragile to them compensates by trying to make it bigger. It was crucial to Nancy Robbins that she became Nancy Davis, Dr. Loyal Davis's daughter. In her mind, she needed his identity. In the same way, being Ronald Reagan's wife bolstered her confidence. Asserting that identity had nothing to do with salesgirls; it had everything to do with her, and with the deep insecurities she was trying to hide.

I managed to sabotage some of the dresses that were bought on these shopping trips. My usual technique was to cut out one tooth of the zipper with manicure scissors, go to my mother, ask her to zip me up, and then act baffled when the zipper broke. Occasionally, I resorted to an eyedropper full of bleach, but that got Anne in trouble because my mother assumed she'd done it. So I went back to the zippers and sometimes unraveling the hem or splitting a seam. My mother never figured out I was behind these mishaps, which surprised me because she is a very shrewd woman. She would go away grumbling about faulty merchandise and sloppy workmanship.

Saturdays were a respite for me. There were no shopping trips, no battles. On Saturdays, I had time alone with my father at the ranch.

I planned all week what I wanted to say to him. I thought if I found the right words, shared enough thoughts with him, he would reach across the distance.

One Saturday, when summer had baked the ground and the fields were golden brown and dry as straw, we turned our horses toward the oak grove. My father always rode in front of me and I remember him best that way—his back muscular and straight, his face turning occasionally, eyes scanning the land.

"When Mom took me shopping this week," I said, "I saw a colored woman with a white man. They were holding hands."

This had impressed me, because all my friends, and my parents' friends, were white. We'd had black maids, but they wore uniforms, ate in the kitchen, received harsh orders from my mother, and always called my parents "ma'am" and "sir." I wasn't sure if this was because they were maids or because they were black, but I didn't like it. So when my mother and I passed the couple on a Westwood sidewalk, I smiled at them. It seemed more the way things should be.

We were passing out of the oak grove when I brought this up to my father.

"Oh?" he responded, and then said something to his horse.

"Yeah," I continued. "I thought it was really great that it didn't matter to them—you know, that they were different."

"Well, Patti, it *should* matter. Those things just don't work."

"They don't?" I said, my voice getting smaller.

"No. They are different from each other. It's not just their skin color—it goes deeper than that. Relationships between the races just don't work out. For one thing, the world isn't ready for it."

I fell silent, let the sound of the horses' hooves and the drone of bees fill the space between us. I couldn't believe what I'd heard my father say; when I was younger, he told me that everyone was the same. "Just like horses come in different colors," he had said, "so do people. It doesn't matter."

But now he was telling me it did.

"Speaking of shopping with your mother," he said as we came to a curve on the trail and then started going downhill, "why do you have to make it so unpleasant for her?"

"I didn't do anything," I argued, knowing it didn't matter what I said. This wasn't how I'd planned our ride.

"Patti—" My father hurled my name at me, reprimanded me with it. "You won't even walk beside her. You trail behind. How do you think that makes her feel?"

"She yells at me," I offered bravely, hoping he might listen this time and believe I was telling the truth.

"Patti, how can she not be upset when you deliberately hurt her? And you know, sometimes women are more easily upset than at other times—certain times of the month—you know what I mean."

We were headed toward the barn and the horses were walking faster, anxious to get us off their backs and get the carrots that always rewarded them after a ride. I didn't say anything else. But I wondered how my father could be so blind to the fact that there wasn't just one time of the month. It was every day, every week, all year. All my life.

There were other Saturdays at the ranch that have stayed with me like treasures, winter days when the fog moved inland from the ocean, when mist caught in our hair and the horses' manes. We would gallop up trails and across fields that had turned green from the rains; cold wind pulled water from our eyes and the gray sky was thick and low above us.

My father taught me about the land, about animals and birds and cycles of nature. Years later, he would wound me when he ridiculed environmentalists.

But on some of these smoke-colored days, nothing mattered but being with him. He gave me riding lessons, and if I fell off, he made me get back on right away.

"Otherwise, you'll be afraid," he said, leading me over to my horse and helping me to remount. "You always have to get back on after you fall off."

The ranch was an escape for me; I could run across fields and climb up oak trees, pretending I was an Indian or a wild animal. My only escape at our house was riding my bike. I would go as fast as I could, pretending I was pedaling to another country. In a sense, I was. I would often go to my friend Cory's house which was about as different from mine as Sweden is from America. It was casual, permissive, usually chaotic, and I loved it there. I brought Cory to my house only once—when my parents weren't there. As I led her through the immaculate rooms, past tables of jade pieces and Limoges boxes, she said, "Wow, everything's so perfect. How do you ever play here?"

"We don't," I answered. That wasn't totally true. We did have a playroom, but that didn't seem to matter. The overwhelming perfection of my house and my mother's determination to keep it that way was all I could grasp. Our childhood was to be confined to one small room.

CHAPTER 7

. . . .

MONEY WAS A big issue in my family—a live wire that always seemed to be sizzling. Later in the White House, scandals erupted because of money. There were news stories about gifts that were supposed to be declared and weren't, designer dresses that were borrowed and not returned, and recycled presents.

Our feelings about money are formed at an early age. Anyone who has grown up with financial hardship expects money to do a disappearing act, because that's how it seemed to them in childhood. Growing up, my mother was better off financially than my father, but her cousins, with whom she lived while her mother was on the road, were, by their own admission, poor. My father saw money eaten up by alcohol and the Depression.

Children in these environments learn to hoard; they throw nothing away, they save everything. My mother held on to clothes that she probably hadn't looked at in years; she saved wrapping paper, ribbons, baskets, and cheap vases that held all the flowers that were delivered over the years. And she was loath to part with money, because somewhere in her was a little girl, frightened that there wouldn't be any more.

For me, money is still a very loaded issue because of the things that were attached to it during my own childhood—particularly approval and judgment.

At Christmastime, for example, we could measure how much our parents liked us by how many gifts we got, and whether or not they came out of my mother's "gift closet"—the closet where she put things she'd been given and didn't want—or whether something had been bought specifically for us. It was never the *things* that mattered; it was the approval or disapproval they represented. When Michael lived with us, he got fewer presents than either Ron or I. Maureen, if she came by on Christmas Day, got a single present. Ron got the most presents and I hovered somewhere in between, depending on my approval rating at the time. I grew to dread Christmas because I associated it with embarrassment and a subtle form of punishment.

It was also a time of tests. We were graded on our reactions to gifts. When I was around eleven, my present from my parents was a silver metallic dress with a round, gathered skirt and tiny puffed sleeves.

"Oh—uh," I stammered.

"Why don't you try it on?" my mother said.

I glanced at my father—a please-help-me look. But I think he was helping Ron put a truck together or something. I took the dress into my room and wondered what would happen if I lit it on fire. I put it on and looked in the mirror. I wasn't sure where I was supposed to wear this, if I was expected to wear it that day, but I knew that I couldn't bring myself to wear it at all.

Tentatively, I walked back out to the living room

"Oh, that looks lovely," my mother said.

"I—uh—I don't really like it," I explained.

"It looks nice," my father said, although I could swear he wasn't looking at me. I'm sure he was looking at my mother.

She returned it, I suppose, because I never saw it again. And somewhere in Los Angeles, some other girl would stare at herself in the mirror and wonder how the hell she was going to get out of this one.

One year, I asked for my own saddle. I rode every weekend at the ranch, and I was learning to jump. One of the horses at the ranch was "mine," and I'd been using an old saddle of my father's. My mother arched one eyebrow and said, "That's a very expensive gift you're asking for, young lady." I blushed and instantly regretted my request. "Well, we'll do it this way," she said after a long, excruciating pause. "The saddle will be your Christmas and birthday present. We'll get it for you for Christmas, but then you won't get anything for your birthday. Understood?"

"Yes," I said, ashamed that I'd asked at all.

When Ron wanted a stereo, he got a similar reaction—comments on the expense of such a gift. But Ron always was more confident and less apt to be shamed than I was. "What's the big deal?" he said. "You guys have money." I cringed at his boldness, but he got the stereo—not from our parents, but from Marje Everett, the wealthy race track owner who was a friend of the family. Marje also used to take Ron to the track and place bets for him; he'd come back with a stack of money, but he'd have to argue to keep it.

The more expensive gifts generally came from our parents' friends, but they were still a reflection of our parents' approval. Frank Sinatra once gave Ron a guitar; he gave me a silver and turquoise bracelet. But there were years when their friends ignored us and this always coincided with times of rebellion. If we weren't certain how our parents felt about us, we just had to wait until Christmas or a birthday, and it would be made clear.

Money became something unattractive to me. I saw it used as a measuring stick, a way to pass judgment. Poverty came to equal integrity, because I thought that wealthy people automatically became greedy and judgmental. It took me a long time to let go of that impression, which is, after all, judgmental in itself. But in my childhood, I didn't witness money and generosity as being connected to each other. That was a discovery I made later in life.

When I was in my late twenties and I went for the first manicure of my life, I noticed extra money on the table from the previous client. Embarrassed at my own igno-

rance, I asked the manicurist if it was customary to tip
for things like manicures.

"Well . . . yeah," she said, looking at me as if I were
from Mars.

"Sorry, I know that sounds stupid," I told her. "But
I didn't grow up learning that. This is all sort of new to
me."

When I was younger, I used to go with my mother
sometimes for her hair appointments and facials, and I
would watch her write out checks for the exact amount.
I never saw her add a tip, so I had no idea that it was
customary to do that.

I can chart the times I was getting along with my
parents versus the times I was shunned by the material
things that came my way. During one of the times we
were getting along, Betty Wilson, a close friend of my
mother's, gave me a dining-room table. Marion Jorgensen, whose husband backed my father financially,
gave me a couch. Mary Jane Wick, whose husband
Charles later became head of the International Communication Agency, gave me a beautiful set of white
eyelet bed linens. This was just before the 1980 election,
when I was keeping my political opinions relatively
quiet, when I was giving interviews in which I presented
the Reagan family as tolerant, close, and supportive—
in short, when I was lying. I was rewarded for dishonesty, for sweeping the truth under the rug and
creating a fantasy. It felt like blood money to me, and
I hated myself for it.

Conversely, the times I have struggled most to make
ends meet were the times I was being the most honest.
There were no material rewards for being politically
outspoken or for being frank and telling my parents,
"We've never been a close family." The only reward
was that I could live with myself. Selling things at pawnshops to get by was just the cost of telling the truth.

Since 1985, I've been able to make a living as a writer,
although at times it's still been a roller-coaster ride. The
idea that I could make a living at being honest and true

to myself was the exact opposite of what I'd come to accept. There was another guideline in my family regarding money. To my parents, children should be fed, clothed, educated and supported as long as they're dependents. Once that status changes, my parents believe their obligation ends. My father told us repeatedly how he worked as a lifeguard, washed dishes, made his own way, came up from poverty. My mother talked about working as a salesgirl at Marshall Field's.

I used to think that, as image-conscious as my parents were, they would be embarrassed if the media ever uncovered the fact that I was usually scraping for money—taking odd jobs, selling things. Or that Ron had a beat-up car that was always running close to empty because he didn't have gas money. But now I see that I was projecting my embarrassment onto them. I would sell things at the sleaziest pawnshops I could find because I knew they wouldn't ask for an I.D. and I could use a fake name. I thought I was protecting my parents, but now I realize it wouldn't have bothered them.

My parents have very puritan ethics when it comes to money, and they are comfortable with those ethics. If one of their kids is having trouble getting by—well, this builds character. This was how they did it in the Great Depression.

I've decided, at this point in my life, that people's attitudes about money are lodged in the marrow of their bones, and the attitudes never really change. I will probably always have to work at equating money with honesty. And my parents will probably always view money as a measuring stick, and as a line of demarcation between youth and adulthood. If I'd figured that out earlier, I could have gone to better pawnshops.

CHAPTER 8

· · · · · · · · · · · · · · · ·

IN 1963, TWO important people in my life died: Dick Powell and President Kennedy.

Dick Powell died in January, and in a pattern that had become familiar to me, June Allyson, Richard, and Pam vanished from our lives. I saw Richard at school, but that was all.

I remember Richard Powell's face when he finally returned to school after his father's death. I'll always remember it because I learned more about death that day than I ever have since. I looked at Richard's eyes and I knew he had retreated, pulled himself in. I saw more sadness than if there had been tears. I knew where the tears were—locked away in his soul.

"I'm sorry," I said to him in math class. I was sitting by him and felt that I should say something. We had grown up together and I felt the loss, too.

"Thanks," he answered. But his eyes told me words were foolish and shouldn't even be attempted. So I was quiet with him, because he was hiding somewhere to heal, and I sensed he shouldn't be disturbed.

Then, on November 22, 1963, we were called out of classes and told to stand around the green field where we gathered each morning to pledge allegiance to the flag. Young, confused faces watched as the flag was lowered to half-mast and the principal announced that President Kennedy had been shot in Dallas. School was cancelled for the rest of the day, and we were told that our parents had been notified to come pick us up.

While we waited, we milled aimlessly around, trying to understand, trying to make sense of a tragedy that had no sense to it. I remember the afternoon as having a dream-like quality, slow and slightly unreal. A photograph taken with the wrong lens.

There are things that stand out, though, stark and brittle. A boy who remembered my parents' diatribe against Kennedy when he was running against Nixon looked at me with knife-blade eyes and said, "Well, your parents will probably be happy."

"They will not!" I shouted back. But I wondered. I was nervous.

I remember my mother's face when she came to get me; I remember where I was standing—in the assembly hall. I saw her walk in and I thought, "Please be crying. Please be sad." But there were no tears on her face, no trace of weeping that had subsided or been brought under control.

We walked to the car and my eyes were red and swollen, my mouth salty with the taste of tears. I wished desperately for my mother's face to soften, to crumble—to share in the anguish that was all around us.

When the car doors closed around us and the sound of my crying was magnified by the small space we now shared, she turned to me and said, "All right, Patti. I think that's enough now."

During the ride home, I pressed my face against the window and tried to swallow my tears before they fell down my face. That night after dinner, my parents and I were in the den, watching Jackie Kennedy walk out of the plane, blood-spattered and numb. I'd seen it several times by then, but I was still mesmerized, stunned, unable to avert my eyes.

"Couldn't she have changed her suit?" my father asked suddenly. "There's blood all over it."

I turned and looked at him, astounded by the question.

"Well, honey, her husband was just killed," my

mother answered patiently, matter-of-factly, as if she were saying, "The pool man is here."

There have been many times when I've heard her remind him of a reality which he couldn't possibly have forgotten, and I've found myself doing the same thing at times. I don't think this is a matter of memory or age. I suspect this dates back to having been a boy with an alcoholic father who learned how to divorce himself from grief. The grief of an entire country was definitely not something my father was willing to deal with.

Not only did I not see anguish on my parents' faces in the days following the assassination, they didn't cancel a cocktail party that had been scheduled for a couple of weeks.

"You're not going to have it now, are you?" I asked my mother.

"Of course. Don't be silly."

"But—"

"Patti, stop being so dramatic," she snapped.

I sat in the playroom as guests were arriving, heard some familiar voices—Robert and Ursula Taylor, Alfred and Betsy Bloomingdale, the Tuttles. But I felt sick to my stomach, and moved into my own bedroom where I closed the door and let the sounds fade to a blend of laughter and voices overlapping.

When I went back to school, my classmates talked about how upset their parents were.

"My mother couldn't even eat," one girl said.

"Yeah—my father cried. I've never seen him cry before," someone else chimed in.

Ashamed, I invented the lie that I desperately wanted to be true.

"My mother cried all afternoon," I said. "My father went in to comfort her and they both started crying."

That night, I lay in my room in the dark and asked God to forgive me for the lie I had told. "Maybe they cried when I wasn't looking," I suggested. "Maybe I didn't really lie."

When my parents were in the White House, my

mother mentioned an exchange of letters between her
and Jacqueline Onassis; she spoke warmly of her, ad-
miringly even. My father quoted John Kennedy in a
couple of speeches. And something cold would go
through me. I'd think, "Don't you remember? Don't
you remember that day? That whole week? The cocktail
party?"

Things were increasingly political in our house at this
time. My father formally changed political parties. That
was when I first started hearing his explanation that "I
didn't leave the Democrats, they left me." The rhetoric
about socialism and the demise of democracy as we
know it was now focused on Lyndon Johnson who,
from what I was hearing around the dinner table, was
primarily guilty of helping too many poor people.

I began seeing more of the people who would later be
dubbed "The Kitchen Cabinet." Holmes Tuttle came
up to the house more often; the Bloomingdales were
more frequent visitors, as were Betty and William Wilson, whom my father later appointed ambassador to
Italy. Justin Dart, who owned the Rexall drugstore
chain, was a name I heard more frequently, but whom
I rarely saw.

By that time, my father had a job on "Death Valley
Days." The job was similar to that on General Electric
Theater—he introduced the weekly show, did commercials for Borax (one of which I did with him), and acted
in some of the segments. But it was more obvious than
ever that this was a day job, not a passion. Politics was
his passion, and it was becoming stronger all the time.

Guns and politics. In my mind, they always seemed
to be connected. I thought of Lincoln and Kennedy and
the gun my father kept in his closet.

He said there were people who had always opposed
his politics, going all the way back to his days as president of the Screen Actors Guild. He said he'd received
threats, letters, anonymous telegrams.

"What did they say?" I asked.

"They threatened my life. For a while I wore a gun in a shoulder holster whenever I went out. But that was years ago. There are just people around who don't want to hear what's happening to this country."

The gun was on the third shelf in a high cabinet that was on the wall above the built-in drawers. My father's shirts were neatly stacked on the first shelf, and sweaters were on the second. There was probably something else on the third shelf, but all I saw was the gun, in a box with bullets beside it.

"Do you remember what you told me when your father was running for president?" a friend named Jamie asked me years later. It was a few months after my father had been shot.

We were in my tiny Santa Monica bungalow, sitting at my piano. He had just played me a song he had written.

"No. What?"

"You said you were afraid that if he became president, he'd be shot. Don't you remember?"

"I'm not sure," I said, but of course I remembered all too well.

CHAPTER 9

. . . .

SOMETIME AROUND THE age of eleven, I became aware of the opposite sex. James Arness moved onto our street. I was infatuated with him, until I saw his son Rolf. Rolf was tall, lanky, with dark hair and a way of walking that suggested he had a monopoly on coolness. He rode a skateboard. I decided I was in love and immediately took up skateboarding, practicing in the driveway until I thought I was accomplished enough to make an impression upon him.

I also liked a boy at school named Peter, although not as much as I liked Rolf. Peter used to call me sometimes in the evenings, and this was when I first discovered my mother's predilection for listening in on phone calls. I would invariably hear her pick up the extension phone, hear breathing on the line.

"I have to go now," I'd say abruptly to this boy who was probably baffled by my quicksilver mood change.

I would march in to my mother. "Why were you listening in on my phone call?"

"I did no such thing."

"Yes, you did!"

"No, I didn't!"

My father would intervene and tell me to stop making things up, stop being so dramatic. "Stop accusing your mother."

I thought about Rolf almost all the time, when I wasn't thinking about Paul McCartney, whose pictures were taped on my closet doors. Actually, any one of the

Beatles could make me go giddy, but Paul was the one I dreamed about. I had other pictures of him I kept in a drawer; at night I took them out and looked at them under the covers with a flashlight. I imagined kissing him, whenever I wasn't imagining kissing Rolf. I was starting to imagine kissing in general—almost anyone could fit into the picture.

Obsessed as I was with all these new feelings inside of me, I didn't care much about the political rumblings in our house, the jokes-that-weren't-really jokes about my father running for office someday. I didn't care that my mother always acted as if we were about to be destitute at any moment, even though our life-style belied that. I didn't care about Communists who, if I believed the talk at the dinner table, were a major threat. And I didn't care that I was failing math. I did, however, care about my math teacher, Mr. Newland, who I, at times, also imagined kissing.

I had no one to talk to about these new feelings. I had pals at school, but no close friends; I kept to myself most of the time. And this was definitely *not* something I could discuss with my mother.

I decided to write a letter. But I had no one to write to, so I left the salutation blank and just plunged ahead. I wrote about liking the boy down the street, daydreaming about him, wondering what it would be like to kiss him. I said that I didn't think he liked me, or ever would, because I was too tall, wasn't pretty enough, and wasn't good at talking to other people. For two pages, I detailed my insecurities, my loneliness, and the more I wrote, the more I found solace in the geography of words. It became unimportant that the letter would never be sent. But still, it seemed foolish to have a letter that began Dear—.

I completed it one night when I was sitting at the desk in the playroom, supposedly doing my homework. I'd seen the Dear Abby column in the newspaper and thought that sounded as good as anything else. "Abby" was the final touch on my never-to-be-sent letter. I slid

it in my notebook and went to the bathroom to brush
my teeth.

When I came out, my mother was standing by the
desk, reading the letter.

"What is this?" she demanded.

"Why did you go through my things?"

"I asked you a question."

"It's something of mine. It's private." I wished that
my anger would hurt her, but I knew it couldn't.

"You're writing to Dear Abby? You're writing to a
stranger?"

"No—I wasn't going to send it. It's for me." I moved
closer to my mother, reached for the pages. "Can I have
my letter back, please?"

"No, you may not. I'm not going to have this kind of
thing going on in my house." And she turned and
walked out with my letter.

That was how I learned to hide my words. But it was
a lesson that would be repeated. A couple of years later,
I began writing poetry and short prose pieces. My writing was dark; it frequently dealt with death, and revealed feelings of isolation and loneliness.

On one occasion, my mother confronted me with a
poem she had found while I was at school. She said she
had come across it while she was putting away my clean
clothes, but the poem had been in my desk drawer. I still
remember it; it was about my wish to live out my entire
life alone, by the sea somewhere, not talking to anyone,
because other people only cause pain. It described the
night's darkness and death as comforts. It was definitely
pessimistic, particularly for a young adolescent.

"This is your goal in life?" my mother asked, holding
the poem out to me, just beyond my reach.

"Could I have that back, please?" I asked.

"No, you may not. If this is how you want to live
your life—thinking about death, and being all alone—
then you'll just have to wait until you're on your own.
As long as you're under this roof, you will be a part of
this family. Is that understood?"

I didn't answer her. I stared at the page, knowing I wouldn't see it again, and I didn't.

Another time, my mother came into my room while I was writing. I quickly covered the paper with my arm.

"What are you writing?" she asked, moving in behind me, looking over my shoulder.

"Nothing."

"Let me see it."

"No."

There was a long moment of silent staring—a standoff—but because I was sure she would reach for the paper, I tore it into little pieces in front of her. I had already developed the habit of memorizing what I wrote as I was writing, so I knew I could re-create it.

"Nothing," I repeated, my poem spread out like confetti on the desk.

I found, over time, places to hide my writing—inside suitcases that were kept in high cabinets, underneath drawer linings.

Now I can understand the insecurity that led my mother to search through her child's belongings, to destroy writings. I couldn't possibly feel that then—I only felt violated. But now I see the desperation behind it. My mother is a woman who needs to control everything around her. Yet, inside, she doubts her ability to do so. I can still envision my mother opening drawers and closets, thumbing through papers, and it looks incredibly sad to me. Had she been more secure herself, she might have been willing to let me mature and keep all those adolescent secrets that seemed so important.

By the age of eleven, I was tall, I had breasts, and I knew that any day I would start my period. My mother had explained menstruation to me; I don't remember the words, but I do remember being frightened of this imminent event. I started to dread going to the bathroom. I was waiting for blood and was relieved every time I didn't see it.

One afternoon, I came home from school with the same trepidation I usually had when entering our house. I never knew what I would be walking into, who my mother would be. I went into the bathroom and locked the door. I can still see the afternoon light slanting across the white bathroom wall and the stain of blood on my underwear. I resolved to conceal this from my mother for as long as I could. She had put a box of Kotex under the sink, but it was already opened so I didn't think she would notice if I used some of them. But for two months, I designed an elaborate plan to avoid discovery.

Several times, while my mother was gone for the day, I walked from my parents' house to Brentwood Country Market to buy Kotex, and hid the boxes in my room. It was a five-mile walk, round-trip. I carried the Kotex boxes out to the trash cans so my mother wouldn't find them in the wastebasket. I threw out underwear if it was stained. At school, I avoided taking a shower after gym class so no teacher could see and report to my mother.

But, like most criminals, I got careless. I forgot to hide a piece of underwear stained with a spot of blood. My mother came into the room with the evidence in her hand.

"What is this?" she demanded.

"I don't know," I answered in a small voice.

"Come with me." My mother turned, walked out of the room and into the bathroom. My body followed, but my mind ran out of the house, down a long road to another city.

I was being locked in the bathroom with my mother again. I commanded myself to stop trembling and hold my ground.

"When did you get your period?" she asked.

"A few days ago," I lied.

"And you weren't going to tell me?" Her voice was getting louder, more shrill.

"I guess I was—I don't know."

She lifted the hem of my school uniform and looked at me, the bulge of Kotex between my legs—proof of my defection from childhood into the enemy ranks of women.

"I do not like lying," she said, dropping the hem of my dress.

"I didn't lie."

"You didn't tell me about this," she shouted. "Don't split hairs with me."

"I'm not splitting hairs," I answered defiantly, not really sure what splitting hairs meant.

"You cannot tell the truth, can you? You have to lie about everything!" My mother's voice resounded in the bathroom.

I didn't answer her because the answer would have been, "Of course I have to lie about everything."

Her hand drew back and slapped my face. Then, she turned and walked out, leaving me listening to the fluorescent hum of the bathroom light. I stared at my face, the mark on my cheek. I sat down on the floor and waited for it to fade—I knew by that time how long it took.

When I walked out of the bathroom, my brother and his nanny, a Scottish woman named Myra, were in the playroom. I knew they had heard everything. But Myra averted her eyes and Ron became more absorbed in his toys. Everyone in our house had selective vision and hearing, even my six-year-old brother. It's a survival technique and can be learned at a young age.

There were only two people on the battlefield—me and my mother. Everyone else had run for higher ground.

That night at dinner, my mother said to my father, "Patti has started her period."

I heard the sharp edge beneath her words, caught her eyes as they glared at me.

My father nodded and said, "Oh," but I saw him move even farther away from me. Now there was embarrassment between us, as well as distance. Instinctively, my mother knew my father would be uncomfortable with my new womanhood, and that would give him more reason to scurry away from his daughter.

I knew the game that was being played; I had mapped out my mother's strategy. Instead of fostering close-ness, she encouraged distance at every turn.

I used to time how long it took her to come in and separate Ron and me when we were playing or just talking. I think our time together peaked out at five minutes.

If I had harbored any dreams of growing closer to my mother as I grew into a young woman, I would have been deeply disappointed. If anything, seeing me mature only fueled her anger. Afternoons were becoming predictable. There was almost always a fight, a scene in front of my bedroom window, a slap across my face. My father would come home at the end of each day, either from the ranch or from working on "Death Valley Days," and my mother would take him into their bedroom and close the door. The low tremor of their voices would leak through the walls, and I knew they were talking about me. All I could do was wait. After a while, there were my father's footsteps and his sad presence in my room.

One afternoon, the argument started as soon as I got home from school. My mother had searched my room and found a tube of lipstick that a school friend had given me.

"What is this?" she asked.

"Someone gave it to me."

"Who?"

"I don't remember." I wasn't going to drag anyone else into this madness.

"I told you that you were not to wear lipstick," she said, moving closer to me.

"I'm not wearing it. Why did you look in my drawer?"

"I was putting away your socks."

"It wasn't in that drawer," I snapped back.

"Are you calling me a liar?" my mother asked, her voice still controlled, her eyes boring into me.

"All I said was that it wasn't in with my socks."

I knew what was coming; I watched her hand draw back as if in slow motion, and I clenched my jaw because I'd learned that it hurt less that way. I only blinked at the moment of impact.

By the time my father came home, the redness had faded from my cheek, and the story had been changed.

He still had his riding clothes on when he came into my room; I could smell hay and horse sweat. His English riding boots had stains on the inside from pressing against his horse's sides.

"Patti," he began, and his tone was so dark, even my name sounded ominous, "what is it with you? Your mother does everything she can for you and all you do is talk back to her and hurt her. She's in there crying right now. Your mother is very fragile—we can't even have an argument because she gets so hurt. All she wants is to have a daughter. She looks at friends of hers, like Mrs. Bloomingdale, and how nice a time she has with Lisa, and she doesn't understand why she can't have that with you. Now, you know you aren't allowed to have lipstick. You broke the rules."

"How do you think she found it?" I was actually asking a legitimate question—I wanted to know what he'd been told.

"You left it out and she saw it."

I said nothing, adding another lie to the ones already told by my mother, putting another secret in my pocket. That's how it works—lies get piled on top of lies.

On one of these afternoons, my father said, "You're affecting your mother's health, Patti. She can't keep weight on. She's very underweight."

"But she doesn't eat." I'd watched her at the dinner table, rearranging the food on her plate, eating little of it.

"Well, of course not," my father answered. "She's too nervous and upset to eat."

I saw clearly what was going on in our family—the strategies and the games—yet said nothing. I often protected my mother's stories with my silence. If I accepted her view of things, maybe I could win her love. I would force myself to stay quiet. Yet, at other times, I would be surly and defiant, inviting her rage. That seemed to be my expected role.

My brother played his role, too. He could make a joke out of almost anything—plug up the holes with humor—and in doing that he made everyone think that nothing was wrong. In time, Michael and Maureen found their roles and they've played them well; they've acted casual and unassuming, choosing to accept their second-class status.

We are a family of performers. Give us cameras, lights, and a national election and we can look like we all get along and are a supportive, nurturing group. But if you leave the lights on too long, something will start to show; makeup melts and wounds become visible.

CHAPTER 10

. . . .

IN 1964, I felt the earth shifting beneath us, tipping us toward the political side of the world. But then, I'd been waiting for that for years. It all revolved around Barry Goldwater's campaign for president. Suddenly, my father's station wagon and my mother's Lincoln Continental had Goldwater stickers on the bumpers; I think even the jeep at the ranch had one.

I had met Barry Goldwater a few times in Phoenix when we visited my grandparents; I used to play with his granddaughter, Sally. But he wasn't a frequently talked-about person in our house until 1964. With fascination, I watched the television commercial with the little girl pulling petals off a daisy and a mushroom cloud consuming her. It was starting to sink in that the wrong person in office could actually destroy the world. Was Goldwater the right person? I wasn't sure.

But I kept quiet, swallowed my questions. Because my father had finally become the spokesperson he'd wanted to be—the voice of conservatism.

The other new word swirling around our house that year was Vietnam. I'd never heard of it before then, and one day when my parents weren't home I looked it up in the atlas to see where it was. I didn't want my father to know I was at all interested in Vietnam because then I'd have to listen to another lecture about the hordes of Communists gathering on the warpath, galloping toward world domination.

I've tried to analyze why I didn't buy into my father's

philosophy, why I wrote it off as alarmist, and the only thing I could come up with is that it sounded too far-fetched. But I knew that a lot of people didn't see it that way and my father was the one they were lining up behind to lead the rebel yell.

In October of 1964, he gave his now-famous campaign speech for Barry Goldwater. It was taped in Phoenix, Arizona, in front of a "canned audience." I was probably the only one in that audience who was not thrilled to be there.

I remember my father molding the crowd with his words—quieting them at moments, inciting them at others, pulling tears from them as a finale. He talked about patriotism and the evils of big government. The speech evoked different emotions in me.

"We can preserve for our children this, the last best hope of man on earth," I listened to him say, "or we can sentence them to take the first step into a thousand years of darkness. If we fail, at least let our children, and our children's children, say of us, we justified our brief moment here. We did all that could be done."

People around me were clapping and crying, blowing their noses and wiping their eyes. My mother's face was streaked with tears. I was completely confused. Was my father suggesting that the only hope for man on earth was Barry Goldwater? And where did the thousand years of darkness come in?

The other thing that confused me was my father's emphasis on children. I was frequently tempted to remind him that I was his child; it seemed sometimes as if it slipped his mind. Often, I'd come into a room and he'd look up from his notecards as though he wasn't sure who I was. Ron would race up to him, small and brimming with a child's enthusiasm, and I'd see the same bewildered look in my father's eyes, like he had to remind himself who Ron was. Michael, at this point, was at Judson, a boarding school in Arizona, and was hardly ever mentioned anymore. Out of sight, out of mind. Maureen had remarried, this time to a man named David Sills, a Marine. But they weren't mentioned very much, either, except on the few occasions they came to the house. On these visits, politics were avidly discussed—it was always Maureen's line of communication with our father. But I sometimes felt like reminding him that Maureen was his daughter, too, not just someone with similar political philosophies.

The night of the Goldwater speech, I lay awake long after midnight, playing back the tears and emotions that had surrounded me in the hall, wondering why I couldn't feel the same things. All I felt was dread—for two reasons. One was selfish: My life was drifting in a direction chosen by someone else, and I had no power to alter its course. The second reason was my father's politics had started to frighten me. The dinner-table discussion regarding Vietnam revolved around hostility toward this tiny country which I had, before this time, never even heard of. I found myself put off, and in fact frightened, by the talk of war and the apparent ease with which my father discussed this possibility. Lyndon Johnson won the election and the world did not plunge into darkness, but my parents kept the Goldwater bumper stickers on their cars just in case.

Goldwater may have lost, but my father won. Almost overnight, he emerged as a viable political candidate, although this was probably just my impression at the time. In hindsight, I think it was a gradual emergence. My mother said that letters were pouring in, urging my father to run for governor of California. Holmes Tuttle and a few other people formed a group called Friends of Reagan which was explained to me as an exploratory group to determine if there was enough support for my father. The group hired the political consulting firm Spencer/Roberts. I didn't sense, though, that there was any hesitancy about my father's plans—I could already envision the new bumper stickers.

Acting seemed, more than ever, a way to pay the bills as opposed to a career of choice. Sometime in 1964 (during the Goldwater campaign, I believe) my father made the last film of his acting career. It was called *The Killers,* co-starring Angie Dickinson and Lee Marvin, and my father said he did it just for the money. When it came out, I was forbidden to see it.

"Everyone dies in it," my mother explained.

In the midst of all this political activity, there was a domestic crisis of sorts. My parents had decided to send me to boarding school. In retrospect, I don't blame them. I'm sure having me miles away as I entered my teens seemed like the perfect way to ease family tensions.

According to my father, the decision to send me to a boarding school was prompted by a psychiatrist who was consulted by the headmistress of my grade school. The way I remember it, boarding school came about by a process of elimination, but the psychiatrist story is an interesting one because, starting at about age ten, the thing I wanted most for Christmas was a session with a psychiatrist. I was always turned down.

"Tony Curtis used to see his psychiatrist six days a week," my father would say, in answer to my request.

"So?" That sounded great to me—six days a week with someone who could help me figure out what was going on in our house.

"Well, he consulted him on everything."

"So?"

"Even his choices of leading ladies."

"So?"

A sigh of exasperation. "You're not going to see a psychiatrist, Patti."

But, according to my parents' version of things, *they* did. Or they at least had a phone conversation with one—details on this are a bit sketchy.

"She said going away might have a positive effect on your attitude, your hostility," my father told me not too long ago.

Well, yes, I could have told them that. I'd have less to be hostile about.

At my next school, I was to repeat the eighth grade. The theory was that my skipping the third grade and being younger than my classmates accounted for my attitude. I was clearly angry, but this was 1965 and teachers didn't ask students about their home environments, or about what could be causing their hostility. They just assumed the age difference between me and my classmates was to blame.

Before the boarding school issue emerged, I wasn't really that unhappy about repeating eighth grade, where my old school ended. It meant I couldn't go to either of the two day schools I dreaded being sent to—Westlake and Marlborough. These were two prestigious girls' schools in Los Angeles; the students wore navy blue uniforms and bobby socks and spent their summers at the Beach Club. I couldn't imagine spending my high school years surrounded by only girls, and I couldn't imagine spending them in uniform.

But since I had the stigma of repeating a grade, my mother told me that neither Westlake nor Marlborough would want me. I was campaigning hard for public school.

"A public school is integrated," I said. Whether it was early social conscience or rebellion, that was how I felt. It didn't seem right to be in a school with only white kids—the world wasn't like that.

"You will absolutely not go to a public school," was my mother's response. "We think it would be best if you go to a boarding school."

"I don't want to go to a girls' school," I said.

There was one close call. My mother drove me to Bishop Girls School in La Jolla to take an entrance exam and be introduced to the principal.

The grounds of Bishop were beautiful—rolling green lawns, tall pines, and colorful flower beds. If it weren't for the fact that there wasn't a boy within miles and the girls wore uniforms, I could have been very happy there.

I was led, with about a dozen other girls, to a classroom for our exams. The first test was a series of essay questions about why we wanted to go to Bishop and what we thought we could contribute to the special environment. The teacher said our answers would remain confidential. "Great!" I thought.

"I don't want to come to Bishop," I wrote. "I want to be in a school with boys, and Negroes, and Oriental people. I don't like uniforms and I don't like girls very much, either."

The next test consisted of multiple-choice questions in four categories: history, science, math, and English. The questions were easy, but this was not a test I wanted to pass. I wanted to make it clear that I was not Bishop School material. I figured if I answered everything wrong, they would either get suspicious or think I had the I.Q. of a frog, so I answered some wrong and some right. I thought I had the percentages down pretty well on that test; they'd think I was just stupid enough not to be considered for admission.

I turned out to be half correct. I was not considered for admission, but they knew I'd faked the test. A week after our visit, my mother came into my room with a letter in her hand.

"Well, I hope you're proud of yourself," she said.

I waited to hear what exactly I was supposed to be proud of.

"You deliberately failed the entrance test at Bishop," she continued.

"No, I didn't," I lied.

"Really? Well, if this is an accurate representation of your intelligence, then you should be in an institution. An idiot could have passed this test."

Finally, somehow, I ended up at Orme School, a coeducational boarding school in the Arizona desert that was also a functioning cattle ranch. I'd gone to summer camp there one year, although the only thing I remembered about it was that every night, thunderstorms rumbled across the desert and by dawn, there wouldn't be a trace of them. I had liked my summer at Orme and I readily agreed that this would be a great school for me; luckily, they had an eighth grade.

The summer before I went away was unusually calm, as though a truce had been declared. We took a week's vacation and stayed at the Hotel Del Coronado, in San Diego, as we had for several summers. I went rafting and bodysurfing with my father, and my mother and I kept a safe distance, which would have been interpreted as a type of closeness by the untrained eye. There was another family who stayed at Coronado in the summers—the Shoenbergs. They were from the South, although I can't remember which state now, and they had four daughters; the youngest, Linda, was around my age.

It could have been the presence of another family that eased the tensions in ours, but in my mind, I always give credit to the ocean. The easiest times in my family's history have taken place by the sea. In later summers, we would rent a house on Trancas Beach, north of Malibu, and I remember the sound of waves and tides filling the spaces between us, not the sound of harsh words and anger.

That summer in Coronado, my brother was seven and was still restricted to the shallow water. I went into the deeper water with my father and learned from him the pattern of waves, and how to position myself so the wave would pick me up and carry me to shore.

"Swim!" he'd yell out to me, with blue water rising between us. And I'd swim as hard as I could to catch the wave, to get a good ride, to not fall off the back or be somersaulted under, to make a perfect landing on shore. To get his approval.

In the evenings, we had dinner with the Shoenbergs in the opulent, chandeliered dining room of the Del Coronado. I was allowed soft drinks and sugary desserts, which were forbidden to me at home.

When we got back from Coronado that year, I set about preparing myself for boarding school. After years of fighting my mother over her wardrobe choices for me, I had definite ideas about how I wanted to look. If Elvira had been around then, she would probably have been my model.

My mother started cleaning out her own closet and bringing me clothes that she wanted me to take to school. They were hardly my style, but I was tired of arguing and she wouldn't be there to make me wear them anyway.

There were no uniforms at Orme; the recommended daily attire was jeans, but girls were required to wear dresses on Sunday nights for dinner and the chapel service. Sunday nights were what my mother was trying to provide for. As usual, I had another idea.

Night after night, I sat under my covers with a flashlight, a needle and thread, and the skirts my mother had handed down to me. I tightened them, shortened them, made them into something only a girl bent on looking cheap would wear. It took weeks of diligence and patience, probably did irreversible damage to my eyesight, but I was determined. When you've been dressed like Little Bo Peep for years, the slut look is very desirable.

In September, I boarded a plane to Phoenix, Arizona. My grandparents met me at the airport for the long drive to my new school. Orme is seventy miles north of Phoenix, off the Black Canyon Highway which cuts through wide miles of desert. As you drive north, you drive into seasons—snow in winter, and in autumn, a bronzing of the shrubs and trees. At the turnoff for Flagstaff, there is another sign, a small wooden one that reads "Orme Ranch," with an arrow pointing to an unpaved road.

In the cold light of that fall afternoon, we drove through the wooden gates of what would be my home for the next five years.

CHAPTER 11

. . . .

I ENTERED ORME School as Patti Reagan, daughter of an actor. But I knew that I would finish out my high school years as the daughter of the governor of California. The atmosphere in my home, just prior to my departure for Arizona, was charged with expectations. My father was saying, "Well, I just haven't decided." But I didn't believe him, because it was obvious that everyone else had decided.

I was at school in the same state as Michael, yet I wasn't encouraged to call or contact him. I put this together from a conversation I'd overheard just days before I left for Orme. My mother was talking to Stu Spencer, one of my father's political consultants; I don't know where my father was, but this conversation was taking place in his absence. My mother was stressing the importance of de-emphasizing the fact that my father was divorced.

"He has *two* children," she said. "It won't be so much of a problem with Michael—he's away at school. But Maureen will want to get involved with the campaign. We just can't have that."

Stu Spencer agreed that divorce was not a good thing to have on one's political resumé.

So I dutifully kept my distance from the brother my mother was trying to hide. In fact, I tried to put my whole family behind me and pretend they didn't exist. It helped to be away from the perfect living room and manicured life. Orme seemed, at last, like the real

world. Anyone entering Orme came through gates into
a barnyard, with rail fencing around it, as though
horses should be standing there, pawing at the ground.
Often, they were.

"Girls Camp" bordered the barnyard—a three-sided
square of wooden buildings. On the other side of the
barnyard was a large dining room, an infirmary, and
some offices, and at the far end was a barn, which was
sometimes used as an assembly hall, a place for school
dances, a theater, or a study hall. "Boys Camp"
couldn't be seen from the barnyard because it was
about a quarter of a mile away, the logic being that
distance would deter boys and girls from sneaking into
each other's rooms, which was no logic at all because
this was high school and what was a quarter of a mile
when adolescent hormones were kicking into overdrive?
Up on one hill was a chapel, on another hill was a horse
corral, and beyond that, a hay barn. Because it was also
a functioning cattle ranch, there was a milk barn, and
cattle roamed the wide desert acreage.

Sometimes we were late for classes if cattle were
crossing the barnyard, which was not an excuse that
would have ever worked in a city school. But it was
normal to us. For required sports, we could take horseback riding if we wanted.

The rooms in the girls' camp were actually two rooms
connected by a bathroom and a large walk-in closet. So
even though there were doors between the rooms, there
were, in effect, eight girls living together. To me, this
was like moving into a lion's den; girls made me nervous, I didn't think I measured up. I felt unattractive,
insecure.

And then I noticed patterns emerging, things I'd
adopted from my mother without knowing it. I found
myself screaming at one of my roommates one day—
shrieking until my throat burned. My mother's voice,
my mother's rage—exploding out of me—and it scared
the hell out of me. Once, a boy said something that
offended me and I slapped his face and watched as my

handprint reddened on his cheek. He slapped me back. I never did that again, but I never forgot it, either.

By the time my mother and father visited at the November "Parents' Day," my hair had grown longer, and I'd perfected the technique of drawing thick, black lines around my eyes and applying pale, almost white lipstick. Jeans that I had tightened under the covers with a needle and thread were, by that time, even tighter because I'd gained weight. With no one to watch over me, I'd started eating candy and cakes and ice cream: forbidden foods, which actually didn't even taste that good to me. It was the forbidden part I couldn't resist. I'd also gotten my ears pierced—a cork and needle operation four of us did to each other in the closet one night.

So I looked a little different when I went out to the barnyard to greet my parents. I remember it was one of those blue and gold fall days when the desert wind was just cold enough to make you check the sky for storm clouds. My mother's eyes when she saw me were colder than the wind. My father didn't appear to notice anything different. Both reactions bothered me.

Students were milling around the barnyard, introducing their parents to teachers who were hovering nervously, hoping to make a good impression. This was a good distraction for about twenty minutes, as I squired my parents around, but then the conversation turned to my appearance.

I can't remember the exact dialogue, but it was along the lines of: My mother was embarrassed to be seen with me, with my hair falling over one eye, Veronica Lake style, my overdone makeup, and my tight jeans. And, of course, my attitude—"chip on her shoulder a mile high"—an observation directed to my father as if I weren't there. My father was baffled, uncomfortable with dissension in the ranks.

The final blow came when I pulled my hair back, exposed my newly pierced ears, and said, "Since you're getting upset, you might as well get upset about this, too. I pierced my ears."

My mother seethed, I stood defiant, and my father said, "Well, before you get your appendix out, do you think you could let us know in advance?" My father always makes jokes when he feels there is tension in the air. Sometimes, it would help, but not then. My mother turned on her heels, announced that she was going to sit in the car for the rest of the afternoon, and walked off. That left my father and me standing there awkwardly, facing each other, close but miles apart. I realized then that we only knew how to relate to each other by bouncing off my mother. Ours is a ricochet relationship. In some way, she has to be there or we've lost each other.

I remember, on that day, that the minutes stretched out interminably. With people all around us, we stood there floundering—two lonely souls with nothing to say.

My father has a scar on his thumb—a dent, really, on the tip, which he says came from a childhood accident when he and his brother were playing with an ax. I've always loved that scar; when I was a child, I used to touch it, although I don't think my father noticed. It made him seem more real to me; it was something tangible, something that said, "I was a kid once, too. I got in trouble, almost lost my thumb." Because there are so many incongruities in my father. Even his hands—they're pale, soft, not rugged at all, not as large as you might expect. But then there's that scar.

And that's what I remember most about standing in the barnyard with him on Parents' Day, with my mother sitting a hundred yards away in the car, windows rolled up on her anger. His hand went up to his face, to smooth his hair or something, and I stared at it until he became a little more real to me. A kid once—"almost lost my thumb."

"Patti, you can't let your mother sit in the car all day," he said finally.

"Well, what am I supposed to do?"

He hesitated, not sure for a second exactly what the best course of action was. "Well, I think you should go apologize."

I did, but only because I preferred the engagement of battle to the disengagement of someone I wanted to be close to, but couldn't find. The scar on his thumb has told me more than anything else about my father.

When I went home for Christmas that year, I resumed my habit of searching my mother's medicine cabinet. There was now a bottle of Librium and a bottle of Valium. The more I checked, I realized that Valium was phasing out Miltown. The tiny Valium pills were disappearing the fastest, and she still put Seconal by her glass of water at night.

During that holiday, I learned one of the reasons for the hesitancy regarding my father's campaign for governor.

"As soon as he declares his candidacy, he can't work on 'Death Valley Days,'" my mother complained. "Because of the equal-time laws. Brown would demand the same amount of time. It's just ridiculous. How are we supposed to make a living?"

The impression I got was that then-Governor Edmund Brown was being blamed for this, even though when I pressed for more information I learned that it was a law that both candidates in a campaign have equal television time.

On Christmas Day, the visitors who stopped by the house seemed to have no doubt about my father's impending candidacy. I remember A. C. Lyles calling him "Governor." My grandfather pulled me aside, looked at me with narrow eyes, and said, "I want you to show how proud you are of your father. You back him up, do you understand me?"

I said yes, knowing I was lying again.

On January 4, 1966, a few days after I returned to Orme, my father announced his candidacy for governor of California.

By that summer, the campaign was in high gear, and I couldn't hide my displeasure—it bubbled out of me, escalating the tensions between my mother and myself.

"I think you could at least show some pride in your father," she would say frequently, and repeated this one morning as she burst into my bedroom, surprising me as I was getting dressed. I hadn't heard her coming, which was odd because I was usually in a constant state of alert, listening for her footstcps.

"Well, what do you want me to do?" I asked defensively, although I knew the answer. Ron, who was all of eight at the time, had "Reagan for Governor" bumper stickers plastered on his bedroom walls. My mother wore "Reagan for Governor" pins, even on formal dresses. She'd given out the pins to the butcher at the market, the gardener, the maid, and her hairdresser.

I was scrambling to put on my clothes, frightened at the thought of being undressed in front of my mother. Too many nights locked in the bathroom with her; too many memories.

"Do you have your period?" she asked, staring at the bulge of Kotex in my underpants.

"No," I lied, tugging my shorts on.

"Don't lie to me, young lady. I asked you a simple question."

My fingers were getting numb, they were shaking so badly, and I was fumbling to do up the buttons. When she grabbed my arm, I pulled back quickly. "Leave me alone!" I said loudly, surprised at the force of my own voice.

"Don't you talk to me like that."

"Okay, I won't. I won't talk to you at all. I'm leaving." I'd managed to get my clothes on and I walked past her, heading for the front door.

"Where do you think you're going?" my mother screamed. "You come back here this instant! Don't you dare walk away from me!"

But I did walk away—a small victory, but I did it. And when I got to the driveway, I started running. I ran to my friend Cory's house, through the front door, which was usually open, and announced, "I ran away from home."

"For good?" Cory asked.

"I don't know. I haven't figured that out yet."

I stayed with Cory all day. She had already introduced me to pot, so we smoked a joint, raided the kitchen, and got seriously into a large bowl of red Jell-O in the refrigerator. I think I ate too much of it, because I got sick and threw up in the bathroom.

By evening, I realized I had to go home. I had no money, no place to go.

My mother heard me enter the house. "Get in your room right now," she said angrily. She stayed close behind me as though she were afraid I'd bolt again.

My bedroom door slammed behind us, and she stood facing me. "Let me tell you something, young lady. Whether you like it or not, your father is running for governor of California and if the press had gotten hold of a story like you running away, it would have been terribly embarrassing to him. You just think the world revolves around you, don't you? You don't think of anyone else but yourself, do you?"

I didn't answer.

"Do you?"

"I guess not."

"You guess not? You run away from this house in the middle of a campaign? It could have been all over the papers!" Almost as an afterthought she asked, "Where did you go?"

"To the beach," I said. I think I lied sometimes just for the practice of it; I'd found it a helpful technique and I didn't want it to get rusty.

"To the beach?" she repeated. "Oh, that would have made a lovely story. The press would have a field day with that. You think the whole world should just stop for you, don't you? Everyone should just think of Patti. No regard for your father, and of course, you have no regard for me. Right?"

I hesitated. I wasn't exactly sure what I would be agreeing to if I said "Right." Sometimes I just tuned out when my mother got like this—waited for it to end— and I lost bits of her dialogue in the process.

"Right?" she said, moving in closer. I knew what was coming.

"I don't know." That was it—the magic words. She slapped my face hard and then stormed out. I went to the mirror and watched as my face grew red. It had become a ritual: The siege would end with a slap, and I'd be left alone, staring in the mirror with hard, tearless eyes.

My father came in later, and I felt my eyes change— soften with expectation.

"Patti, the press is really looking for ways to embarrass me. I thought I'd gotten used to it because of Hollywood and the picture business, but politics is much worse. Any sort of family dirt, like this running away thing . . ."

He didn't finish his sentence. My father is a master of incomplete sentences.

That evening, I wandered into the kitchen while Anne was preparing dinner.

"Hi, Patti. I'm glad to see you," she said. "I was worried."

"You were?" I hoisted myself up on the counter and took a piece of parsley off the silver platter she was garnishing.

"I was afraid you wouldn't come back. You were gone all day."

I munched on my parsley and watched Anne bustle around the kitchen, pouring water into crystal goblets, filling serving trays. "Yeah, well, I couldn't figure out where to go."

That November, I stood in the phone booth at Orme, listening to my father tell me he had just been elected governor of California. His voice was elated, confi-

dent—a voice meant to move a nation. What it moved
in me that night was fear.

Politics, slick men in dark suits who had started to
huddle around my father and talk in low, conspiratorial
voices; a family that had just turned a corner and would
never go back . . . I wanted none of it. But here it was,
a choice I had no part of, a destiny that had swept me
up in its currents and changed my life.

This is how my parents remember that night: I was
crying and said, "How could you do this to me?" They,
by their own accounts, were shocked and disappointed
by my reaction. How could I not be proud, happy,
congratulatory?

This is how *I* remember it: Tears choked my throat.
I heard sounds of laughter and talking behind my father's voice. I knew what I was supposed to say, but I
couldn't because that wasn't how I felt. Someone
walked by the phone booth, his footsteps crunching
along the gravel path, and I thought, "Lucky kid—his
life didn't change tonight." I might have said, "How
could you do this to me?" I'm not sure. It certainly
sounds like what I was thinking, but I remember more
the rush of feelings and fears, the sense of things spinning out of control.

There was another girl at Orme, Nikki Williams,
whose father had been elected governor of Arizona that
night. Someone told me that she just withdrew from
everyone and went to bed. Later, her roommates heard
her crying quietly into the night.

Christmas was different that year, although not so
different that old tensions didn't arise. There were our
usual fights, the usual finales of my mother's hand aiming for my face. No matter how our lives changed, that
was a constant. One change was that everyone except
the immediate family was calling my father "Governor." And there were meetings—suit meetings for everyone except my father, who wore whatever he
wanted.

This is when I remember first noticing the men who

would remain attached to him for years: Mike Deaver, Ed Meese, Bill Clark. What happened after a while, though, was that these men seemed to converge into one. I would see one of them talking to my father, I'd turn away and suddenly not be sure which one it was. Even when he was president, and Jim Baker melted into the equation, the same thing would happen to me. I'd see a newspaper photo or watch a soundbite on the evening news and moments later, I'd wonder, "Wait, which one was it?" There was something so similar about all of them; maybe it was the way they related to my father—warmly, almost paternally, but tentatively, as though they weren't sure who he was. So they all started wearing the same look in their eyes, like "I really like Ronald Reagan, but I'm confused. I can't figure him out."

Lyn Nofziger was different—he always stood out to me. It wasn't just that he was more rumpled than the others; he was usually in his shirtsleeves and left his jacket somewhere and forgot about a tie. But I always thought he knew things the others didn't. Significant things, like what my father was thinking, which was something I could never figure out. And Nofziger's eyes were always sad, too, as though there was some dark painful area of his life no one had ever bothered to ask about. So he just locked it away, kept it to himself. Only those things always seem to leak out through one's eyes.

I sensed my mother didn't like him as much as the more pulled-together, Brooks Brothers–suit men. She commented once that he smelled like cigars. I suppose it's possible, I don't really know, but I don't think that was the reason for her coldness toward him. I think it was that Lyn Nofziger was just different—which is what I liked about him.

When Kitty Kelley's book came out, I saw her book party in Washington, D.C., on TV. There was Lyn Nofziger, smiling gently at the reporter, side-stepping questions, those same sad eyes, that same uncomplicated manner. I thought, "That's pretty brave; he must know he won't get a Christmas card from the Reagans this year." I know there was probably something behind his attendance at the party, but he was too polite to let anyone know what it was.

Something else happened over that Christmas vacation which would have far-reaching consequences.

My mother had taken me shopping because my wardrobe by that time consisted of jeans and men's shirts. I'd manage to persuade boys who weren't that attached to their clothing to let me have them. I had nothing to trade for the shirts. Usually they just gave them to me.

"What happened to all the clothes I gave you?" my mother asked.

"I don't know."

"What do you mean, you don't know?"

"I guess they got lost in the laundry or something."

"All of them? What kind of laundry do they use there?"

"I don't know. One that loses clothes, I guess."

So we went shopping. No more birthday cake dresses, but conservative ones. We'd come back, pulled into the garage, and when I got out of the car, my mother said, "Patti, you have a fat butt."

I stopped, turned around, and faced my mother, small and slim in her perfectly coordinated outfit. She was smiling. I suddenly felt so large, so cumbersome, that I half-expected the asphalt to crack beneath my weight; I couldn't say anything.

But later, I did say something to a friend. She was a friend my mother approved of, probably because I'd met her at church one Sunday when I'd gone with my parents. Occasionally, I spent nights at her house. Shortly after my mother had commented on my weight, I sat on one of the twin beds in her room and cried.

"I'm fat," I said between sobs. "And I feel so ugly."

"You're not ugly," she said, taking my hands in hers. "My sister could help you lose weight."

"She could? How?" I'd have done anything right
then. I couldn't stand sitting at the dinner table with my
mother's eyes following every forkful of food as it went
into my mouth.

"She lost a lot of weight. She took some diet pills."

I'd seen her sister—she was slim, pretty—I couldn't
imagine that she'd ever been fat, but according to both
of them, she had been.

She didn't have any diet pills right then, but she
promised she'd get some for me. Rainbow pills—the
diet pill of the Sixties. I went through the rest of that
Christmas vacation dreaming about this magic potion.
Just knowing I would soon have it made me feel better.

The holidays ended with our trip to Sacramento for my
father's inauguration. The atmosphere was one of high
drama and upheaval. Ron was asking where he would
go to school, who his friends would be. My mother was
planning how she would divide her life between the
house in Pacific Palisades and the governor's mansion
in Sacramento. The arrangement, which remained
fairly consistent throughout my father's terms as governor, was that both my parents and Ron would come
back to the Palisades on weekends and holidays, and
during the time when the legislature was in recess. Ron
would go to school in Sacramento, and my mother
would be there during the week, unless something pressing brought her back to Los Angeles.

My father's inauguration in Sacramento was the first
time I had seen that much activity surrounding my
parents. Everyone was nervous. Cameras and crowds
were everywhere. Ron and I were often pulled along,
told to keep up. Sometimes, it just became a blur, and
I would imagine myself somewhere else, far away—like
Greenland. Other memories I have are in vivid color—
the heavy purple drapes of the governor's mansion, the
dark polished wood of the floors, the brass lamps,
the winter gray of the sky outside. I tried to absorb the
enormity of what was happening, but it was over-

whelming to me. From almost every window in the mansion, I could look down and see crowds pressed against the fence, staring in. There was a part of me that just wanted to go back to boarding school, get on a horse, and ride out into the desert.

My mother hated the governor's mansion. "Where will Ron play?" she worried. She hated the gas station across the street, the downtown traffic on all sides of the property.

The American Legion Hall was right behind the mansion, but it was a while before she noticed that, a while before she decided "orgies" were going on inside the hall. My father didn't seem at all upset about the old mansion; he'd played at gas stations and in vacant lots when he was a kid. It seemed fine to him.

By this time, most people know that my parents have made decisions based on astrology. This seems like an appropriate moment to say that I had no idea about this. I had no idea why my father was being sworn in as governor one minute after midnight.

I knew my mother was anxious to start redecorating his office. I'd been listening to her descriptions of the "horrible faded wallpaper" and the "dingy carpet" and the "god-awful furniture." So maybe the decorator was going to start work at two minutes after midnight; I didn't know. And I didn't ask.

Now I know it had to do with an astrologically propitious hour. I'd heard my parents read their horoscopes aloud at the breakfast table, but that seemed pretty innocuous to me. Occasionally, I read mine, too—usually so I can do the exact opposite of what it says. But my parents have done what the stars suggested—altered schedules, changed travel plans, stayed home, cancelled appearances.

The evening of the propitiously planned inauguration was spent at the Firehouse, a Sacramento restaurant. John Wayne, who had been invited to the inauguration, was sitting at one table, drinking cup after cup of coffee. No one had been able to find him earlier that day, and finally someone did. He was having a few drinks—a few too many, according to my mother. So people were assigned to keep a full cup of coffee in front of him at all times. The rest of the faces were familiar to me—the Bloomingdales, the Tuttles, the Jorgensens, the Deutsches. My grandparents were there, too, and my grandfather, at one point, came over to me and grabbed my arm tightly. His fingers dug into my flesh and he said, "I want you to look happy." He scared me when he got like that and I probably smiled out of terror. With his fingers bruising my arm and his face tense and angry, I'd have danced in place if he told me to.

We rode in limousines to the rotunda where the swearing-in was to take place; I remember staring out the car window at the lights of the city which looked better by night than it did by day.

After the swearing-in, everyone filed past my parents. Ron was ahead of me and when his turn came, my father picked him up, lifted him high in the air, and kissed him. The lights bounced off them and my father's eyes were watery with tears.

My grandfather, who was behind me, said, "Keep it moving, come on." His life ran on schedule; he didn't make exceptions.

Trying to avoid his grip on my arm again, I said timidly, "We're supposed to keep going."

"I don't care," my father answered, still holding Ron in the air.

Then, blinking against the hot lights, I thought I saw something that I'd never seen before, nor have I since. I thought, for the briefest of seconds, that my father really looked at Ron—focused on this small boy held high in the air as his son, the product of his sperm, the beneficiary of his genes. It was as though something dawned on him, quickly, fleetingly.

When Ron had moved on and it was my turn to stand in front of my father, I couldn't find that glimmer of recognition. Maybe it had never been there, maybe it was just a trick of the lights, or something that I wished into reality. But I'd like to think that for that brief instant, a few minutes after midnight, my father left his solitary world, looked at his child, and said, "Oh, that's who this small person is."

CHAPTER 12

. . . .

THE DIET PILLS arrived in the mail, in small matchboxes with pretty pictures on them. There were pink, blue, and green tablets, color indicating potency. My mother's comment about my weight was echoing in my ears as I counted the pills, but now I know that if she hadn't provided me with that excuse, I'd eventually have found another.

As soon as I took one of those pills and felt it kick in, felt the rush like electric currents lighting up my blood, I knew I'd found my drug. I told myself they were just for weight loss. But the truth is, I was thrilled with the way they made me feel. I was on my way to addiction.

It was the perfect drug for me. Amphetamines are like revving up an engine—they make you feel like you own the road. They chase away the sadness. Suddenly you feel on top of things: I don't need to be depressed or angry. I've got these pills to take. Life is good. I don't even have to sleep. I can work, write, get things accomplished. I'm really alive now, nothing can drag me down. I have more self-esteem, more confidence.

The panic sets in only when you think you might run out of pills.

A friend said to me once, "You mean you didn't 'Just Say No'?"

"Are you kidding?" I answered. "I said, how many do I take and how long does it last?"

My schoolwork got better, at least in those classes that I liked, because I couldn't stop writing. I couldn't stop my brain. Not even drugs could get me interested in geometry or in dissecting worms, but were I asked to write a four-page essay on the French Revolution, I would produce seven pages. I stayed up all night. Asked to read *Heart of Darkness* by the next week, I would read it overnight.

By the time I headed home for Christmas, I had punched many holes in a new belt to keep my jeans up. My hip bones jutted out. My face was sunken, and I had adhesive tape around a ring that kept falling off my finger. Even my shoes felt too big.

There was a photograph ("was" because it ended up in the trash can with the other pictures) of me sitting on the couch with Ron and my parents. I was wearing a long red dress that hung on me as though I were a coat hanger.

But no one in my family said a thing. I'd gone from being somewhat zaftig to being conspicuously anorexic, but this transformation was neither mentioned nor, apparently, noticed.

By Easter vacation, when I met my parents in Phoenix for the annual pilgrimage to my grandparents' house, I'd stopped getting my period, and there were nights when my jaw clenched so much it ached, and when I'd stare, wide-eyed and jumpy, into the darkness and hallucinate all sorts of things—strange, willowy figures, crouched animals, you name it. I never thought, "I should get off these pills." What I thought was, "Maybe I should lower the dosage."

I did and the hallucinations stopped, and I started timing the pills a little better so that I could get some sleep and my jaw would relax. But then I found another drug that fit right into my anorexia. In my mother's toiletry bag, I found diuretics—water pills—every anorexic's dream because you can lose something like a pound of water in a day and a half and then go racing to the tool chest to punch another hole in your belt.

I found them when I was following my historical pattern of counting my mother's drugs. I have this image of me methodically calculating how many tranquilizers she must be taking and clucking my tongue in judgment, as if I weren't doing the exact same thing. I probably did not do that but, metaphorically, I did. I think my mother was taking Valium at the time, so I'd count those, feel judgmental, and then steal a few diuretics while I was there.

The medical consequences of what I was doing are serious; you can die from excessive doses of the combination of drugs that I was taking. Diuretics deplete the body of minerals (especially potassium), which weakens the heart, and my poor heart was being kicked into overdrive every day with all the amphetamines I was taking. This is what, eventually, almost did me in, but it would take a while—years, in fact.

Also, on that vacation, I found that a childhood friend, a girl who lived near my grandparents, had drug connections. She could get "whites" (white-cross Methedrine, street speed).

"I had about a dozen the other night," she told me, "but we were driving along and we'd had too much to drink and they fell out the car window."

"Where?" I asked, a little crazy at the fact that perfectly good drugs were scattered over someone's front lawn, waiting for the lawnmower. "Do you remember? I mean, do you remember exactly where you were when they flew out the window?"

So that night, in the warm Arizona dark, two girls who had made up excuses to get out of their respective houses were walking up and down a quiet neighborhood street with flashlights, combing the ground for drugs. We never found them, but it gives a good indication of how desperate you can get when drugs are driving your life.

By the time I got home that summer, I hadn't had my period in about six months. In a rare moment of sanity, I decided it might be a good idea to find out why. Of course, it never occurred to me that it could have something to do with the fact that I looked like a skeleton with my skin stretched over the bones.

"I think maybe I need to go for a checkup," I told my mother.

"Why? What's wrong?"

"Well, I—uh—haven't gotten my period for a long time."

I read the thoughts that raced through her mind. Or rather, one thought—pregnancy. I was still a virgin, but I knew she probably doubted that.

"For how long?" she asked.

"Six months." Which ended the pregnancy concern, because nothing could have been growing in my emaciated body for six months.

There was something unusual about that summer— my mother and I had this nice sort of easiness between us. At the time, I thought it was because I had removed myself as a threat, at least in the realm of sexual rivalry, by starving and drugging myself into a completely unsexual-looking person. I'd starved away my breasts, my hips; from the back, I could have been a boy. But I think there was something else going on in this warm summer air that seemed to hang over my mother and me—no storms, no hard winds, just the lull of smiles and kind words. I think that because I was rail-thin, I no longer stirred up memories of a time when my mother was unhappy with her own appearance. The year before, when she called me fat, her anger wasn't aimed at only me. Memories came back up for her, old insecurities. Anger was her first response to this unwelcome tide.

By that summer, I was as thin as she was, and perhaps that was easier for her to take.

But I think there was something else, too. In our use of pills, we had converged. Even though we chose opposite drugs, even though we didn't admit to addiction, we shared a common secret.

One evening, I was watching television with my mother. We were in Pacific Palisades and my father was

in Sacramento. The news program we were watching
had a segment about withdrawal from Valium. It
showed someone having convulsions and seizures. If
you didn't know, you'd think you were watching someone in the throes of an epileptic seizure. I turned to my
mother and said, "You should pay attention to this."
She glanced at me and didn't answer. Of course, I
should have paid attention, too, but neither of us
thought we had a problem. Even if the program had
shown someone withdrawing from diet pills—zombie-
like, disoriented, desperately depressed—I wouldn't
have seen it—not with any clarity of vision.

I noticed that Miltown hadn't been entirely dis-
carded. We flew back and forth between Los Angeles
and Sacramento a few times that summer. On one plane
trip, my mother shook two Miltown into her hand and
asked the stewardess for a glass of water.

"Do you have a headache?" the stewardess asked,
thinking they were aspirin.

"Yes," my mother lied.

I thought about the pills hidden in my suitcase in an
empty shampoo bottle, and wished they were white and
could be mistaken for aspirin.

On another plane trip, my mother complained of
indigestion, so she pulled out two Miltown.

"That helps indigestion?" I asked.

"Yes."

To determine why I hadn't had my period in so long,
my mother said she was going to make an appointment
for me with her doctor, since I didn't really have one of
my own. But it was said matter-of-factly, with no hint
of judgment or suspicion.

She drove me to the doctor for an examination. I
remember lying on the table, my feet in the stirrups,
thinking, "Oh God, all these years I've been riding
horses . . . what if the stories are right? What if riding
horses can break things and make it look like you're not
a virgin?"

But the doctor completed his examination, turned to

my mother, who had stayed in the room, and said,
"Well, everything seems to be fine." We all knew what
that meant.

The next day, mysteriously, I started my period.

We flew up to Sacramento, planning to stay there for
the remainder of the summer, but as soon as we arrived
at the leased house which had become the official governor's mansion, we were told that Robert Taylor had
died. It wasn't wholly unexpected; his body was
ravaged by lung cancer from years of smoking, and he'd
been hospitalized for months. We turned around and
flew back to Los Angeles.

I remember that week like a dream—Ursula Taylor's
face transformed by grief, my mother trying to comfort
her, unable to hold back her own tears, my father's
eulogy for a man who had been one of his best friends.
I remember Barbara Stanwyck, Robert Taylor's first
wife, so shaken by sobs she had to sit down in the
entryway and gather her strength. I remember the confusion of children who didn't quite know how to fit
death into their lives. We moved through the hours with
bewildered faces and questions we didn't dare ask because we knew no one had the answers.

A few days after the service, we flew back to Sacramento. My father came home from the Capitol every
day at around five, but he didn't seem part of those
months. What I recall most clearly of that summer is
spending time with my mother, sunbathing, sitting by
the pool, exchanging books, laughing. Emotionally and
physically, my mother and I have been at war for a very
long time, but spiritually, we've understood each other
in ways that we wouldn't admit, even to ourselves. Both
of us have used drugs, anger, and defensiveness as a
buffer against pain. And both of us have been capable
of truces, of reaching out to one another for periods of
time until some event, some source of pain, would again
wrench us apart. That summer was one of our rare
cease-fires.

When I went back to school that fall, I'd put on a little weight. I still looked like I'd been in a prison camp, but I looked as if some kindly guard had been giving me extra rations.

When my grandparents picked me up at the airport, my grandmother was the one who finally noticed my weight loss.

"You must have to run around in the shower just to get wet," she said.

But my grandfather didn't seem to notice, which was a bit unusual because his surgeon's eye generally recorded everything.

The first night back at school, after dinner, I helped clear the dishes from my table and on my way through the kitchen I noticed a new addition. A young man in his twenties, lean, with sandy hair and blue eyes, looked up from the stove where he was cooking; he smiled at me. I dropped a plate and had a vision of the rest of the year as one long obsession, which turned out to be pretty accurate.

A couple of months later, I had an opportunity to put myself right in his path. I and four other girls were crowded into the bathroom one night, smoking with the shower on hot so the steam would mask the smoke, and the window open so both the steam and the smoke would pour out. We also had a can of Right Guard in case a teacher came by.

A teacher did come. I had just left the bathroom, so according to what she saw, I was innocent. But I was guilty and more important, I wanted to be found guilty because punishment would mean working off "hours" in the kitchen. So, the next day, I turned myself in, confessed, and got exactly what I wanted: one hundred hours of kitchen duty.

Because I knew the school would notify my parents about my crime, I decided to write my father myself and tell him that I had turned myself in (although I omitted my ulterior motive). It was also a part of my continuing effort to get my father's attention.

He wrote back and told me that turning myself in was the right thing to do, but that punishment was necessary because I'd broken the rules. He then went on to describe how important honesty was, how there would be chaos and anarchy in society if dishonesty were tolerated. He said that I would undoubtedly be disturbed if I felt that he wasn't honest in his job as governor, and if the news reported that he had broken the laws and lied.

My father and I exchanged very few letters; they always had to do with a specific subject, never casual news or inconsequential updates. One subject I was informed of, through letters, about this same time, was the sale of our ranch. The ranch was the sweetest memory of my childhood and I was heartbroken to see it go. I was made to feel a bit better, though, by the fact that my father had sold it to Twentieth Century–Fox, which owned a large piece of land next door and promised not to develop the property.

My mother's letters came more often and just gave me news of our dog, descriptions of the weather, and assorted bulletins. It was through one of her letters that I learned that Ron, who was then going to school in Sacramento, had been beaten up by three boys because he was "the governor's son" and rode to school in a state car.

I wasn't sure that the car really was the reason, but I didn't argue. These were volatile times. There was a war in Vietnam, a war in everyone's living room—right there on television. And there was a war on college campuses, like Berkeley; my father wasn't holding back on his rhetoric. He said that if Berkeley students wanted a bloodbath, they'd have one. I'm sure that not everyone at Ron's Sacramento school came from a Republican family, and that more than a few people were opposed to my father's disdain for anti-war protesters. Much later, Ron told me about the incident and said the boys were saying things like "warmonger" as they were punching his face and giving him a black eye.

I was definitely far from the fray, being out in the middle of the Arizona desert. My political feelings were still fairly undeveloped. I fantasized about being in Haight-Ashbury, plaiting flowers in my hair, or at Berkeley, protesting the war. Instead, I was sneaking poetry books into geometry class, riding horses, and getting up at five every morning to work off "hours" in the kitchen.

CHAPTER 13

· · · · · · · · · · · · · · · ·

DIET PILLS CAME in handy on my new schedule. The night watchman would rap on the window to wake me up at five so I could start working in the kitchen at five-thirty. The kitchen man's name was Don and it didn't take long before we were making out on the stairway in back of the kitchen, in the walk-in freezer, the trash can area, and eventually his room. The room part got a little tricky; I had to get a nurse's excuse to get out of the evening study hall. Then I would sneak across campus. That's where I finally got careless.

It was probably starting to look suspicious that I was coming down with illnesses at night, but would be racing between classes the next day and galloping around on my horse in the afternoons. One night, when the nurse decided to check on me in my room, I wasn't there. I was in Don's room, and it was the night I'd decided that we'd taken foreplay about as far as we could. I wanted to lose my virginity. I thought: "I'm sixteen, I'm old enough." So I crossed the campus dressed like a flasher in a raincoat with nothing underneath, though it wasn't raining. I didn't want to waste time removing clothes.

We were on the bed, he was on top of me, and I was about as close as anyone can get to not being a virgin anymore when there was a knock on the door and the nurse's voice said, "Hello in there!"

"Yes?" said Don, trying to sound calm.

"Is Patti Reagan in there?" she asked.

"Who?"

"Oh, God, he's not even convincing," I thought. I pushed him off me, grabbed my raincoat, and hid in the closet. I heard him fumbling to put his pants on, heard the door open and then the nurse's voice again.

"Patti is not in her room where she's supposed to be, and I think she came here."

"Why would you think that?"

"Because the other morning, early, I saw her coming into your room. I decided to let it go, but now . . ."

"Well, I don't know what you saw, but you're mistaken," Don said.

"I'm afraid I don't believe you," she said, and stormed out.

Don came to the closet, opened the door, and said, "You better get out of here."

I didn't even get fifty yards from his room before she caught me.

"Come to the infirmary with me, please, Patti."

She led me through the infirmary to her room in the back and told me to sit down on the couch.

"What are you wearing under that?" she asked.

"Nothing." I crossed my legs self-consciously.

"What were you thinking of?" she said, shaking her head sadly.

"Well, I, uh, don't know," I said, assuming it was obvious.

For the next thirty minutes, she lectured me on the necessity of remaining chaste until marriage. I nodded, apologized, nodded some more, and waited for the ax to fall. But when she finished, she said, "This stays between us. But if you try this again . . ."

"I'm not expelled," I thought as I walked back to my room. I was still a virgin, which troubled me, but at least I was still in high school.

I didn't write my father about what happened. But he would find out—everyone would.

Don and I eventually continued our illicit meetings with a little more discretion. Before the end of the school year, Don left and went to Alaska. He wrote to me often, and I decided I was going to run away to Alaska to be with him. At the time, Michael was in his last year at Judson, his boarding school in Scottsdale, Arizona, and I had the brilliant idea of eliciting his help. I needed someone to "sign me out" of school "for the day." It would look like I was just leaving for the day, but I was planning on a permanent departure. In a number of detailed letters, I told Michael how, just before the end of the school year, he should pick me up and drive me to the airport where I would board a flight to Alaska, and once I got there, I would take off my braces with a screwdriver or something so I'd look older, and then I'd get a job and live with Don and never be heard from again.

Michael said he'd help me, but he never put it in writing; he said it in phone calls, which is significant because the only written evidence of this plan turned out to be my letters, sent to him, but passed along to my parents.

Two days before I was going to take flight, my father showed up at school. My mother had made the trip as far as Prescott, but had let my father go the rest of the way. I remember a long, silent car ride to Prescott because my father never was good at these things. He wasn't a good emissary.

I don't know what Prescott is like now, but in the Sixties it looked sort of like Dodge City. The women wore stretch Wranglers, tailored Western shirts, cross-your-heart bras, and sported beehive hairdos held in place with Spray Net; everyone smoked unfiltered Camels.

That night in a Prescott hotel dining room, with pinafored waitresses serving up steaks and french fries, sat the governor of California and his wife, who were far more accustomed to dinner at Chasen's. Beside them was their sixteen-year-old daughter, who had desperately been trying to lose her virginity to a kitchen worker and who'd decided to put a few thousand miles between herself and her parents.

In most families, this would have been a scene of high drama. But aside from the fact that my parents had come to Arizona, the whole thing was treated as if it were nothing. Cataclysms had rocked our household because of things as trivial as hairstyles or clothes or a wrong facial expression. But this—the fact that a sixteen-year-old was planning to take off to Alaska, lie about her age, move in with an older man, and get a job slinging hash—was not a crisis. In fact, we didn't even really talk about it; we talked about the fact that Michael had turned me in. My parents applauded his action. We actually had an intellectual, philosophical, detached discussion about the merits of such an act. But no one asked, "By the way, why did you want to run away? And what about this guy? And why Alaska?" In our curious family dynamics, we had simply skirted the issue.

Years later, it was almost a family joke. "Oh yes, remember when Patti was going to run away with a dishwasher? Now that was a good one. Crazy kid."

That was the Alice-down-the-rabbit-hole aspect to our family. Things were always the wrong size. Little skirmishes took on major proportions, and big dramas were tossed aside over dinner.

In the summer of 1968, in the wake of the Martin Luther King and Robert Kennedy assassinations, my parents were assigned Secret Service agents. By this time, my father was being discussed as a possible presidential candidate, and he needed protection.

There were two camps of rhetoric on this possible candidacy. Press statements released by the Reagan strategists and statements made by my father himself indicated that he hadn't made up his mind. But there were constant discussions at the dinner table and endless meetings at the house. Richard Nixon and Nelson Rockefeller had already declared their candidacies.

And there was my father—or there wasn't my father, depending on whom you listened to. If someone had asked me, I'd have directed them to my mother's demure smile, the kind of smile that says, "Oh, we both know the answer to that, don't we? But let's not talk about it just yet."

The strategy, apparently, was to keep everyone guessing. Meanwhile, my father was making these short little trips to different states to make speeches. When someone crocheted a pillow with an elephant walking toward the White House, it was promptly displayed on the living-room couch.

I knew my father wouldn't become president that year, and all I can attribute it to is intuition. I also knew that it was only a matter of time before he would be president.

Michael and Maureen were never around then. I overheard my mother giving an interview in which she was asked about her two daughters. "I have only one daughter," she answered tersely. The family image was being trimmed, reworked, varnished into something more acceptable for prime time. However, the "one daughter" she acknowledged had Eldridge Cleaver's *Soul On Ice* by her bedside and dreamed alternately of going to Haight-Ashbury and handing flowers out to tourists, and throwing rocks through the windows of ROTC buildings.

And Ron, who until then had been far more reliable, was borrowing my Jefferson Airplane albums and refusing to go to the barber and have his hair cut. And he had discovered that he wasn't immune to having my mother listen in on his phone conversations; there were a few loud arguments about that—accusations and denials.

It was clear to me that my mother loved having Secret Service protection. She never drove anymore; she was, instead, driven. And she became good friends with one of the agents, spending hours in conversation with him. There were evenings when I had to call her in for dinner.

It was one of those strange role-reversal things—calling my mother in from the driveway where she was talking to some guy.

My father did not return from the Miami convention a winner, but he was quick to note that he didn't really lose, because he was still governor of California. My mother, upon her return, took her anger out on the maids. Everything in the house was wrong; too many newspapers were piled in the kitchen, the refrigerator wasn't full enough, and she didn't like what we were having for dinner.

The new cook's name was Bobbi, and I had spent a very happy few days hanging around in her room, watching television, and talking to her. She was a calm, intelligent black woman who never seemed intimidated by my mother.

"She's really on the warpath since he lost," Bobbi said to me under her breath. But then she laughed and shook her head, as if all that drama were so silly.

"How does she do that?" I wondered. "Why isn't she scared?" I'm still looking for the answer.

CHAPTER 14

· · · · · · · · · · · · · · ·

WITH THE CONVENTION behind us, life returned to normal. Back at Orme, a junior now, I found a new focus for my existence. This was my English teacher, a handsome, muscular man with blond hair and blue eyes that narrowed, teased, and seemed to see everything.

"You keep getting in trouble with men," some inner voice said. "Didn't you learn anything from Don?"

But I didn't listen. I'd already fallen in love with writing. I had my life mapped out. I was going to be a poet, live hand to mouth the way most poets did, probably drink too much the way a lot of poets did, have painful, dramatic love affairs, write about them, and only get recognized after I was dead. I was entranced by Sylvia Plath, Dylan Thomas, Anne Sexton, and beat poets like Gregory Corso and Lawrence Ferlinghetti.

Jim, my English teacher, called me over after class one day to discuss some of my poetry, which I'd handed in for a creative writing assignment.

"Can we meet tonight?" he said. "We can use this classroom. This is good stuff, and I want to work with you on it."

That was how it started, although at first I was caught between being attracted to him and being ecstatic that he was taking an interest in my poetry. The poetry-ecstasy won out for a while, until the two things merged and one evening in the library I walked over and handed him a poem that was about him. He read it, looked at me, and that was that. I ended up entangled not only with my teacher, but with his family. I liked his wife; I liked his two children; I started babysitting for them and became almost an adopted member of the family. Kay, Jim's wife, started to confide in me about the tensions between them, about Jim's unkindnesses, his temper. The deeper into it I got, the more I realized what I felt for his wife and children was love, and what I felt for him was love. It was not just a triangle, it was a spider web, and I couldn't get out of it. I didn't *want* to get out of it.

We passed poems back and forth, but those only recorded the emotional journey. There were afternoons when Kay took the kids somewhere, and I went over to their house and did everything with Jim just short of intercourse. The trick was doing as much as we could, but leaving on as many clothes as possible. That way, if someone came home, zippers and buttons could be done up quickly. Through our panting and moaning and soft commands, we were always listening for footsteps.

The window of my dorm room looked down on his house; I could see who came and went; I could tell when he was alone. One day, I saw him walk through the front door, but I knew Kay was there so I couldn't go over. I was lying on my bed reading a book, but thinking about him made the pages blur.

What we were doing was dangerous. It was all mixed up with fear and guilt and wanting the forbidden. Jim could be cruel, taking me to the edge sexually and then backing off, leaving me dangling there helplessly, trembling and flushed, not knowing what to do with the fireworks going off inside me. And he'd watch me, deliciously enjoying the control he had over me. One night, he took me out riding through the desert on his motorcycle, and when we got far from campus, he stopped and we both got off. We stood there kissing and grinding our bodies together. I could have done it right there, out in the dark desert. I wanted him that badly. But he backed up, got on the motorcycle, and took off before

I could climb on. I walked back to campus, angry and crying, but not willing to let go, not willing to end it. It was a game to him, but he had me. I was hooked, not just on what I thought was love, but on the fear, the risk, the danger zone he'd taken me to.

For a few days, Jim had me teach his freshman English class for him. They were studying *The Once and Future King,* the Camelot tale by T. H. White. What Jim wanted was a class discussion on the love triangle between Arthur, Guinevere, and Lancelot. Is it possible to love two people equally, to be torn like that? Does anyone survive it?

"Why are you having me teach this?" I said to him one evening when we were going over the class notes and instructions he'd made up for me.

"Because you need to learn it."

"Are the answers here, in this book? It ends in heartbreak, tragedy. Is that what I need to learn?"

No response, just a half-smile. I was going to learn whatever he felt like teaching me.

I learned one thing I never forgot—that love isn't always simple and clear, and sex is even less so. I loved Kay, not sexually, but strongly. When she cried over Jim's treatment of her, tears came to my eyes, too, and it didn't matter that this seemed contradictory.

Control is the only explanation I can come up with for Jim's teasing. He was willing to have sex with me, but was predictable about stopping short of making love. Perhaps he'd convinced himself that as long as we didn't make love, he wasn't really committing adultery. But my money's on the control theory.

Much later, when it all came out and my mother talked to me about it, she said, "It's terrible that he took part of your youth from you. You should have been going to school dances, going steady." But I couldn't imagine giving those years to acne-faced boys with sweaty palms who wanted to make out in the backseats of Chevrolets.

That Christmas, he brought Kay and the children to

Los Angeles, and with the boldness of someone who was dancing on a slippery edge and loving it, I invited them to my parents' house. Not only were my parents there, my grandparents were also. I felt I could hide what was going on because I was getting good at it. I was one person when I was with his family—the adopted member, the babysitter, the friend—and another when I was with him.

But my mother saw it. She saw everything, with all of us standing around in the living room by the Christmas tree. I wouldn't realize that she'd seen it until my first year in college. But for whatever reason on that December day, she chose to become an accomplice rather than an interrogator. She took it all in, figured it all out, and never said a word.

On Christmas Day, my grandfather sat in an armchair, drawing on a cigarette, and said, "Your teacher seems very interesting, Patti, but I think you should be careful about being too influenced by one person intellectually. It's a common pitfall among young students."

My mother stood back from the conversation—passive, neutral. I noticed, but didn't wonder at it; I was too deep in my own deception.

That summer, she would hand me letters from Jim, her eyes giving nothing away.

That was the summer the whole family took a trip abroad. "The whole family" meant, in our language, Ron, me, and our parents. This was the edited family, without Maureen and Michael. My father, for reasons that were never explained to us, had been asked by President Nixon to go to the Philippines and meet with Ferdinand Marcos. We were given one of the presidential planes for the trip—an Air Force plane that had bunks, spacious seating, and white-jacketed men to serve food.

In Manila, we stayed at Malcanang Palace. Ron and I slept in a suite with lacquered capice shell walls and a piano covered in shells. My parents were in a suite down the hall that was so full of expensive antiques, I was afraid to turn around too quickly. Heavy velvet draperies hung over the windows.

The second day we were there, while my father was meeting with President Marcos, Ron, my mother, and I went on a bus tour of Manila.

"This is one of Mrs. Marcos's projects," the tour guide said, indicating a long green field filled with neat white marble crosses. "For Philippine soldiers who died bravely." Then the guide said, "And her next project is to clean up this area on your right." The area he referred to was a riverbank, littered with garbage, where people were living under propped-up pieces of corrugated sheet metal. I looked out the bus window at children playing in the greenish water, women filling pails with it, other women nursing babies, and men sitting on boxes, smoking. One man was knee-deep in the river water, urinating. I thought of the capice shell suite I'd be sleeping in that night, of the lavish meals we could never finish.

"Don't you feel guilty about how we live when you see this?" I asked my mother, who was sitting beside me.

"Of course not," she answered, turning to me with an expression that mocked my concern.

My impression of Ferdinand Marcos was of a quiet, reticent man—until I looked at his eyes, which were like steel. Imelda Marcos was fluttery and silly, chattering about her priceless collections of everything in the world. I was sorry, years later, that I didn't visit her closet and view her shoes.

The last night of our stay there, the Marcoses held a party for us. We were encouraged not to finish any particular course of the seven-course meal, because we wouldn't have room for the next one. It was as though wasting food was state policy.

The only amusing thing about that party was that my mother was told by Imelda Marcos that she would have a dress made for her, and that was what she would wear. A seamstress came to my parents' suite and fitted

her for a typical Philippine dress. Apparently, Mrs.
Marcos didn't want American fashions at this particular party. What astonished me was that my mother
went along with it. Telling my mother what to wear is
sort of like telling John McEnroe what racket to use—
it's one of those things that most people wouldn't try.

Of the whole trip, my memory of the riverbank was
the most lasting. I will never forget my mother's comment, which reflected an attitude I didn't even want to
understand.

I wrote Jim a letter when I got home and said, "I have
a feeling that the Philippine Constitution, at least as it's
been rewritten by the Marcoses, starts out with the
words 'Let them eat cake.' "

I only kept one secret from Jim—my addiction to diet
pills. I still got my drugs by mail, but my tolerance was
getting higher, so I needed more. I found out that a girl
who was a year ahead of me had a prescription, and I
started stealing them from her when she wasn't in her
room. We walked in and out of each other's rooms
freely—it wasn't that difficult. But it was unusual to
walk out with your pockets full of someone else's pills.
Finally, she must have figured it out. One night she
confronted me. I opened my eyes wide, stared right at
her, and lied.

"I never took anything from your room. Whoever
told you that is wrong. I don't even know anything
about any pills." I was an accomplished liar; I'd been
raised on it and it was a way of life at that point.

I turned eighteen in October of my senior year and
made a concession to my parents over Christmas to be
a debutante, just to avoid a fight. But that didn't mean
I was going to act or feel any differently. I was still dying
to lose my virginity.

I thought eighteen would be the magic wand waved
over Jim that would make him stop torturing me with
sex that was never completed. But it made no difference.

I decided, somewhat unilaterally since I never actually discussed this with him, that my virginity was the reason. Maybe he didn't want responsibility for being the first, so I made up my mind to let someone else fill in for him.

The someone else turned out to be my tennis coach, whom I'd met on Easter vacation at my grandparents' house. We went out a few times and he was wholesome enough that neither my parents nor my grandparents asked too many questions, or set down too many curfews.

We were making out one night in his car, when I said, "I want to lose my virginity."

"Right now?" he asked incredulously. It was difficult enough even kissing with the damn gearshift in the way.

"Well, no, we can do it tomorrow night. What about in your room?" His college dorm room was small, with cinder-block walls and one window. Not a very romantic setting, but I wasn't after romance. I was a girl-on-a-mission.

The next night, I told my parents we were going to the movies and we went straight to his room. I insisted on darkness. With Jim, it was always daylight, and I loved looking at his body—I wouldn't have wanted darkness with him. But I didn't really want to be making love with this tennis coach who undoubtedly thought I cared more than I did, and I needed darkness to mask what I was doing, and to let my imagination change the cast of characters.

We were on his narrow dorm-room bed, naked, with not even a streetlight flickering through the curtains on the small window.

"Are you sure you want to do this?" he asked.

"Of course I'm sure."

"I don't have anything."

"What do you mean?" I said, wanting it to be over.

"I should go get a rubber."

"Oh . . . okay."

He got up, put on his clothes, and said, "I'll be right back—I'll get one at the gas station on the corner."

He was back in about three minutes and we picked up where we left off. I felt a burst of pain inside me, the leakage of blood. For three days, there were spots of blood and I was sad when they stopped, because they reminded me of this great passage.

"I have something to tell you," I said to Jim when I came back from vacation. We were in his house, alone, but I sat down across the room from him on the couch. He was in an armchair where, on too many afternoons, I'd knelt between his legs, feeling them locked around me, holding me prisoner and reminding me that I didn't want to escape. On this day, though, I stared at his face, not wanting my eyes or my thoughts to wander.

"I lost my virginity while I was away. It doesn't matter who it was. I wanted it to be you. I didn't even want light in the room because I wanted to pretend it was you . . ." I was rambling and starting to cry. Dammit, I'd practiced this, I wanted to be in control for once. I lowered my eyes, stared at my hands, tried to pull in the tears. But when I looked up again, there were tears in his eyes, too.

I'd wonder later how I ended up crossing the room because I wouldn't remember crossing. I would only remember being against him, his arms and legs holding me, our hands tugging at clothes . . . and still not making love. But the tears mattered more right then. It may be the only honest emotion that Jim ever gave me.

Before my senior year was out, I'd been accepted at Northwestern University in Illinois, which was my first choice, partly because I didn't want to go back to California, and partly because I thought Jim was going to be teaching there. He was leaving Orme at the end of the year to return to college teaching, and Northwestern had been mentioned. My understanding was that we would be together then—really together. But this had never actually been stated; it was woven into obscure poems and murmured between kisses.

Our communication was as vague and circuitous as the communication in my family. Like a homing pigeon, I'd flown right toward the familiar—the vocabulary I'd grown up with.

My father gave the commencement speech that June, but I don't remember a word of it. I only remember crying, and not really knowing why. I guess I felt a kind of closure at leaving what had been my home for five years. I also was planning a life no one else knew about. I didn't let myself doubt that Jim and I would be together; I took it as a certainty. Northwestern was just a stop along the way—he was the rest of my life.

There had been one other man in my life during that last year of school, but it wasn't a romantic involvement. Tony had left Orme without graduating, joined the Marines, and was in Vietnam. I hadn't known him that well at school, but through our letters a friendship grew, and through his words and descriptions, I started to feel like a witness to war. I still have his letters, tied up neatly with string, his military picture on top.

Tony came back from Vietnam that summer between tours of duty. He came to visit me in Sacramento at the governor's mansion.

At the dinner table that night, there were four hawks and one dove. The dove, feeling the unmistakable defeat of being hopelessly outnumbered, chose to keep her mouth shut. Most of the conversation was supplied by my father and Tony. A sample:

"They've really got our hands tied over there," Tony said. "The government isn't backing us up. We should be wiping out all those gooks."

Gooks? I thought back to one of his earlier letters, when he questioned his ability to kill another human being and, more important, questioned the wisdom of being asked to.

"Well, that's true," my father answered, beaming at this new alliance he'd discovered right there at his own dinner table. "That's what I've been hollering about all along. I wish all these flag-burners and Communist sympathizers would stop spreading lies and propaganda."

"Why don't we just nuke 'em?" Ron piped up. He was twelve.

"That wouldn't be a bad idea," my father agreed.

"We just need stronger leadership," my mother contributed.

"Damn straight," Tony said, and went on to tell war stories which didn't ring true to me because I'd memorized the stories in his letters. Those were the real ones, not the John Wayne tales that were being tossed around the dinner table that evening.

"Why have you changed?" I whispered to Tony later. He was staying the night, and we were standing in the hallway outside the room he'd been assigned. He pulled me to him and kissed me, and I knew that if it weren't for what I'd heard at dinner, I probably would have snuck into his room later. The lure of the forbidden was tugging at me again, but the dinner-table dialogue had pushed me away.

"Answer me, Tony." I pushed back from him and stared at his face in the shadows—blue eyes, freckles, not the face of a killer.

"It's war, babe," he said, a little too casually.

I was too upset to sleep that night. If my political consciousness had ever been in doubt, it no longer was. I hated how the war had changed Tony. I was standing fast against my father's politics, and I knew I would oppose him on every front.

"Now, the student body president at Northwestern is a very radical black girl named Eva Jefferson," my father said to me, weeks before I was to leave for college. My mother sat next to him, nodding her head in agreement. "Just be aware of that and stay away from her."

I went back to my room, took out a piece of paper which had things to do listed on it and below "buy a warm coat for winter" I wrote, "look up Eva Jefferson."

The plane lifted off from Los Angeles airport, taking me to Illinois, to a new home, and closer to Jim. He hadn't ended up at Northwestern; he was teaching at the University of Pennsylvania. "Doesn't matter," I thought, taking out his last letter on the plane and reading it for the hundredth time. "Pennsylvania is just a short plane flight."

CHAPTER 15

· · · · · · · · · · · · · · · · ·

NORTHWESTERN WAS EXACTLY what I imagined a college campus would be. There were ivy-covered buildings and tree-shaded paths. My roommate was from New York and couldn't understand why I'd chosen the Midwestern winters over California's year-round sun.

"It's a long story," I said, shrugging it off.

I wasted no time finding Eva Jefferson. She was soft-spoken, intelligent, and seemed to be respected by everyone. The year before, when students across the country were striking in protest of the Kent State shootings, and campuses were frequently erupting, she had kept Northwestern's protest nonviolent.

She asked me once what my father had felt about the Kent State shootings, since he was famous for his diatribe against anti-war protesters on campuses.

"I didn't talk to him about it," I told her.

But that wasn't true. My father had said that the students were hurling rocks and bottles at the National Guardsmen, as though that were a justification for aiming loaded rifles at students and firing. Not once did he express regret, or acknowledge the shootings as a tragedy or a crime. I couldn't bring myself to repeat that conversation, and in fact, this is the first time I've related it at all.

Through Eva, I met a group of women who exposed me to feminist thinking, still new and controversial then. We were all rebelling against mothers who advocated "letting the man wear the pants in the family."

So we made a point of wearing pants, of not wearing bras, leaving our legs and underarms unshaven, and dressing in black. I immediately threw out my Lady Schick razor and my bras, and loaded up on black turtlenecks.

I never planned to graduate; I didn't care about required courses. I took poetry, creative writing, and literature classes and a course in Greek mythology with a teacher who used to jump on the desk and act out the parts.

My parents were giving me a small allowance, and I saved every penny of it. Before Thanksgiving, when snow had already fallen and icy winds were blowing across Lake Michigan, I took the El into Chicago and got on a plane to Pennsylvania. "You're a liar," something in my head told me as I got closer, and found myself hoping that only Jim would be there to meet me at the airport. "A liar and a traitor and this is wrong."

"But I love him," was my only response to my conscience, and it was starting to feel like a feeble one.

It was a Thursday. The plan was that I would go to school with Jim on Friday and read some of my poetry in his creative writing class. He was still my mentor; that hadn't changed. But everything else between us was falling apart, and I knew it.

The whole family met me and we drove back to the two-bedroom house they were renting. I slept on the couch that night, listening to hear if Jim and Kay were making love in the next room. I heard nothing.

"What's going to happen with us?" I asked Jim in the car the next day, on the way to campus.

"What do you mean?" he said. He was looking at the road, but his eyes played with me even though they weren't on me. Green land stretched out around us, wet with rain.

"Come on, can't we ever be direct with each other?"

He pulled off the road and turned to me. "I'll come into Chicago next month, and we can stay the night together, okay? We'll talk about all this then. I just don't have the answers right now."

I held on to that promise like a lucky charm.

Jim was supposed to arrive in Chicago late one night, call me when he got to whatever hotel he was staying at, and I would take the El into the city to meet him.

"You're out of your mind," my roommate told me. "You're going to take the El into Chicago in the middle of the night? Do you know what kind of people ride the El at that hour? It's not safe. It's crazy. You're crazy."

"I don't care—I've been waiting for this for over two years," I said, suddenly feeling very old.

He never came, he never called, at least not that night. I sat up waiting, dressed, ready to go, until two A.M. and then I slept for a few hours with half my clothes still on. At dawn, I got up, went downstairs, and smoked a cigarette, watching the sky get light. I felt ragged and used, and I decided I couldn't do it anymore.

I avoided Jim's calls for a couple of weeks, but finally I picked up the phone one day and his voice cut into me. I told him not to call me anymore. It was as if he were a book I could put down and never open again. He didn't call anymore, but he wrote me letters I never answered, but didn't throw away, either.

Within a few weeks, I ended up in New York with my mother, who was visiting the city. I told her the whole story. She would seem the unlikeliest person to turn to, but that's the complexity of our relationship. My mother was the only one I could run to. We'd been isolated for so long on our private battlefield that there was almost no one else in my world.

It was my first trip to New York. My mother had a suite at the Waldorf Astoria, and I woke up in the morning and looked down at the Manhattan streets choked with yellow cabs. It's an unusual sight for someone raised in Los Angeles, where a cab is something you phone for. I sensed at breakfast that my mother knew

I had something on my mind and she was waiting for me to get around to it.

"I've been involved with Jim, the English teacher you met, for the last couple of years," I began.

Her expression said, "I know." Her words followed.

"How long have you known?" I asked.

She shrugged. Her eyes and face were soft, warm. "I guess since he came to the house."

The story tumbled out of me with only a few omissions. I said nothing about the afternoons in his house, about feeling that I would have done anything with him—anything he asked. But there was a sense that I could have told my mother these things. As much as her morality was formed in the Fifties and reflects the conservatism of those times, she has an ability to move up through the decades and appear modern and liberal. There have been comments in the media that she is more liberal politically than my father, but I don't think her ideology or her morality are rooted in either liberalism or conservatism. One of my mother's complexities is her ability to transform, adapt to situations for personal reasons. I was bringing her a personal crisis, showing her I needed her, and she adapted to that, became gentle, nurturing, and nonjudgmental.

"Did you make love with him?" she asked softly.

"No." I only answered what she asked; I offered nothing more, although I realized and appreciated that I could have.

"Well, that's good. It would be more difficult if you had—you know, more painful, I think." Her words broke off. She probably wasn't sure she was right.

"I don't know," I said. "I wanted to."

"Well, I have to decide how to handle this with your father. I really don't think I want to tell him about it, at least not all of it. He'd probably want to kill Jim. You know, men are very protective of their daughters. Their daughters are always their little girls, and something like this . . . well, your father just wouldn't take it very easily. I just think that the less said, the better." I felt as if she were talking about someone else—not my father, not the man I'd been searching for all my life. But I liked the image of him coming to my rescue, defending my honor. I didn't believe it, but I liked it.

That day at the Waldorf-Astoria, and for the next few days in New York, I felt like I really had a mother. It was a sweet and unfamiliar feeling, like a gift someone hands you for no particular reason.

When I returned to school, I didn't really know how to recover from a long relationship, and a long illusion, so I became even more self-destructive. I began taking more diet pills, living on coffee and one Snickers bar a day. I smoked grass sometimes to take the edge off the speed, and smoked cigarettes when nothing would soften the edge and I was jumping out of my skin. I was still taking diuretics. There were days I couldn't get off my bed because if I did, blackness would seep into the edges of my vision; my equilibrium would go, and I knew that if I didn't lie down quickly, I'd be on the floor in a dead faint. The spells usually lasted about twenty-four hours, and then I'd be back on the same regimen of speed, caffeine, nicotine, and my daily candy bar.

Falling asleep began to feel like actual falling—as though I'd been dropped off a cliff. Somewhere along the fall, voices would start and I'd force myself awake, frightened that I was slipping over the edge into madness. The voices frightened me the most. I told no one. I just started looking for distraction. I began a relationship of sorts—the relationship being confined mostly to sex and sleeping—with a guy who was a poet and musician.

I slept better when I was with him; the voices left me alone. We didn't talk about emotional involvement; we didn't really talk about anything. We just had sex and slept together, read books in his room, and watched television. I was using him to fill up an emptiness that I didn't fully understand yet, and it would become a pattern in my life, another addiction of sorts.

I think I do understand it now. I have blamed my

father for being there but not *really* being there and have expected other men to make up for that absence.

The truth is, it wasn't my father's fault—he did the best he knew how—and it's not the responsibility of any other man to fill in the blank spots of my childhood. It's my responsibility to stop lugging around these expectations.

For years, I didn't see how I invited romance into my life just to sabotage it. I was on a mission to punish not only my father, but the entire male sex. In truth, I wasn't letting a man anywhere near my soul. Whether the involvement was casual or serious, I'd decided the guy was going to abandon me before he'd even thought of it. So of course he would and then I could blame him, and continue my pattern of being a little girl whose father never noticed her.

One February night, I was sitting downstairs in the dorm, talking to a friend who was on desk duty. She was a tall, intelligent woman who for some reason was dating an unintelligent campus security guard who had adopted racism as a religion. Aside from his appalling mutilation of the English language, which was like fingernails on a blackboard to me, Tim doubled his use of the word "nigger" whenever I was in earshot simply because he knew it got to me.

A little before ten on this night, a black man came into the dorm with a cardboard clothes box.

"Hi, girls, want to buy some hot pants?"

"I don't think so," I said, since my friend had a policy of not talking to black people, in deference to her boyfriend's prejudice. I never thought she was a racist, but she was frightened of Tim's anger and she bent to his ways.

"Oh, you'd look real nice in them," this man said, leaning over the desk and staring at my legs. I probably wouldn't have looked nice at all, since my legs were about as thin as his arms.

I was starting to get nervous for him. This dorm, on

this particular night, was no place for a black man selling clothes out of a box.

"What's your name?" he asked me.

"Snow White."

He laughed. "Well, you are sort of lily-white, I'll give you that. And what's your name?" he asked my friend.

"None of your business," she snapped.

My eyes were telling him to run, get the hell out of there, but the message didn't get through.

"Now, you could go right back there and try these on," he persisted. "Come out and model them. You might like them. You might want to buy them."

"I'm going to call security," my friend said. This meant that at any moment, Tim would come barreling through the door.

"You'd better leave," I said to the man with the hot pants.

But he was having too much fun, and at this point he wasn't taking anything I said seriously. I probably should have been more emphatic, but I was strung out on pills.

Suddenly, Tim and another security guard burst in.

"You a student here, asshole?" Tim said.

"No."

"Then you're trespassing. This is a private campus."

He then snapped handcuffs on the man and ordered me to accompany them to the security office and make a statement.

"We were just mouthing off," I said to the three men in the small office.

"Just tell us what happened."

By the time I got back to my dorm room, it was about one-thirty in the morning. My roommate had taken the phone off the hook.

"What the hell is going on?" she asked, tired and irritable. "Reporters have been calling here asking why you had a black man arrested. Something about selling hot pants?"

"I didn't really have him arrested. Oh, never mind,

I'll explain it tomorrow. We'll just leave the phone off the hook."

I didn't quite understand why all these reporters were so on top of this news story a couple of hours after the event, but then I remembered the head of security saying to me, "I've called your parents and informed them," as I walked out of the office.

At dawn, a security woman showed up at the dorm and said I was to come with her.

"Why? Am I under arrest?"

"I have instructions to board you with me until further notice. Until the danger passes," she said.

"What danger?"

"Just come with me, please."

Her apartment was beige with a dingy green carpet, Formica furniture, and magazines like *Road and Track*.

"Mind if I make a phone call?" I asked her. I wasn't even going to try to be pleasant.

I called my parents in California; my mother answered.

"We've talked to the head of security there," she said. "Now, you do everything he tells you. You did the right thing reporting this man it must have been terrible."

"I didn't report him, and it wasn't terrible at all. *This* is terrible. Everyone's making up a story, something that never happened. What the hell is going on here?"

"You watch your language, young lady. Your father wants to speak to you."

That's one thing about my mother—you could break your leg in five places, but if you said, "Shit," she'd forget about the leg and chastise you for using profanity.

"Now, Patti," my father said. "Don't go changing your story because someone has gotten to you—some of these radicals you like so much. You did the right thing. This man needed to be arrested."

"Because someone has gotten to me? Who could get to me? I'm under house arrest!"

"It's for your protection."

"So you're not going to believe me, right?" I asked.

"Just do what the campus security office tells you. It's for your own good," my father said.

I went into the bathroom in my temporary prison and opened the medicine cabinet (I opened everyone's medicine cabinet in those days). She had a bottle of diet pills there, which happened to be my favorite kind, and I emptied half the contents into my pocket. Under different circumstances, I might have visited this woman more often.

The next phone call I made was to Eva Jefferson, who knew the story behind the story. The hot pants man's name was Mickey and his brother was running for alderman in one of the districts. Apparently, there were factions at Northwestern who were opposed to his brother and this whole event was like a gift dropped out of the sky right into their Republican laps. A liberal black candidate could be discredited by playing up the fact that his brother offended the governor of California's daughter and was arrested.

"I want to call Mickey," I told Eva.

"I only have his brother's phone number."

"Okay, I'll call him."

I waited until the security woman left the apartment before I made the call. I could have just walked out of the apartment, but I didn't have any sense of control over my own life. My parents had controlled me, then Jim, and now my parents along with Northwestern's security office were calling the shots. I couldn't find myself in all of that. I didn't even know who I was anymore, if I ever had.

The only thing I was certain about was that Mickey was being railroaded. While it was true that Northwestern was a private campus and could bring trespassing charges against unwelcome visitors, it was not a law that was enforced with any regularity. People came and went freely from the dorms and the Student Union and were never asked if they belonged there, or if they were enrolled. And Mickey had not refused to leave when

Tim came on the scene. He wasn't given a chance to leave. He was pushed, harassed, and handcuffed.

Mickey's brother sounded cautious on the phone, stunned probably that I was calling him, but after a few minutes we were busily planning a media strategy, in which Mickey and I would give interviews together and tell the real story. And on top of that, when the case came to trial, I'd walk into the courtroom arm in arm with Mickey.

When my captor returned, she told me that the head of security wanted to see me. She drove me to his office and stood outside the door while he talked to me.

"I know this is hard for you," he said when I came in and sat down. "But we have to do what we think is best."

"Who is 'we'?" I asked.

"I can't really answer that."

"So there are more people in on this decision-making process than just you and the other security people, right?"

"I can't answer that," he repeated. "But it's important that you do what we say. You'll have to stay where you are a little longer. You can't go back to your dorm yet."

I didn't say anything, and suddenly his expression softened a little. "You must feel like you're trapped in a plastic bag, and the more you struggle, the more you suffocate," he said, almost to himself.

"Yeah . . . that's exactly how I feel."

"I understand, I really do. But there's nothing I can do. My hands are tied. You'll have to stay there longer."

For the rest of the day, I couldn't get the plastic bag analogy out of my head. The more I thought about it, the more my entire life felt like that. Suffocation waiting to happen.

Late that night, while my guard was sleeping in the next room, I got up and went into the bathroom, locking the door behind me. I took a single-edge razor blade from the medicine cabinet and sat down on the edge of the tub.

I had left the light off; there was enough of a glow from the outside streetlamps coming through the window for me to see. I touched the blade to my wrist and felt how easy it would be—not much pressure, even, the skin's so thin there. Just a quick movement—that's all it would take. I'd heard you just get sleepy as the blood drains out, that it was not that painful. I think that I sat there for nearly an hour, imagining my death. But this is what was getting in my way: anger. I was angry at everyone—my parents, the college, the entire state of California for electing my father governor, and myself, for having no control over my life. The more anger stood in my way, the more disgusted I felt at myself for sitting there with a razor blade poised over my veins. I got up, put it back in the medicine cabinet, and brushed my teeth, because suddenly I had a horrible taste in my mouth.

I've returned to that bathroom several times in my thoughts and realized how easy it would have been. I was so young, I had no sense of myself, so I wouldn't even have known who I was killing. I think of it every time I hear about teenage suicides. I know the anonymity they must have felt, because I felt it. I was alive, but I had no grip on what my life was about, or on what *I* was about. I wasn't grounded in anything. It makes death look so easy.

The next day, I did what I should have done long before. I just walked out of the woman's apartment—after I'd put some of her drugs in my purse. The first person I looked up was Mickey. We started trying to set up some interviews, to tell the real story, but I was about to learn something: When it comes to the media, if the real story isn't as scandalous as the false one, don't even bother.

The only reporter we could get to talk to us was someone from the local Evanston paper. Meanwhile, I was getting letters from racists all over the country congratulating me on the capture of a dangerous black man armed with hot pants.

The second part of my plan worked better. The trial was scheduled, and when the head of security called me in again to go over my testimony, I said, "I'm not going over it with you. I've gone over it with Mickey."

"You what?"

"Yeah, and we're going to walk in together, too. So what do you think? Most of the major papers, plus *Time* and *Newsweek*? They should all be there, right?"

A few days before the scheduled trial, my mother called and said that, just by some odd coincidence, she was coming to Chicago, and could I meet her and Frank Sinatra that night for dinner? She had flown in with him on a private plane, but there was no reason given for either of them being in Chicago at that particular time. I seriously considered taking Mickey along with me to the Drake Hotel, walking into the dining room and acting like nothing unusual at all was taking place. But I didn't have quite that much courage.

Over dinner, Frank Sinatra said a few things about law and order, and citizens standing up for their rights. And my mother added that you can't let people influence you to back down from positions that are correct. Then they both got tired of it and just talked to each other for the rest of the meal, which was fine with me because I thought the whole thing was ridiculous.

If it weren't for this story, I probably wouldn't even comment on Kitty Kelley's suggestions that my mother and Frank Sinatra had an affair. Because I think that was ridiculous, too. But since I've put them together at dinner in Chicago, I have an obligation to say, So what? People can have dinner together, fly on a plane together and not be sleeping together. And I don't think they were. Not then, or ever.

The trial was postponed, to no one's surprise. I can only assume my parents had something to do with it. In fact I have no idea if there ever *was* a trial. If so, I was never asked to testify, which isn't surprising, either.

In 1986, when I was on a book tour for my first novel, *Home Front,* a man walked up to me after the Oprah Winfrey show, handed me a rose, and said, "Do you remember me? The hot pants?" Words never come out right in surprise moments like that. But if they had, I'd have told Mickey then that inadvertently, he had helped me grow up. I had been filled with anger and self-pity at the time of the hot pants incident. But after it was all over, after my moment in the bathroom, I had put some of my feelings aside. I was still angry, but I knew the value of being alive.

CHAPTER 16

. . . .

BY THE TIME spring came, I'd decided three things: First, I wasn't going back to Northwestern the next year. I was still upset over the scandal that had engulfed me. Second, I needed to think in terms of some sort of career to bring in money because it's only okay to be a starving writer if you don't actually starve. So I decided that acting, which was the only other thing I had an aptitude and a fondness for, might pay the bills. And third, I never wanted to have a child.

This last decision took shape one evening in a pizza parlor near campus. I was there with some friends when a mother began yelling at her son, who was maybe eight or nine. He'd been waiting in line at the counter, but had hung back and let other people go ahead of him. His mother finally noticed this, went over to him, and in a voice that filled the place and bounced off the walls, started yelling at him for not just stepping up and ordering as he'd been told. The woman was unrelenting and the child just stood there, looking at a spot on the wall—getting through it. I thought about cycles, about history repeating itself, and I was terrified that I could find myself one day in a parking lot or a market, shrieking at my child. Then I thought about women in the Bible who were ostracized and pitied because they were barren—it seemed like an enviable state to me. A guaranteed break in the cycle.

As to the other two decisions, they resulted in my return to California, my transfer to USC, and my deci-

sion to study drama, because if I wanted to earn a living
acting, I needed to learn the craft. I could confine my
writing to the late hours of the night, since drugs usually
nibbled into my sleep time anyway.

Most parents would be less than enthusiastic over
their child's choice of acting as a professional goal. But
my parents probably didn't feel entitled to object since
they had both been actors. I think that my mother had
two other reasons for endorsing my choice. One was,
she undoubtedly assumed I'd given up writing, and
since I'd learned by that time to hide my pages as well
as my true ambition, her assumption was understand-
able. Any career choice was preferable to writing. The
other reason was, I think my mother was more enam-
ored of her own acting career than she had ever admitted. When she reminisces about acting, her face lights
up and her eyes sparkle with nostalgia. She is a little too
emphatic in her assertion that a woman can't have both
a career and a family life, a little too insistent when she
says it was never difficult to quit her career. I think the
idea that I might have an acting career appealed to her
in a vicarious way, because she adopted the same tone
that she did when she shuffled through her own memories.

"Well, it's in the genes," she said, sounding girlish
and bubbly. "Your grandmother and your great-
grandmother were both actresses, too. So you come by
it naturally. I think it's wonderful. Don't you think so,
honey?" The question was addressed to my father.

"Huh? Oh yes—uh-huh," he answered in the vague
way he has, that tone that leaves people wondering if he
heard the question.

Before transferring to USC, I went to England to take
summer courses at Oxford. The summer-school part
was just a way to get to England—I really wasn't too
concerned with the courses. I fell in love with England
the moment the plane landed; I loved the tiny room on
the Oxford campus where I spent foggy afternoons

reading by the heater and writing poetry. I loved the campus, with its old stone buildings and narrow passageways, and Oxford's cobblestone streets.

Some of my friends from Northwestern had also enrolled in this summer course and we went to London whenever we could. London was an amazing place to be then. It was 1971, and American teenagers were traveling through England with backpacks and almost no money, because there were youth hostels where they could sleep for a few dollars a night. Trafalgar Square was crowded with American kids wearing peace symbols and tie-dyed shirts. On one trip to London, I met a guy who was hitchhiking through Europe; he followed me back to Oxford and stayed with me for the next week. We rented a motorcycle and rode out into the countryside, stopping for beer in small pubs. We bought fresh bread and cheese and ate by the river with so much quiet around us, it was like another world.

It was a great summer romance, both with him and with England.

At the end of that summer, I returned home and drove to Palm Springs for the weekend with a girlfriend. There, we had dinner with Truman Capote. It had been arranged for me by a producer friend named Aram Saint-Suber, whom I'd met years before in Arizona and had kept in touch with. I brought along a tattered copy of *Other Voices, Other Rooms,* Capote's first novel, which I'd read twice; I returned with it autographed.

He took us to a Mexican restaurant where we sat until after midnight, listening to one story after another. However unusual Capote's mannerisms and voice might have been (and many people, including my father, have had a great time imitating him), I think he was one of the most intelligent, perceptive men I've ever met. He looked at everything as a writer; it was either a good story or it wasn't. Manson and his band of killers apparently didn't constitute a good story.

"Boring," Capote said, taking a sip of his margarita.

"They're just drugged-out kids who got into killing. There's no complexity there. I went and interviewed them because I was approached about writing a book on them. Boring as hell."

The one thing he said that I'll always remember was, "If you want to be a writer, you have to be willing to use everything. Everything that's interesting, of course."

I was careful in my questions about writing because I knew he was friendly with my mother, and I didn't want him to unknowingly alert her to the fact that I was still writing. When I returned from Palm Springs, I repeated the Manson story to my parents, but left out all the advice about writing.

USC was about as far from Northwestern as any school could get, in every imaginable way. Freeways circled the campus, and the buildings looked like an aluminum plant. The drama department was a small island of creativity (there may have been others, but I didn't get to them) at a university where football games and frat parties were taken as seriously as world events. Actors like John Ritter, Paul Linke, John Ashton, and Laura Owens were taking graduate drama courses and were around much of the time, examples of success for young hopefuls. Even then, John Ritter was the undisputed star.

At first I lived in a dorm on campus, but the cement and smog surrounding that area of Los Angeles started getting to me. I decided to move into my parents' house and commute to school; on the surface that could be judged as masochism, but I think it was more complicated than that.

There is a reason why abused children return to parents, abused wives return to husbands, or lovers remain with tyrannical partners. You think that, next time, it will be different. You don't return for punishment, you return for love. I was in bad shape right then; I was doing a lot of drugs and I wasn't exactly filled with self-confidence. I knew that living at home would mean being there with my mother much of the time, because my father was in Sacramento during most weeks, and Ron was away at boarding school. But I didn't think about our long, battle-torn history as much as I thought about the love that might be there this time around.

What happened instead was that everything came to a head. If my insecurity was excessive right then, so was my mother's. She eavesdropped on all my phone calls. She opened my mail "by mistake." My mother's remarks on my unshaved legs and underarms or my bra-lessness would send me storming into my room to put on something even more revealing. I was matching anger with anger. In this, my mother and I were intertwined, but we were intertwined in another area as well, although I didn't see it that way then.

I started stealing tranquilizers from her medicine cabinet and trading them for diet pills. I had friends with access to diet pills, but who preferred tranquilizers, so it was a good arrangement. I was using her habit to support mine.

One day, I found a bottle of Quaaludes—it was new and I hadn't heard of it yet.

"Do you know anything about Quaaludes?" I asked one of my friends.

"You can get Quaaludes?" she said, her voice going up an octave in her excitement.

"Well . . . yeah," I told her, wondering what gold mine I'd stumbled onto. "How many Dexedrine is it worth to you?" I think I ended up getting five Dexedrine for one Quaalude.

I don't know why Quaaludes were concocted, or in what madman's laboratory. And I certainly don't know why they were prescribed. I can only hope that the accompanying literature and the doctor's warnings included information like, "This might make you lose your balance, bump into walls, slur your words, and lose your motor coordination." That's exactly the effect Quaaludes have.

It's not surprising to me that people looking for a

recreational drug would go for this, but I suspect that anyone who was prescribed Quaaludes by their doctor wouldn't go back for a refill.

I don't know if my mother ever took any. I only found that one bottle, that one time. I hope she didn't. I never took a Quaalude, but I babysat a friend once who had taken two, and it was like trying to get a rubber band to stand up straight and behave itself.

I was getting some diet pills from a reputable doctor, which is proof that even good doctors can be seduced by an addict's stories, and from a disreputable doctor, recommended by a friend.

"This guy will give you whatever you want," my friend said. And he did.

I also continued to quietly steal drugs from my mother. I still don't know why she didn't figure this out. If she did, she never confronted me. In a pinch, I had street connections. I never actually went to out-of-the-way locations late at night, or to garages behind un-marked houses, or to strange cars in parking lots. I just called a friend.

An odd incident happened while I was living at home, commuting to USC. One of the more popular street drugs at the time (if you were into uppers, which obvi-ously I was, heavily) was "black beauties." Most of us divided the black capsules in half because if you took a whole one, you'd be up for a week. The guy I got them from bought them in Mexico; they were made by a pharmaceutical company, but I don't know of anyone who ever got them through a doctor.

I had this pill bottle full of them; the label was written in Spanish, and it looked very authentic—pharmaceuti-cal, in fact. I'd hidden the bottle in my room, in the space beneath the bottom built-in drawer and the sub-flooring. This would seem to be an exceptionally good hiding place, except that I was never more clever than my mother. She found it.

When my parents confronted me, my father was stern

and upset, but my mother looked at me with what could only be called compassion. I saw it, my mind recorded it, but it would be years before I understood it.

The day of the confrontation, I came home from classes in my usual attire—long denim skirt, leather sandals, thrift store blouse, no bra, and a brass peace symbol dangling around my neck. I was called into my parents' bedroom. By this point in my life, the two chairs bordering the fireplace might well have had straps and electric wires attached to them; I always seemed to be getting executed in one of those two chairs.

"Patti, sit down," my father said in his most severe voice.

My mother was sitting on the edge of the bed, but I didn't see any accusations on her face. Her expression was soft, distant.

My father sat in the other chair, facing me, and held up the bottle of black beauties. "Shit," I thought, "there are at least ten pills left in there. What am I going to do?" That was my whole stash—it might have lasted me a month. (A druggie measures time by quantity of drugs.)

"What are these?" he asked.

"Pills. Diet pills."

"The label's in Spanish."

"Yeah, well, they were sort of a foreign import."

"Where did you get them?" my father asked.

"From a friend who'd lost all the weight he'd wanted to and gave them to me. He's from Mexico; that's where his doctor is." In fact, he was from Beverly Hills, but I was an adept liar by then.

My father believed me. I didn't get executed, I didn't even get probation. I was so thin that my skirt hung off my hip bones, and my ribs were painfully visible. But no one asked why, or what kind of diet I was on, or what I was doing taking pills for weight loss. My father just said, "Well, we'll keep these." Which of course meant that I spent the next three days searching through every wastebasket and trash can, in vain.

My mother never said a word. She just looked at me with this sort of kindly expression. With understanding, is how I see it now. There was a bond between us, and maybe it's the only bond we'll ever have, which is sad and lonely for everyone, but there it is.

A single event led to my departure from my parents' house, and also marked the last time my mother would ever raise her hand to strike me.

The assignment in one of my drama courses was to watch Marlon Brando in *A Streetcar Named Desire* on television that night. I'd tried to get home in time, but the freeway was jammed and I'd already missed fifteen minutes of the movie.

"Hi! I'm home!" I yelled, running through the front door.

"Come in and say hello, please," my mother called out from her bedroom. My father was in Sacramento.

"I have to watch this movie for a class and it's already started. I'll come in after." I was heading for the den to turn on the television.

"You'll come in here now." I knew by the edge in my mother's voice that there was no specific reason for her request. She was only demanding my presence because I'd said I had to do something else.

I walked to the door of her bedroom, and she got up from the bed, pulled me into the room, and shut the door behind us.

"You can't even say hello without making a federal case out of it?" she demanded.

"I said I have to watch this movie for school."

"I don't care! I told you to come in here!"

Her hand drew back, but this time, *my* hands came up and I pushed her. As she fell back on the bed, I started screaming—loud, louder than she had ever screamed at me, a sound meant to punish her for all the years I'd held it in. I frightened myself with the rage exploding out of me; I knew I was in a danger zone.

People did terrible things with rage like this. I left my mother on the bed, her face shocked, her voice silent.

The next morning when I woke up, my grandfather was there; he had flown in from Phoenix. He sat on the edge of my unmade bed and told me that anyone who would assault her mother had to be disturbed.

"Assault?" I said.

"Don't interrupt me. And don't dissemble." My grandfather frequently talked like a dictionary come to life. "You could have seriously hurt your mother."

"She fell on the bed," I pointed out.

"And your complete lack of control, this screaming and shrieking . . . I will not tolerate this kind of violence against her."

My mother stood in the corner, looking wounded. I sat across from my grandfather, wishing I were stoned, because with everything I could have said in answer to him, nothing would have made any difference.

The good thing that came out of this was that I got to see a psychiatrist, which was something I'd been requesting for years. I desperately wanted an analytical perspective on the chaos of my home.

But when my parents brought up something at dinner one night that they could have learned only from the psychiatrist, and when the psychiatrist said something that could have come only from my parents, I stopped seeing him.

It didn't discourage me from analysis, just from that particular analyst. And it educated me as to the risks of asking my parents to pay the bills. Over the years, I've taken jobs as a delivery person for a gift shop, a waitress, and a bartender to get money for therapy.

CHAPTER 17

. . . .

DURING THE SUMMER between my sophomore and junior years at USC, I rented a room at a friend's apartment in Beachwood Canyon, in Hollywood. I was getting $180 a month as an allowance from my parents; my rent for the room was $50 plus my share of the utility bills, so I was just getting by. But I had my own room; I could do what I wanted with it, hang whatever pictures I liked on the walls without having to ask anyone. And I didn't have to worry about leaving pages of my writing around.

I bought a ten-dollar bed from the Salvation Army, made curtains from Indian print bedspreads, and retreated at night into the world I'd created in my small room. There, in the soft amber lights, I listened to Leonard Cohen on the record player, burned incense, smoked grass, and wrote poems.

I had lovers sometimes, but I wasn't as desperate for contact or romantic illusions as I had been at other times. I never let any man get close to me during this time, and always made them leave before dawn.

It was the first time that I had felt free of my parents; even though my father was still governor and was mentioned almost daily in the news, I didn't have to go to Sacramento, and with the way I looked, I wasn't exactly first choice for photo opportunities. I seldom spoke to my mother and had completely lost touch with Ron, Michael, and Maureen.

I had a dream one night, which was probably a more

involved dream than the fragment I remember. I
dreamed that my father and I were walking on the
beach, talking—really talking—and more important, I
saw his eyes actually focus on me.

It's a risky practice, looking for messages in dreams.
But I did. I thought the dream was telling me to get my
father alone and finally tell him the truth about our
family, tell him what happened whenever he was away
from the house.

Through the Highway Patrol men who protected
him, I found out when he would be landing in a private
plane at Santa Monica Airport.

As my father came down the steps of the plane, I
waited for him to notice me, wondering if my dream
would come true right then. He met me with the same
surprised, startled look that I'd grown accustomed to.

"Well, hello, Patti."

"I came to talk to you," I said. My hands were shaking and sweat was running down my sides.

Someone graciously vacated his office for us, and we
went in. My father sat behind the desk, a wall of windows behind him, and I sat on the other side, squinting
into the light that poured through the glass.

"What I wanted to talk to you about was what's gone
on in our house when you were not there," I began,
having the vague sense that I'd just stepped off a high
diving board without checking to see if the pool had
water in it. "You've been lied to for a long time and I've
taken the blame for a lot of things that weren't completely my fault."

The whole story tumbled out—the hitting, the
manipulations of the truth, the collision course that my
mother and I always seemed to be on that had started
when I was still so young. I don't know how long I
talked; it felt like hours, but was probably minutes.
When I stopped, I noticed I was crying; I didn't even
know when the tears had started.

"Well, Patti . . ." my father said, and the tone of his
voice made my heart sink. "What the hell is it with you?

Why do you make these things up about your mother?
She is the most loving, caring person in the world, and
you've caused her nothing but unhappiness. She has
never done these things you're accusing her of. All she's
ever wanted is to have a happy family and be a
mother."

"You think I'm lying?" I asked, my voice choked and
thick.

"You've always made things up, invented things,
usually about your mother. But this is inexcusable.
Your mother would never hit you and all these other
things you're saying . . . well, they're just not true."

My crying exploded then, and it sounded like a
child's sobbing—that ragged, out-of-control wail. I
heard it as if it were someone else's, but I knew it was
mine.

"I feel like I'm in some glass, soundproofed room,"
I said when I could catch my breath enough to speak.
"You can see me but you can't hear me."

"Patti, what I'm hearing is simply not the truth," my
father answered. He scraped back his chair and stood to
leave.

I can't remember walking out, or saying good-bye, or
leaving the airport. I recall driving back to Hollywood,
telling myself that I would never again try to put the
truth in front of my father, because he didn't want to
see it, and it hurt too much to try. I remember feeling
broken, like a fool for reading meaning into a dream.

"It was just a stupid dream," I told myself. "It didn't
mean anything."

I auditioned at school for the play *Look Back in Anger*.
Jim had first introduced me to this John Osborne drama
in high school, and I wanted to be in it. In fact, I was
determined to be in it. I read for the part of Jimmy
Porter's wife and had most of the role memorized so I
could audition without reading from the text.

I had to read several times in order to get the part
because the student who was directing it didn't want me

in it. He told everyone in the drama department that it wasn't my acting he objected to; it was the fact that my father was governor. It would look as if I were getting special treatment if I were cast in the role.

But he told me something else. "I didn't want you for this play. You probably wouldn't have gotten it if your father weren't governor. So you better act the hell out of this part."

At rehearsals, he'd send the rest of the cast off the stage and make me go through these method-acting absurdities like "pretend you're an ape defending your food" or "pretend you're bacon frying in a pan."

But I did the exercises because I was too insecure to refuse. Years later, I was in New York in a Greenwich Village restaurant, and this same guy who had made my life miserable walked up to the table wearing an apron and carrying a waiter's order pad. I wanted to say, "Well, there's justice in the universe," but instead I said, "Hi, nice to see you again. Could I have a glass of wine?"

One morning, just before the play was to open, I went to a second-hand store on Santa Monica Boulevard. I'd parked on the other side of the street and to get back to my car, I didn't bother going to the crosswalk—I just jaywalked. I didn't see a motorcycle coming up fast behind a Cadillac. He hit me and knocked me through the air. Then I found myself sprawled in the middle of a lane, with cars speeding by on either side. Blood poured from my face onto the street. A man was kneeling beside me, trying to help me up, but my body felt frozen, immovable.

"Come on," he said. "Your nose is bleeding. It's not that bad, but we gotta get you out of the street."

The police came and a crowd had gathered. When my leg buckled under me from the pain, I looked down and saw that it was so swollen it looked like a tennis ball had been implanted under the skin. The skin was black, not only from the bruise that was blooming there, but from the black rubber where the tire had made contact.

"You better have that X-rayed," a cop said to me. "It could be broken."

"No, it can't be," I answered. "I have a play to do."

My leg wasn't broken, but the ball of swelling turned sickening colors. I limped through final rehearsals, hiding the pain that shot through me in the scenes where the actor portraying Jimmy Porter threw me to the floor and grabbed me roughly.

Two days after the accident, I called my mother and told her what had happened. I expected a familiar pattern—a truce brought on by a crisis, as well as concern and sympathy. But her voice was wintry and stiff.

"Well, I hope you feel better," she said in a tone that could have cut glass.

I went through the play wearing two pairs of support hose to cover the bruise, and I ignored the pain in one of my ribs, even though it was occasionally so sharp it took my breath away. Only after the play had closed, and the director had grudgingly told me that I'd done well, did I go to the USC medical center and find out that I'd separated the cartilage on one rib, and had probably made the injury worse every time I got thrown around on stage.

I moved out of Hollywood and into an apartment near campus, which I shared with a girl who was also in the drama department. Wendy's career aspirations were hyphenated, as in singer-dancer-actress. We both played guitar; we shared the same taste in music and books; we shared bags of grass and cartons of ice cream, and occasionally we shared lovers, although not on the same nights.

I wanted to go into therapy again, but I thought if I asked my parents to pay for it, I might end up with the same situation as before—a psychiatrist reporting to the people who were paying the bills. Because the allowance I got from my parents barely covered my half of the rent bills, I had to come up with another idea for money. So I did what any self-respecting left-wing hippie would do—I started selling drugs. I bought grass in bulk, divided it up into pounds, tied them neatly in plastic baggies, and made enough of a profit that I could start seeing a gestalt therapist my acting teacher had recommended.

Wendy was the only person in whom I confided, and some of what I confided had to do with my therapy sessions. It would be the undoing, not only of those sessions, but of our friendship.

One day, I forgot about an appointment with my mother. (My parents have always organized their lives by appointments, even with their children.) Around three-thirty or four, my mother called and said, "You were going to be here at two."

"Oh, I forgot," I said. "I'm sorry—it just slipped my mind. I can't come now because I have a class in about an hour."

"Fine," she said, and hung up.

Wendy came back shortly after that and said, "I thought you were going to see your mother."

"I never told you that." I couldn't have told her. I'd forgotten about it.

She stood there stunned; her expression made it clear she had blown it.

"What's going on, Wendy? How did you know I was supposed to meet my mother today?"

After a few moments of discomfort, she said, "She told me."

"Excuse me?"

"Your mother's called sometimes when you weren't here," she explained. "So we've had these conversations. She asked a lot of questions about you and seemed really concerned. She doesn't understand why you treat her so badly. She said you've lied about her to your father. I felt really sorry for her, and I've gone up to the house to see her a few times. I think she's right, Patti. She's a very nice woman. Why do you make things up about her? I don't think she deserves that."

It was like déjà vu. I thought I was listening to my

father, or my grandparents. Whenever this has happened to me, I feel a terrible exhaustion. I knew my mother had timed her calls so that she would be able to talk to Wendy, not me, and could win another convert over to her side of a battle which seemed to have no end.

"Well, I might as well tell you everything," Wendy continued.

"There's more? I can't wait."

"I went in to see your analyst, also."

"You what?"

Wendy looked at me defiantly. "I wanted to find out why you don't get along with your mother. I wanted to help her."

"Wendy, it's none of your goddamn business why I don't get along with my mother. And whatever goes on between me and my analyst is none of your business either."

"Well, he didn't tell me very much," she admitted.

"It's called doctor-patient confidentiality. But of course, whatever he did tell you, you passed along to my mother, right?"

"Yes," she said.

Wendy moved out after this and years later, when my parents were in the White House, she went to Washington, D.C., to work for my mother.

Wendy was probably one of many people who were swayed by my mother's side of the story. One Christmas vacation, when I was working in a Beverly Hills gift shop, Fred Astaire came in several times. Out of the blue, he pulled one of the saleswomen aside and said: "I'm so surprised to find that Patti is a nice girl. Her mother has told me terrible things about her." The saleswoman repeated the conversation to me afterward and wondered why I wasn't surprised, why I seemed exhausted instead.

I had expected some resistance when I told my parents I was quitting college at the end of my junior year, that I had neither the intention nor the desire to graduate. But their reaction was calm; I assume this was because a degree in drama wouldn't have made that much difference in my ability to get acting jobs.

"Well, I can't say we're surprised," my father said. "But you know, this means that you won't get any more allowance. You're on your own now."

My allowance was still $180 a month, and I probably had nothing saved up. I can't really remember. But if I'd had a small stash of money somewhere, I would remember that.

"Maybe I'll go back and finish college someday," I suggested. "I'm not sure."

"No, you won't," my mother said.

I kept my apartment near campus for most of that summer, paying the rent by working at Brooks Brothers Men's Store in downtown Los Angeles. Usually, I worked upstairs doing the bills and credit card verifications. I'm sure that their books were probably incomprehensible when I left—numbers are not my strong point. There were days when I was asked to fill in on the floor and help men pick out suits, which was even more disastrous.

I quit as soon as I had enough money to leave town on a camping trip with a man named Randy, who lived near me, and his friend Tad, a soft-spoken musician. I was attracted to Tad, but there was something about him that kept me from following my usual pattern of translating everything into sexual terms. Maybe it was that he didn't talk that much; he would play his guitar and sort of drift off into his own world. Also, since I was going to be traveling with the two of them, it was better to keep everything simple and non-sexual.

We camped out below Mount Hood in Oregon and then went to Washington; we hiked during the days, drank Gallo wine at night, played guitars, and cooked food over campfires. We talked about going as far as Canada and decided that we would return to L.A., wrap up our lives there, and then we would drive into

Canada. We would let life just carry us along, not make too many plans, drift. We were so young.

We were gone almost two weeks and pulled into L.A. late one night. The plan was that Randy and Tad would go back to Oregon so Tad could take care of some things; then they'd drive back to L.A., get me, and the three of us would be gone—nomads leaving the world behind. I imagined living the rest of my life in Canada in some tiny cabin by a lake, writing by the fireplace.

Randy was back in three days. He called me and said, in a voice that frightened me, "Patti, can you come over? I need to tell you something."

"Tad's dead," he told me when I got there. His hands were on my shoulders, but suddenly I couldn't feel them. "We stopped at King's Canyon on the way up and he wanted to hike up this mountain. It started to rain and the trail was getting real slick so I told him we should go down, but he didn't want to. He thought that the trail would go over the top and down the other side, and he said, if I wanted to go down, he'd go up and around and meet me in a while." Randy's voice had that flat monotone quality that people get when they recount something so painful, it deadens everything inside them. "I waited until nightfall," he continued, "and by then it was really raining. I got someone to call the rangers because I thought I could hear his voice. I could hear him screaming, but he was way the hell up there. By dawn, they'd figured out that he'd fallen from one ledge onto another and the way the mountains were—like columns close together—the helicopter couldn't get down close enough to drop a rope. And there was no way the search and rescue guys could hike up to him from the ground. They were trying to get a longer line somewhere—that was his only chance, but just as it was getting dark the next night, we heard him scream again as he was falling."

"You heard him?" I asked, trying to imagine it.

"Yeah—we knew he'd fallen."

I remember us holding each other and crying; I remember the numbness that gripped my whole body. And I remember Randy saying, "You know, he always said he'd die in the mountains. Remember he told us one night when we were sitting around the campfire?"

I walked home in a daze. And I called my father, because I needed to reach out to someone and I thought maybe, this time, he'd be there. My friend was dead; he was twenty-one, and I wanted a reason, even though I knew no one could give me that.

I told my father the story, in as flat a voice as Randy had used. The tears were there, but my voice sounded distant and detached.

"Well, I know it's hard," my father said. "But this is where faith comes in. God has his reasons. He's told us that."

"He has?"

"In the Bible. He said, 'In my house there are many mansions.'"

When I hung up the phone, emptier than I'd been before, I was angry at God that a twenty-one-year-old guy—my friend—just fell off a mountain in the middle of the night in the rain, and got smashed to bits on the rocks.

Randy and I took off together, not to Canada, but to Oregon to plant a tree for Tad at the University of Oregon, where he had planned to go someday. It's still there, I guess, with a plaque that tells passersby how short Tad's life was.

CHAPTER 18

. . . .

I RETURNED FROM Oregon in September with no place to live, no job, about a hundred dollars left to my name, and an almost-empty bottle of diet pills, which made everything else pale by comparison. The rest of my life could wait—I needed more drugs.

But when I went to the doctor who had bought my stories before (lost my pills, dropped them in the toilet, dropped them in the garbage disposal, etc.), he put me in an examination room, took a blood test, ran an electrocardiogram, and said, "We have to talk."

I got dressed and followed him into his office.

"Are you trying to kill yourself?" he asked. "Your electrocardiogram looks like a sixty-year-old's," he continued. "And I suspect your blood test is going to show a potassium deficiency. I can put you on a high-potassium drink for that, and I'm not going to refill this prescription, but the rest is up to you. I know you can get amphetamines somewhere else, but if you want to see your twenty-fifth birthday, you won't."

I left his office more frightened than I'd ever been before. All the symptoms I'd been ignoring—heart palpitations, dizziness, nausea—were possibly fatal if I kept doing what I'd been doing. As I drove back to my friend's apartment, I thought, "Okay, I have to stop this. I'm hooked on diet pills. I've got to get off them. I'm messed up, I'm destroying my body, and I don't want to die."

I quit, and even though there would be occasions

over the next few years when I'd slip and get a diet pill from someone, I never returned to my former addiction.

My resolution was limited to the one drug that I was addicted to, though; it didn't include all drugs. I made a distinction between addictive drugs and recreational ones. To get me through the weeks of mood swings and depression that came along with quitting diet pills, I saw nothing inconsistent about smoking a joint.

Withdrawal would have made me sleep at least eighteen hours a day, except I didn't have that luxury. I had to get my life together. Every morning, I had to drink a thick, cherry-flavored potassium drink which almost made me sick. I got it down by reminding myself that this would save my life. I could have become a statistic.

To get some money, I sold everything that was worth anything. I took a couple of pieces of my grandmother's jewelry to a pawnshop on Western Avenue, where the man ahead of me was selling a gun, and the man who walked in after me looked like he wanted to buy one. At another place, I sold clothes, a table my mother had given me, and a few books. I was able to bring my bank balance to three hundred dollars, which seemed like a lot of money to me then. I drove to Santa Monica; the trunk of my Pinto was crammed with my guitar and all the clothes I had left, and the backseat was piled high with books. Amazingly, I got a job at a restaurant called The Great American Food and Beverage Company, where all the employees were required to entertain. The amazing part was that I wasn't very entertaining—I only knew two or three songs, and I played them very badly. The same day I got hired, I found a tiny single apartment for eighty-five dollars a month. I bought a cheap bed at a second-hand store and made bookshelves from bricks and boards.

The theme of the Great American was sort of Henry VIII hedonism; food was heaped onto platters, inviting gluttony, and the music was not meant to be background. Some incredibly talented people worked there:

Katie Segal, who is now famous as an actress; Jeff Altman, the actor and stand-up comic, honed his act there and could command everyone's attention when he acted out all the key figures in the Watergate scandal. Rickie Lee Jones lived down the street in a small apartment and would sit at the bar on some nights, occasionally getting up to sing. She'd close her eyes, get lost in the song, and people would stop talking, forget about eating, and sit with forks poised in midair, mesmerized by her voice.

I started seeing someone who worked at the restaurant. I had to sneak him into my apartment at night because the landlady ran the building like a schoolmarm. So we'd tiptoe past her door and then try to keep our lovemaking quiet because she frequently patrolled the building.

After a few months, I found another apartment up the street—two bedrooms, two bathrooms for $114 a month; a girl I'd once worked with at a gift shop agreed to move in. My romantic involvement ended, but that really didn't matter. I was finally living someplace I liked, where all the tenants were my age; everyone smoked grass and played their stereos too loud.

The couple who managed the building were only a few years my senior and were close friends of Dennis Wilson. The first time I saw him walk by my window, I almost spilled coffee on myself. I'd grown up listening to the Beach Boys; they were the music of summer, the music of teenage romance and teenage loneliness, and Dennis was always the one my eyes had gone to on the album covers. The second time I saw him go visit my landlords, Tricia and Eddie, I made up some excuse to go up there: a leaky faucet or something. I learned right then how the expression "knocked off my feet" came about, because his eyes almost knocked me off the stairs. When Dennis looked at me, I temporarily forgot that the rest of the world wasn't blue like his eyes. They just locked me in and all I could see was this color like the ocean on a perfect day. I walked back downstairs to

my apartment, sat on the couch, and said to my roommate, "He's the most beautiful man I've ever seen."

I started finding myself alone in the apartment a lot
because my roommate had a boyfriend and usually
stayed with him. I was working about four or five nights
a week and had my days free. Dennis walked by one
afternoon while I was playing guitar. I didn't see him,
but he heard me and knocked on the door.

"Hi, I heard you playing," he said.

"Yeah, well, I'm not very good." I could feel my face
getting red. "Do you want to come in?" He was hovering there in the doorway as if he felt awkward and shy.

He came in, but didn't sit down; he walked around,
almost pacing, looking at everything, his hands in his
pockets. From the very beginning, and for years after
that, Dennis was a contradiction to me. He was tense
and more than a little crazy at times; but something
smooth and almost serene came through once in a
while, as if there was this one calm pool in the middle
of a raging river.

"Do you write songs?" he asked, picking up my guitar and looking at it.

"Yes, I just started. I've written poetry for a long
time, but I'm trying to write songs now."

"I'd like to hear some of them."

I didn't answer because I knew there was no way I
could play anything in front of him—not right then.
But Dennis's mind jumped from one thing to another.
As soon as he said that, he was at the door, telling me
he had to go up and see Tricia and Eddie.

"You want to go out sometime?" he asked—almost
over his shoulder.

"Yeah, okay," I said, trying to sound as if it didn't
mean anything.

The problem was, it did. And we didn't really go out;
he picked me up after work one night and we went back
to his house. As wired and unpredictable as Dennis
could be, that's how he was that night, and I knew I

shouldn't stay with him, I knew I'd get hurt, but when did I ever listen to myself about things like that?

He had black satin sheets on his bed and I left tear stains on the pillowcase because I cried myself to sleep, with Dennis practically snoring next to me. I'd had the feeling, in the middle of making love with him, that he didn't even know who I was. This was probably true because months later, when we both knew each other better, he told me he barely remembered that night.

I had hoped Dennis would pursue me after that night, but he didn't. "God, what do you expect?" a friend of mine at the restaurant said. "He probably has a different girl every night. I mean—Dennis Wilson— one of the Beach Boys! I'd be happy for just an hour with him. Do you have any idea how many girls would like to be with him?"

It was probably the first time I had really stopped and thought about celebrity and the effect it has on people. I'd grown up surrounded by well-known people and had gone to school with the children of movie stars. What impressed me about Dennis was Dennis; it meant something to me that I'd spent years listening to the Beach Boys' music, but it had little to do with my feelings about him.

I avoided Dennis for weeks and nursed my hurt feelings. I hid when he walked by. Once, when he knocked on the door, I didn't answer.

Then I decided to drop acid. I followed my usual pattern of hey-I-don't-need-anyone-I-can-do-it-myself and did it alone. I was sitting in my apartment, and the lamplight was splintering into tiny shards which started whirling around my head, making me feel like they were aiming for me. "I think I'm in trouble," some thin voice of sanity said from inside my head. I walked upstairs to one of my neighbors, a girl who was well acquainted with acid.

"I'm tripping," I said, when she opened the door.

"By yourself?"

"Uh-huh. I don't think I'm having a good time."

"Okay, I'm going to get something to show you that will make you feel better," she said. "And we'll go back downstairs. I think you'll feel better in your own place."

She brought me coloring books of Disney characters and talked to me for a long while. When she left, I was having a great time watching the lights dance around me. I spent the rest of the time playing my guitar. I wrote a song that seemed to write itself. When the lights started slowing down, and I felt more in control, I realized that the song was about Dennis and about love, and letting go, and a lot of things that probably made no sense to anyone but me. As I stood up, trying out my legs which hadn't felt too steady for the past four hours, I heard Dennis's truck pull into the driveway. Then I heard his footsteps passing by my window, and it seemed very significant that I'd just written this song about him, and I'd just come back to earth, and at that exact moment he walked by. I went upstairs to Tricia and Eddie's to find Dennis.

Their door was open and when I walked in, I collided with his eyes, just as I did the first time we'd met. It was a feeling I'd have throughout the years, when Dennis and I would reconnect after long absences.

"Are you okay?" Tricia asked.

"Uh—yeah—I think so. I mean, yes I am. I dropped acid tonight, but I'm back now. I guess I'm just a little spaced out."

I sat in Tricia and Eddie's living room, telling them about my Disneyland books, and the lights, but when I mentioned I'd written a song, Dennis took my hand and said, "Come on." He led me out the door and down to my apartment.

"Let me hear it," he said, sitting down on the couch.

I played it for him, amazed that I wasn't nervous, and I wondered if he'd figure out that it was about him. I knew he probably wouldn't.

"I like it," he said when I finished. "How can you remember something you wrote while you were tripping?"

"It's all I've been doing for the past few hours."

We talked for a while but I didn't tell him how hurt and angry I'd been at him, because I was having trouble locating those feelings. When he got up to leave, I was surprised to hear myself say, "You could stay."

He came over and kissed me. "I don't think I should. You should get some sleep." And then he said something that I'd remember for years, because it turned out to be true. He said, "We're going to be in each other's lives for a long time."

"I know," I answered. And I did.

But I knew something else, too. I knew that Dennis would move in and out of my life, unpredictably, that there would always be a connection between us, and that I had to be content with that. I couldn't ask him for more. I'd fallen in love with him the first time we met, but I knew we would never be together, and we shouldn't be. Dennis's crazier moods weren't something I wanted to be around. I had to just let him come and go as he wanted, and expect nothing. I don't think I'd felt that way about anyone before. I'd had an idea that love was something to invest in, for some sort of gain. With Dennis, I just left it alone. And for years, whenever I was with him, I kept getting knocked over by his eyes, which was strange because things like that usually fade after a while. But it never did.

I had been avoiding my parents' house, mostly because of the Watergate scandal. I couldn't bear the dialogue I was hearing within my family.

My father would say, "Nixon should have destroyed the tapes. All of them."

My mother would add that it was "terrible what they are doing to this man." And, "It's wonderful that his daughters are sticking by him."

"He broke the law," I offered on one of these occasions, and immediately regretted including myself in the discussion.

"It's a witch-hunt," my father answered. "It's just

because he's a Republican. And he should have destroyed the damn tapes."

I gave up and stayed away from the house. There was another reason, too. My father had announced that he wouldn't seek a third term as governor, which told me that he was going to run for president in 1976. I assumed that had to be the reason why an FBI agent paid a surprise visit to my apartment building.

He didn't visit me; he walked right by my open door with a file under his arm. I listened as he went from apartment to apartment, knocking on doors, but I couldn't hear what he was saying when he announced himself. When he left the building, it suddenly sounded like a stampede; everyone who had been home came running to my apartment to tell me that an FBI agent had just questioned them about me. What were my habits? Did I have men over a lot? Did I do a lot of drugs? Did I attend demonstrations?

"What pisses me off," one of the tenants said, "is that I heard him next door say he was FBI, and I ran in and flushed an ounce of grass down the toilet. I didn't know he just wanted to ask about you."

I gave him an ounce of my grass, which I'd been planning on selling, just to make it up to him.

My mother must have sensed that I was deliberately staying away; whenever this happens, she gets very insistent about calling. She began phoning me at eight in the morning, when I was almost always sleeping, since I worked until after midnight on most nights.

"You're still asleep?" she'd ask at the sound of my groggy voice.

"Uh-huh."

"Well, I thought you got up early. You always got up early when you were younger. I thought that was your usual schedule."

"I wasn't working nights when I was younger. I am now."

These morning wake-up calls would end with my mother saying, "Well, call me back when you get up."

Which I would do, except there was never any specific reason for the call she'd placed during alarm clock hour.

"Why does she do that?" my roommate asked, because it was becoming a regular thing.

"I don't know," I told her, though I really did.

I knew it had to do with control, and insecurity, and the fact that I'd just slipped away into my own life. But trying to explain this to anyone else would have required going into our long history, and I didn't have the patience.

When my roommate told me she was moving out, I said, "My mother's calls?"

"No," she said, laughing. "I'm going to move in with my boyfriend."

"Because if it is the phone calls, I could always get the number changed."

"And you'd have the nerve not to give it to your mother?"

"No, I wouldn't," I admitted.

I had an unexpected visitor at the restaurant one night—my brother Ron. He strolled in, came over to the desk, where I was working as a hostess, and laughed at my surprise.

"What are you doing here?" I asked, hugging him. It had been a long time since I'd seen him and we'd never really spent much time together, so my reaction was a mixture of things—surprise, happiness, awkwardness.

"I ran away from the folks' house," he said.

"You . . . what?" I have to confess that what first went through my mind was, "Oh God, I really don't want to get involved in this."

"Can I stay at your place?" he asked.

"Yeah, sure. You want to hang out here until I get off work?"

He did, and I introduced this unfamiliar person, my brother, to everyone. It was a strange sort of rush to be doing something that other people take for granted; to

We are a family of actors. Despite our disagreements, on cue we could always smile happily for the cameras: this was taken on Christmas, 1983.

I now realize how much my mother and father were shaped by their parents, Nelle and Jack Reagan (left) and Edith and Kenneth Robbins (shown holding my mother, right).

My mother sometimes looked like a very lonely little girl; her father walked out on the family, and my grandmother, a working actress, left her with relatives.

Believe it or not, I wasn't aware of my father's marriage to Jane Wyman or of their children, Michael and Maureen, until I was seven. At that point, my father was forced to tell me about his other family because Michael was coming to live with us for a while.

Bill Holden and his wife, Brenda, were attendants at my parents' wedding, and Bill was later my godfather. Yet, he drifted out of our lives, and I'll always regret that.

My christening appears to have been a joyful occasion: l-r, Dr. Loyal Davis, my mother, Edith Davis, Nelle Reagan and my father.

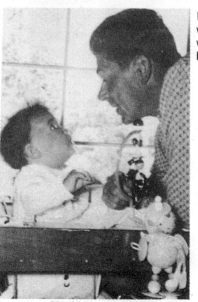

I think *both* my parents were more comfortable with me early on; the trouble came later.

We always seemed to be happiest near water. Summers in Pacific Palisades revolved around the pool.

AP/WIDE WORLD PHOTOS

PRIVATE COLLECTION OF PATTI DAVIS

ARCHIVE PHOTOS

PRIVATE COLLECTION OF PATTI DAVIS

I was thrilled when my brother Ron was born, but my mother
kept us apart most of the time.

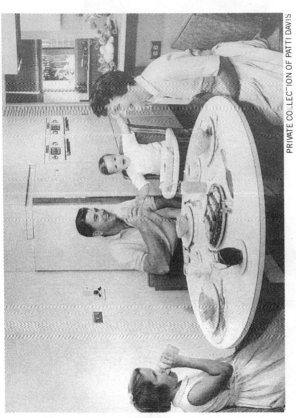

In the perfect electric house built for us by General Electric when my father was host of "GE Theater," we were the perfect family—at least for the camera.

As a child, I was confident, even cocky. But I felt large and awkward as a teenager and being next to my fashionable, petite mother made everything worse.

My parents were jubilant when my father announced his candidacy for governor of California in 1966. I was miserable, which shows in this Christmas portrait the next year.

JULIAN WASSER/TIME MAGAZINE

UPI/BETTMANN

To appease my parents, I agreed to a coming-out party in
1970. Edith and Loyal Davis helped present me to society,
but after that, I refused any part of the debutante circuit.

Addicted to diet pills in the Sixties, I could be fairly thin if the supply was good (top). If not, I grew a little more zaftig, as I was here with my parents and Michael, Maureen and Ron.

PRIVATE COLLECTION OF PATTI DAVIS

PRIVATE COLLECTION OF PATTI DAVIS

In my days as a folksinger-waitress, I moved in with Bernie Leadon (shown onstage with the Eagles in 1974).

This is one of the photographs my father points to when he wants to prove we were a happy family. Yet, the 1980 Republican convention was filled with plenty of backroom family politics.

I was both proud and tearful as my parents left Los Angeles for the move to Washington. Later, as I watched my father's inauguration, I worried about his policies. I figured I could use my new role as "First Daughter" to sway him.

Even *I* had to admit Inauguration Night was a great, shining moment. Here we are: l-r, back row: my cousin Jeff Davis, Maureen's husband Dennis, Michael holding son Cameron, Neil Reagan, my uncle Richard and Ron. Seated: my cousin Anne Davis, Maureen, Michael's wife Colleen, my aunt Bess Reagan, Patricia Davis (my uncle Richard's wife), me, Doria. Center: my parents.

During one of our truces over the years, I tried to get close to my father at a family picnic.

I was nearing the end of my twenties before I realized how small and fragile my mother actually is. Here we are together at the same picnic.

TONY KORODY/SYGMA

What you don't see here are my agents following me as I walked my dog on the beach. Craving my privacy, I eventually requested an end to Secret Service protection.

From the time I was a little girl, I had premonitions someone would try to assassinate my father if he entered politics. Here my mother and I escort him home from the hospital after the shooting in 1981.

My participation in two Survival Sunday anti-nuclear events made my parents irate. I'm pictured here onstage with Graham Nash and backstage with Mike Farrell.

PETER C. BORSARI

UPI/BETTMANN

Though people told me my continued activism would harm my acting career, I insisted on being in an anti-nuclear bene-fit with Jack Nicholson and another with Stevie Wonder.

Tim Hutton and I were drawn together by our newfound fame: his from *Ordinary People*, mine from being the president's daughter. But our relationship was over quickly. Peter Strauss and I lasted longer.

Suddenly, as the president's daughter, I got co-starring roles in a T.V. movie, *For Ladies Only* with Gregory Harrison, and in a stage production of the play *Vanities.*

I shocked my family when I wanted a traditional wedding to Paul Grilley in 1983. Everybody gathered at the Bel-Air Hotel: l-r, Ron, Dennis, Paul's brother Michael, Neil, my father, Paul, me, my mother, Doria, Aunt Bess, Maureen.

PETER C. BORSARI

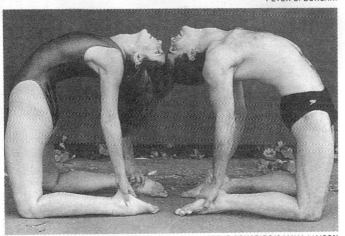

STEVE SCHAPIRO/GAMMA LIAISON

Paul studied Eastern philosophies along with Yoga and quickly won a convert. Even though we're divorced now, we're still good friends.

MARY ANNE FACKLEMAN/THE WHITE HOUSE

My relationship with my family was relatively peaceful for a while after I married Paul. Here we are at the ranch in 1984: l-r, Michael, my father, holding Cameron's shoulders, Michael's wife Colleen, their daughter Ashley, my mother, Ron, Doria, Paul and me.

ROGER SANDLE

THE REAGAN PRESIDENTIAL LIBRARY

In the calm before *Home Front,* I joined my parents for an evening out. My mother, Doria and I got together at Thanksgiving. I always liked Doria and wished we could have been closer.

Working on my first novel, *Home Front,* I was ecstatic. I could finally earn a living writing. In truth, *Home Front* was too innocuous a novel to have caused so much commotion.

My parents left the White House alone. Some people
thought it was a sad image, but I realize that they don't
need anyone else to make their world complete.

After years of tormenting myself about my family situation,
I've finally come to some understanding and acceptance.

me, it was like some sort of holiday event. My brother's here, I kept telling myself, and he's meeting my friends.

When we got back to my apartment, I got the story. Home from boarding school for the summer, he'd had an argument with our mother about her habit of listening in on phone calls. In fact, he was finding himself embroiled in one argument after another.

"She's always on me about cutting my hair, she's always coming into my room," he told me. "She found a bag of grass."

"Oh yeah?" My memory is that we were smoking a joint when he told me this.

"Uh-huh. She called Maureen and asked her what grass looks like. Maureen said it looks sort of like oregano. So I guess she figured it had to be grass, since I haven't shown any overwhelming interest in developing my culinary skills. So anyway, things blew up tonight because I confronted her about listening in on one of my phone calls. She raised her hand to hit me, and I blocked her hand with my arm. She's never tried to hit me before, but I have all these memories of watching her do it to you. I used to look in your room and see her slapping you, and I remember thinking that I was never going to let that happen to me."

"What happened when you blocked her hand?" I was always fascinated with my brother's confidence in sticking up for himself.

"She was completely shocked. She told me I'd hit her, and I said, 'Don't be ridiculous. I blocked your hand.' And then I told her never to try and hit me again. Then I left."

Since Ron was sixteen and didn't have a driver's license yet, he'd gotten a neighborhood friend to drive him over to the restaurant.

"Don't you think we should call and tell Mom where you are?" I said. "I mean, I won't do anything you don't want me to do. But I think it would be decent of us to let her know you're not dead, or on your way to the Mexican border."

That took some discussion, but we finally agreed that we should act like responsible human beings and consider the possibility that a mother whose sixteen-year-old storms out of the house just might be concerned about his welfare. I don't know how we decided that I should be the one to call, but somehow I found myself dialing my mother's number to tell her I had her son.

"He's with you?" she asked in a tone that suggested she'd have been happier if he'd joined the circus.

"Yes. He came to the restaurant. He's going to stay with me."

"For how long?" Icicles were forming along the phone line.

"I don't know."

"Let me speak to Ron, please."

I knew this was coming. "He, uh, he doesn't want to speak to you right now. Maybe he'll call you tomorrow," I said, ignoring my brother, who was sitting on the couch shaking his head no. I wanted to be off the phone more than anything in the world.

"She doesn't know where you live, does she?" Ron asked when I was finally able to hang up.

"No, she's never been here. But if she wanted to find out . . ."

Ron slept on the couch that night, hung around the next day for a while, and then did decide to go home. But before he left, Wendy, my former USC roommate, phoned and said, "I just want to tell you I got a strange call from your mother last night. She said: 'Patti's got Ron.' She sounded really upset. I just thought you'd like to know."

I drove Ron back to our parents' house and let him off at the bottom of the driveway. "I'm sure you understand," I told him.

"Sure. You might get arrested for kidnaping," he answered, and then got out of the car and walked up the driveway with that same casual air that he had when he'd come into the restaurant the night before. It's just life, his walk said—no big deal.

• • •

My next roommate was a girl who had started working at the restaurant after relocating from Arizona. We played music together at work and liked each other; she was staying at her parents' house, so I asked her to move in. It didn't matter to me that she was gay. Homosexuality wasn't discussed as openly then, but she told me and asked if it bothered me. It didn't.

Shortly after she moved in, I allowed myself to think about the fact that she preferred having sex with women instead of men. I wondered if I could have that attraction, or if I wanted to experiment. I thought about it at night as I lay in bed, imagined a woman's body against mine. It didn't bring up any violent feelings of rejection; it didn't bring up any feelings at all. After mulling this over for a couple of weeks, I concluded that this wasn't an attractive idea to me. But I didn't mind when my roommate began seeing another woman that they sometimes slept in her room. I've never thought anyone should judge another's sexual preference.

My mother had apparently forgiven me for harboring my brother when he ran away, and we were on relatively good terms again. She mentioned seeing my apartment several times, so I finally said yes and invited her over. It was late in the afternoon and my roommate was there, getting ready to go to work at the restaurant. As I introduced them and they shook hands, my mother changed the climate in the room with her expression. I don't know how she picked up on the fact that my roommate was gay; there was absolutely nothing spoken or indicated that would have given it away. But she knew.

When I walked her out to the car, she said, "Why are you living with a lesbian?"

"Because she's my friend," I answered defensively.

That evening, my roommate and I talked about my mother's reaction, since it had been very obvious.

"Why don't you have any judgment about this?" she

asked. "You haven't even objected when I've had someone come back here with me."

"People are entitled to make love with whomever they want," I answered. Then I told her about the questions I'd asked myself, the fantasies that just didn't draw me in. She listened intently and then smiled at me.

"I'm glad you told me about that—some people would have kept it to themselves. I think you're destined for a relationship with a guy—no question about it."

Her prediction came true shortly after that conversation.

CHAPTER 19

. . . .

In 1974, THE Eagles were one of the most popular groups in the country. Their third album, *On the Border,* had just been released and it was the only thing playing on my stereo, hour after hour. I was looking at the album insert one night, at the photograph of Bernie Leadon, and I had a feeling, somehow, that I was going to meet him.

Two days later, I drove over to a store called Westwood Music to get some guitar strings. The store was frequented by a lot of well-known musicians, including Jackson Browne and some of the Eagles. As I pulled up to a parking meter outside the store, Bernie's song "My Man," from the new album, came on the radio. Then, a minute after I walked into the store, I turned around and Bernie was coming through the door.

He walked right over to where I was standing, and I felt like I had to say something. "I like your music," I said, and thought, "Oh God, that sounded really lame."

"Thanks," he said. "What's your name?"

"Patti." I deliberately left off my last name because at that time it was still Reagan.

"What are you doing right now? Do you want to go to the beach?" Bernie asked.

"Okay." I think I forgot all about the guitar strings I'd come in there to buy.

Today, I probably would never have gone off with a stranger, but this was the early Seventies. We still had some of the innocence of the Sixties. We still passed joints down the row at rock concerts and took rides from people we'd just met.

Bernie followed me home; I left my car there, and we spent the day on a small section of private beach where Bernie knew one of the homeowners. At one point when we were out in the ocean, we ended up with our arms around each other, treading water, with sunlight and white sea-foam around us. It didn't feel as if we'd just met; there was the easiness of not feeling the need to keep talking, which usually comes after knowing someone a long time.

He drove me up to Topanga Canyon, to his tiny house balanced on a hillside; from the backyard there was a view of the canyon. We made love outside, with an acacia tree spilling yellow blossoms around us and the sun falling behind green hills.

It was dark when Bernie took me home, and he told me he'd just gotten off the road—he'd need about four days to recover and catch up on sleep. He'd call me then. And the odd thing was, I never doubted he would.

"This is a change for you," my roommate said, after I told her every detail of the day. "A guy says he'll call you in four days and you believe him?"

"I've known from the beginning with him," I told her. "And there's something else I know. We're going to be together a long time."

Bernie did call in four days, and we were together for a whole day before I told him who my parents were. The way he remembers it, I had mentioned my father a few times, and Bernie had gotten the impression that he was someone powerful, but assumed he was the head of a corporation or something like that.

We were driving along the Coast Highway when he asked, "So what does your father do, anyway?"

"He's the governor," I told him.

"Of what?"

"California."

"Your last name's Reagan?"

"Uh-huh."

"When were you going to tell me this?"

"Whenever I decided it might not make any difference. Maybe never. I don't know."

"What do you mean you're going to Europe?" my mother said over the phone.

The Eagles were going to play some concert dates in Europe and I was going to be with Bernie. For a couple of months we'd been together constantly, staying either at his house or my apartment. I had considered just going, not announcing the trip beforehand, or getting there and sending a postcard. But I didn't dare.

"I'm going with Bernie," I told my mother, in a stubbornly cheerful tone, as though that could defuse her displeasure.

She had met Bernie once. We had gone to my parents' house for a few minutes to pick something up, I think. It was a brief, agonizing interlude spent standing in the living room introducing a rock musician to the governor's wife, who still played Frank Sinatra on 78's.

"Well, you're going to have a separate hotel room, aren't you?" she said.

"Uh, no. Why would I do that?"

"Have you any idea how this is going to look—traipsing off to Europe with some rock star? The press will just love this."

I knew part of my mother's concern had to do with my father's unannounced candidacy for the presidency in 1976.

"I'm going to let your father handle this," she answered, and hung up. Which meant that she would continue to handle it as soon as she thought of something else to say.

But I was doing more than just going to Europe with Bernie. We were going to live together, which Bernie remembers being more my decision than his, and it probably was. But I figured we were getting to that point anyway, so why not speed things up? Besides, my roommate was moving out to live with her girlfriend. I'd been laid off from work and I was on unemployment. I couldn't afford the rent by myself, and Bernie and I were in love. So it seemed perfectly logical to just push things along and move in together.

Bernie kept his tiny house on the hill, rented it to his brother, and bought a large A-frame on Old Topanga Canyon Road where Charles Manson used to park his bus. We planned on moving in after we got back.

I was in love and felt compelled to spread the news, share the joy. I told all my friends at the restaurant and bragged that I didn't care I'd been laid off. I also decided to tell Dennis, but as I drove over to see him, I questioned my reasons. Maybe part of me wanted him to be bothered by the news.

The Beach Boys had a recording studio in Santa Monica, called Brother Studios. I'd phoned ahead; Dennis was there, and I drove over after quickly putting on makeup and wondering why I was bothering. I was in love with someone else. Why was I nervous, and why was I fixing my eyes, changing my clothes, putting on perfume? There was always an element of confusion when it came to Dennis.

When I arrived, the group was having a meeting. Brian was there, which was unusual, and I could feel tension as soon as I walked into the air-conditioned world of the studio. "Bad timing," I thought, but I plunged ahead anyway.

"I'm going to be moving soon, to Topanga. I wanted you to know," I told Dennis, pulling him aside. We hadn't seen each other in months, and I explained to him about Bernie. He was distracted and jumpy, but he hugged me and said, "I'm really happy for you." I felt the same battle I would always feel with Dennis, especially when he touched me. The battle was between "This is your relationship with him, so be happy with it" and "But I want more—just for a minute." Dennis was already with Karen Lamm then; they would end up marrying, divorcing, and then marrying each other again.

"I'm happy for you, too," I told him as I headed for the door. I ignored the voice inside me that told me I might not be so happy after all.

I hadn't spoken to my mother since she'd hung up on me, and I was leaving the country in a few days. I took a deep breath, dialed the number, and made an appointment to go talk to my parents that evening.

"Why don't you come up around seven-thirty, after dinner?" my mother said.

I was about ten minutes late, which was noted; then we sat in the den, choosing chairs spaced well apart.

"I wanted to tell you that when I come back from Europe, I'm going to be moving to Topanga with Bernie. He bought a new house." I felt the words rush out.

My parents sat stunned, staring at me. Finally, my father spoke.

"Well now, Patti, we weren't prepared for this. We'd expected to talk to you about this trip you're planning, but this is a real shock."

"How can you do this to your father?" my mother asked.

I didn't answer her; I've never figured out a suitable response to that question.

"This is just immoral, what you're doing," my father continued. "Living together without the benefit of marriage is a sin in the eyes of God. He tells us this in the Bible."

"He does? It's in the Bible that you shouldn't live together?" I figured I must have missed that.

"Yes," my father said emphatically. "God wrote that men and women should get married."

"But God didn't write the Bible. The disciples wrote the Bible," I pointed out.

"No, they didn't. God wrote it."

This is the most aggravating aspect of discussing anything with my father. He has this ability to make statements that are so far outside the parameters of logic that they leave you speechless. You sit there with your mouth open, thinking, "This is ridiculous. There's a perfectly sane rebuttal to his statement." Only you can't think of what it could be.

"The point is, you are committing a sin," my father said. "This is a fact. It's a sin in the eyes of God. And if you do this, this young man will not be welcome in our house."

"Well, if he's not welcome, then neither am I," I answered. "But you and Mom will always be welcome in our home." I haven't the slightest idea what made me say that, except that it sounded like a very Christian thing to say, and since we'd been talking about God and the Bible, I must have been inspired. But I couldn't imagine entertaining my parents in our house. Furthermore, I didn't really think they'd take me up on it.

The day we left for Europe, Bernie and I got to the top of the escalator at the Los Angeles airport with a couple of the guys who worked with the Eagles. Suddenly, two photographers jumped in front of us and started snapping pictures. I tried to get away from them, but the escalator was behind me, and then I heard Bernie say, "We'd better do something." Two guys who were with us shoved the photographers back and herded them into a corner. "Open the camera," I heard one of them say. "Give me the film." The photographers were young and looked scared; they opened the cameras, handed over the film, and watched as it was ruined by the light. A week later, an item appeared in *People* magazine stating that I was traveling to Europe with Bernie Leadon of the Eagles; there was no accompanying picture.

Everything seemed to move quickly during this period, and everything was infused with drama and excitement. Our world was rock and roll, crowds screaming at concerts, limousines speeding away from backstage doors. I didn't really notice at first that Bernie's relationship with the group was starting to fracture, but it

would soon become apparent, and it would result in his
being the first one to leave the group. I didn't know,
when I sat on my bed one night writing a song, that it
would increase the tensions that already existed.

The Eagles were getting ready to go back into the
studio and record another album, which would become
One of These Nights. Glenn Frey and Don Henley were
the writers in the group, and the majority of the songs
were theirs; but Bernie and Randy Meisner always had
songs featured on the albums. Bernie hadn't come up
with anything he liked, and when I played him a song
I was writing called "I Wish You Peace," he wanted to
help finish it and record it as his cut on the next album.
I knew that the group had made a decision not to use
any outside writers anymore (they had, in the past,
cowritten with Jackson Browne and J. D. Souther,
among others).

I suppose it would have shown strength of character
for me to say, "Oh no, you guys made this pact. I'll just
keep this song and play it in the living room when no
one's around." I did not have the strength of character,
and I don't even know if I would now. Bernie's insis-
tence that they make an exception to their new rule
didn't help his relationship with the rest of the group,
and I felt guilty about it. But I was also ecstatic that I
was going to have a song on an Eagles album.

This brought up a new dilemma, though. What was
my name going to be on the album credit? I'd been
using Davis sometimes, but Reagan wasn't entirely out
of my vocabulary. I decided that this was the turning
point. I'd change my name and no longer answer to
Patti Reagan.

There was an underlying reason for choosing my
mother's maiden name, but I wouldn't admit it for
years, even to myself. It was a child's way of asking for
a parent's approval. It makes perfect sense to me now
that I would take my mother's name; for all our enmity,
all our battles, she was the only parent who was there.
My father's emotional unavailability made it easy to

relinquish his name; in a way, it had no identity to me.
My mother's did, just as she had a certain identity as a
parent. It might not have been a nurturing identity, but
at least it was something tangible.

During this period, when I was pondering my name
change, I spent an evening with my brother Michael,
which I'd never done before. I don't even remember
how it happened, but I went to Michael's apartment for
dinner. Michael and Colleen weren't married yet, and
I'd met her only once before. Most of the evening's
conversation revolved around my name change; Michael said he didn't see what difference it would make
if people knew who I was anyway.

"I need something that's mine," I explained. But I
knew he didn't understand. When I left that night, we
said we'd get together again, but we never did. Perhaps
the separation of our childhood was ingrained in us. I
had been taught not to seek him out, so I didn't. The
following year when he and Colleen got married, I
heard about it after the fact from my mother.

For about two weeks during this same time, which
was the spring of 1974, Maureen and I began talking on
the phone occasionally. We had lunch once. When I
flew to meet Bernie in Miami, where the Eagles were
recording, she drove me to the airport. But we were still
strangers; it's all any of us have ever learned to be.

My parents didn't get angry about my name change,
which I'm sure was because I had taken my mother's
maiden name. Their reaction was just to ignore the
whole thing.

I made yet another trip to Europe, when the Eagles
played at Wembley Stadium with Elton John, Linda
Ronstadt, and the Beach Boys. I was standing in the
backstage area with Bernie when I saw Dennis and
Karen Lamm walk in; this was the first time I'd seen
Dennis since I'd moved in with Bernie. I went over to
him, introduced him to Bernie, and noticed that he was
uncomfortable and self-conscious. He introduced me to

Karen and the look I received from her froze me. I said, "Well, it's nice to see you again," and walked away.

"She hates me," I said to Bernie. "Did you see how she looked at me? Like she wanted to hit me or something."

"Why do you care this much?" he asked. I hadn't fully explained Dennis to Bernie, and wouldn't until years later.

"Because I do," I said, and left it at that.

I think there are houses that bring good luck and houses that harbor bad luck. The house that Bernie and I had moved into had something very dark and ominous about it. There were strange things that happened there, some of them just feelings that would sneak up on me. I would wake up at night and for some reason be drawn to the top of the stairs, even though there was nothing I needed from downstairs. But I knew that if I went down, I would meet whoever it was who was sharing the house with us—some strange presence that frequently made me turn around sharply, certain I was being watched. One night, while Bernie was away on the road, I'd gone out and left on the outside lights and the inside living-room light. When I came home, the house was dark. I went in and the light switches had been turned off. The doors were locked; no one had broken in, no fuse had blown. I had no concrete explanation for this.

You can't blame a house for splintering a relationship, but I've wondered about its effect on Bernie and me and on Bernie's with the rest of the Eagles. Both relationships seemed to disintegrate while we were in that house. We began arguing more often, and I didn't know how to resolve arguments, or even how to have them. I'd never seen my parents argue with each other; I'd never learned from them how two people work things out in a relationship. My experience with arguing came from my mother, and it had only to do with rage and fear, not with working things out.

The Eagles were four different personalities and from

what I saw, their relationship was affected by their success. The more famous a group becomes, the smaller
their world gets, and the more personality differences
are magnified.

One night in our Topanga house, I decided to try
peyote for the first time, by myself. Bernie didn't come
back until I was well on my way to another galaxy.

He found me sitting in our upstairs bedroom, staring
out the glass doors that opened onto a deck. The house
backed up to a ravine and through tall trees, stars were
dancing in the sky. I was sitting there watching the stars
and thinking about death. This had to do with something Bernie and I hadn't talked about, but had both
been thinking about.

A couple of weeks earlier, we'd flown into L.A. in a
thunderstorm that rocked the plane and made everyone
aboard turn religious. In that same storm, while we
were landing, another plane was crashing and hundreds
of people were killed—just like that. We learned about
it when we walked into the terminal. Since that day, I'd
been afraid for Bernie, afraid because he took so many
planes. While I was tripping on peyote, these fears became enormous.

I told Bernie about this and he said he'd been worried, too. In fact, he'd had a will drawn up a few days
earlier. And the most frightening thing was, he was
leaving on tour the next morning. He was supposed to
be packing because he had an early flight, and we were
sitting there talking about death-by-airplane and these
premonitions that we both had, that if he got on a
plane, he'd die.

Sometime after midnight we got into bed, but I don't
know if we slept at all that night. The conversation had
turned to Bernie leaving the Eagles, which he'd been
talking about doing anyway. Since we both thought
that if he got on the plane the next day he'd die, it
seemed as if right then was a good time to leave. There
is no way to describe this and make it sound rational,
because it wasn't.

The next morning, Bernie called Irving Azoff, who was managing the group, and said he wasn't going on the tour. Panic erupted; one of the lawyers for the group wanted to drive up to Topanga right then and discuss it, but within a few hours, logic returned. Finally, it was agreed that if Bernie thought that particular plane was going to crash, then he could come the next day without missing a show; surely twenty-four hours would be enough time that whatever hex had been put on him would be gone.

This is what he did, except I decided to go with him because I didn't have that much confidence that this hex was really so fickle, and if Bernie was going to die, then I would too. Obviously, neither plane crashed; but just to play it safe, we rented a motor home and drove between concert dates along the East Coast. We stuck with that for nearly a week, and then Bernie started taking planes again. That was, however, his last tour with the Eagles.

My parents and I were not speaking during this time, mainly because I was living in sin. The house Bernie and I moved into after we sold our haunted A-frame was magical. It was a two-story redwood house with so many windows it was like living outside. It was built into the side of a hill and looked down on the canyon; the terraced garden had plots for vegetables so that after a while, we could fix dinner from our garden. Neil Young had once owned the house; there was a detached studio where he had done some recording, and Bernie redid it and turned it into a complete recording studio where he could produce albums.

It seemed like an idyllic life. I gardened, worked on my songwriting, hung out with friends who lived down the hill at the beach; Bernie worked in the studio. I felt far removed from the looming reality of 1976: My father was making another bid for the presidency. He was holding off on his announcement, but the entire country knew he was a candidate.

"Well, if he wins, I'll just leave the country," I'd say to Bernie on the occasions when the reality did crash into our peaceful Topanga life. "I'll go to Canada."

Bernie would just stare at me, with a slightly astonished look, because what response is there to that kind of immaturity? We'd committed ourselves to each other, we were living together, we loved each other, yet when the facts of my familial situation were introduced, I was suddenly on my own again, planning to flee the country.

Around this time, I was at a friend's house on Topanga Beach when Bernie called me from home.

"Your brother's here," he said.

"My . . . what? What are you talking about?"

"Ron—he's here to see you," Bernie said. I noticed that he sounded perfectly casual about this. He was from a family of ten. Didn't brothers and sisters always drop by, participate in your life, come over and spend the day? Well, yes, but not in the Reagan family. We just send Christmas cards.

I hadn't seen Ron in years. He had already become interested in ballet, although our parents didn't know it yet, and I remember he was wearing white and he looked like ballet dancers usually do—sinewy and graceful, his muscles long and defined.

It was awkward at first. I asked him how he'd found me, because our house was so tucked away. Ron had gone to the tax-assessor's office, looked up Bernie's name, gotten the address, and stopped a few residents of Topanga to ask for directions. I was so moved that he'd gone to those lengths to find me, and had been careful not to tell our parents, that I had to turn my face so he wouldn't see my eyes fill with tears.

He spent the afternoon and much of the evening with us. Ron and I took a hike as the sun was going down, and talked about our parents.

"It's strange, isn't it, that you had to go through this to find me?" I said to him. "Why do you think Mom was always so intent on keeping us apart?"

"Well, you were such a bad influence," he teased.

"Seriously."

"She probably thought we'd gang up on her, marshal our forces."

"So it was insecurity?"

"I guess. You know, I remember hearing the fights the two of you had. I wasn't exactly sure what they were about, but I didn't want that to happen to me."

"I don't think you were ever at risk for getting as much anger as I got—over anything," I told him. "Mom liked you."

"Yeah, I know. I had it a lot easier than you did." Ron never shied away from admissions like that; some people would. But that's the way it was—he was the favored child, and we both knew it.

I learned that he was living at home that summer, but coming and going as he pleased, sailing over conflict as he always had. He had a beaten-up car that he usually drove too fast. Because he hardly ever had enough money for gas, he ran the car almost on empty. I don't know if he was still receiving money from our parents at that point, but it couldn't have been much.

"What about the election?" I asked him that night when the three of us were having dinner. "Do you want this to happen? The presidency?"

"It's what Dad wants," he said. "I don't have the right to stand in his way."

Shortly after my brother's visit, I got a letter from my father which read, in part, "I'm sorry you didn't choose to come to the family meeting the other night when I told everyone that I'd decided to run for president."

I hadn't been notified about the meeting, but it was typical of our family that this would be discussed only after the rest of the world already knew.

"Something's going to happen to take him out of the race," I kept telling Bernie every time my father's name was mentioned on the news. "I just know it. I feel it."

"Well, I hope so," Bernie said. "Otherwise I guess you'll be going to Canada."

As far as primaries, the tide was turning for my father—he had started to win some states, but as the convention drew nearer, neither he nor President Ford had the nomination locked up.

It was summer; the sun beat down on our house and the breeze didn't come up until evening. I'd look at the canyon and wonder if my life was going to change—I'd always had a fear that it would. But then I'd keep coming back to the same feeling that something was about to happen.

That something turned out to be my father's announcement of Richard Schweiker as his running mate. It angered conservatives and reversed the tide that had started to move his way.

At the Republican Convention in Kansas City, which Bernie and I watched on television, it was already fairly obvious that Ronald Reagan would not be the candidate in 1976. Because I was "living in sin" and so outspoken about my father's politics, no one wanted me at the convention. Far away from all that high drama, I sat in Topanga and saw Ron, Michael, and Maureen in the box with my mother, and Betsy Bloomingdale, their hairdresser Julius, and Jerry Zipkin in the seats behind her. I could read my mother's expression even on television. She knew my father had lost; she was angry, upset, and determined not to slink away unnoticed. The most telling moment, even to me, was when Betty Ford arrived on the convention floor and was greeted by earsplitting applause. Moments later, my mother came onto the floor, also generating applause; that prompted Betty Ford to get up and dance with Tony Orlando, pulling the applause back in her direction.

I was relieved that my father wouldn't be running for president that year. He would go back to doing a weekly radio show in which he explained his views, and things would be quiet for a while. But it was only the calm before another storm. He was going to run for president until he made it, and I never doubted that eventually he would.

CHAPTER 20

· · · · · · · · · · · · · · ·

ONE THOUGHT THAT had been nagging at me for years was that I didn't want to have a child. Ever. At twenty-four, I was terrified that if I became a mother I would become like my mother and abuse a child in the ways that she abused me. So many years later, I can look back and see that if I'd had a child then, I probably would have done just that—continued the cycle. I wasn't as clear about this then, however, and I had an impressive collection of reasons built up to mask the real one. For example, I felt the world was an unattractive, messed-up place and why bring a child into over-population, nuclear proliferation, environmental destruction, etc. Besides, I had my writing, which was like creatively giving birth, so who needed to have children on top of that? There were probably more reasons, but those were the top few.

A gynecological problem turned out to be the catalyst. I was one of the million or so women who'd had a Dalkon Shield put in, only my doctor was slow in letting me know there were warnings to take them out. By the time he got around to telling me about this, I'd already started bleeding when I shouldn't and having cramps at the wrong time of the month. He told me there was a possibility the IUD had scarred me and I could have a tubal pregnancy if or when I got pregnant.

"I don't want to have a child," I'd answered and had let him put another kind of IUD in me.

I was still under his care four years later, when I

started bleeding and cramping at odd times again. This time my doctor suggested the pill, which I refused, and I left his office with no birth control, no desire to get pregnant, and a fear that if I did, I could have a tubal pregnancy.

Then I heard about an operation in which the Fallopian tubes are cut and cauterized. That was it. I'd found my answer, and nothing was going to stop me.

I called my doctor and said, "I want to have this done."

He replied, "I will absolutely *not* give a twenty-four-year-old girl a tubal ligation."

"But you said I might have scarring—I might never have a healthy pregnancy anyway. So what if I got pregnant by accident and had a tubal pregnancy?"

"Then I'd have to operate," he said.

"Right. So you can just operate now and prevent the whole thing."

"Absolutely not."

I had become so determined to do this that I lost all objective reason. One thing that got blurry was my responsibility to Bernie and our relationship. I didn't discuss this with him. I didn't consult him. It was more like, "Listen, I want you to know I've decided to get sterilized as soon as I find someone who will do it. So, what do you want for dinner?" It wasn't quite that abrupt, but close.

In my heart, I knew I was causing irrevocable damage to our relationship, because what other effect could that have? But I was very myopic about this and saw only what was closest to me.

Bernie remembers my saying that I was afraid I'd become like my mother and repeat her sins, which I don't remember saying, but I hope it's true because it would mean that insight wasn't completely buried.

I arranged to have the surgery done at a county hospital, ignoring the admonitions of friends who tried to point out that at twenty-four, I might not have my whole life mapped out as well as I thought I did. There

was, they suggested, a possibility that I could change
my mind about having kids. But I didn't want to hear
that, so I didn't listen.

The hospital was downtown, near USC. It was a
familiar drive, but not a familiar environment that I
was walking into. WASP girls from Pacific Palisades
whose parents are rich and send them to private schools
don't usually end up at county hospitals.

There was a small group of us who wanted to get
sterilized, and I was by far the youngest. They gave us
a few instruction sessions about exactly what the procedure entailed, blackboard drawings and detailed descriptions. There was a moment, when the nurse was
explaining about an instrument going through this tiny
incision in the navel and cauterizing each Fallopian
tube, when I thought, "Whoa—this sounds scary." I
almost left, almost gave up the whole idea, but I quieted
that voice and stayed.

There would be one other moment when I would
almost change my mind, and Dennis would be the reason.

I was writing a lot of songs then and was playing
sometimes as an opening act for a songwriter I knew.
We played at a club in Venice that had brick walls and
poor ventilation; the smoke got so thick at times it
looked like clouds of dry ice.

I was playing there one night, about a week before I
was scheduled for surgery. The songwriter I was opening for was also a friend of Dennis's and in the middle
of his set, Dennis walked in. We saw each other, collided in the middle of the crowd, and somehow through
the noise and the smoke we stood there talking as if no
one else were around.

Because my sterilization was about the only thing on
my mind, I told him I was going to do it in a week;
suddenly Dennis's face changed to an expression I'd
never seen on him before. He almost started crying.

"Oh God, don't do this," he said, his hands tightening on my arms. "Please—you can't do it. You haven't

thought this through. Listen to me . . ." But right then someone came up and interrupted us. "You and I are going to talk about this tonight," Dennis told me. "Don't you dare leave."

My relationship with Bernie was so strained at this point that I didn't call and say I'd be home late. I followed Dennis back to his house and I don't remember us saying anything at first. We walked through the dark living room and into the bedroom, as if we'd come to a mutual agreement without needing to talk about it, which is probably exactly what happened. One of the effects that Dennis always had on me was that he blocked out everything else. He could narrow the world, pull in its boundaries, keep my focus only on him. I would feel guilty later for what I was doing— cheating on Bernie—but right then there were only the lights coming through the window into the bedroom, the white sheets, Dennis's body against mine, and wanting him.

One of the instructions we'd been given at the hospital was to refrain from sex before the surgery so there would be no danger of becoming pregnant. It was the one thing that even Dennis couldn't block from my mind.

"I can't do this," I whispered to him, which was slightly foolish, since I already was doing it. "I'm not supposed to be having sex because . . ."

"I know why," he interrupted. But he didn't stop and I didn't want him to, but then a part of me did. I was getting confused, and scared that my plans were being ruined which was, I'm sure, his intention.

We did stop before there was any danger of my getting pregnant because I insisted. As I curled up beside him and put my head on his shoulder, an inner voice told me he was right. I was about to do something I would eventually regret, and what Dennis knew best about me was my stubbornness. He could try to talk me out of it, and he did; we lay there talking for almost two hours. But I could block out words—he knew that.

Dennis and I got to know each other better that night than we ever had before. We talked about our childhoods, about growing up with a parent who taught us to fight. Dennis told me there were times when he was so angry at his father, he felt as if he hated him, and then the inevitable guilt would follow.

"Brian was his main target," Dennis said. "But then I'd get in the middle to try and protect Brian. Our father used to beat the shit out of him. The beatings I got were nothing compared to what he got."

"But you did get hit, Dennis. You can't minimize the effect of being hit as a child."

"I don't," he said. "I know it's why I get so crazy sometimes. I just get pissed off so easily."

Seven years later, when I heard over the television that Dennis had drowned after a day of too much drinking and drugging, I thought: That night, he said that the Beach Boys were so young when they became successful that, to him, money had started to feel like a burden. "I have so much money, I'll never have to worry about it—ever. It feels like a prison in a way. I mean, it just doesn't feel right." By the time he died, Dennis had spent, wasted, or given away everything. He died broke. His death was an accident, but I've always suspected his poverty wasn't.

I was supposed to go down to the hospital the following day for my final appointment before the surgery. I was required, because of my age, to talk to a psychiatrist.

"Please think about this," Dennis pleaded with me when I left his house sometime after midnight. "Call me tomorrow—I'll be at the studio all day. Promise me you'll think about it."

I promised him and drove back to Topanga. When I turned into the canyon, into the black fold of mountains, I started crying. I couldn't focus on only one reason for my tears—it was everything. I'd fractured my relationship with Bernie, and now I'd cheated on him. I'd made Dennis stop making love with me, even

though I'd never really gotten over wanting that from
him—all because I'd made a decision to get sterilized.
But that decision had its roots in a much deeper place
than any man could reach; it had to do with a young girl
locked in the bathroom with her mother, waiting for the
blow of her mother's hand.

The psychiatrist was in his forties, dark-haired, with
glasses and an easy smile. I knew what he was looking
for. I knew he wanted to see if I was making a rational
choice, or if I was just upset about something—a broken love affair, for example. One of the nurses had told
me this, in a vague way, but I had enough information
to be confident that I was going to get exactly what I
wanted. After all, I'd been getting what I wanted from
doctors for years. I had a long, impressive resumé in
this game of manipulating doctors. The only difference,
this time, was that I wasn't hustling drugs, I was getting
permission to have a tubal ligation at twenty-four, with
no history of abortions or miscarriages or even any
pregnancies at all.

I was perfectly calm when I sat down across the desk
from the psychiatrist.

"You're very young to have a tubal ligation," he
said.

"Yes, but I've always known I didn't want to have a
child. I'm a writer and I feel my writings are my children. That's where all my nurturing goes."

"Well, a number of creative people feel like that. But
don't you think you might change your mind?"

"I never have. I've felt this way since I was very
young. For as long as I can remember, in fact."

"You were young when you began writing?" he
asked.

"Thirteen. Also, I don't know whether I can have a
healthy pregnancy anyway, because I had a Dalkon
Shield for a long time and there's a chance I could have
some scarring. So it doesn't make sense to expose my-

self to that kind of risk if I know I don't want to have a child anyway."

I knew at that point that he would say yes, and moments later, he did. "Well, you certainly seem rational and clear-headed about this."

Yes, I did, but *seem* was the operative word, although he didn't know it.

I called Dennis from a pay phone outside the hospital. "I've thought about it some more, and I'm going to go through with it," I told him. There was silence for what seemed like a very long moment.

"I guess there's nothing else I can say about it if you're that sure," he said. "I just wish you wouldn't."

Bernie drove me to the hospital the morning of the surgery, and he had the same air of resignation that I'd heard in Dennis's voice. I kissed him good-bye. He said he'd be back in a few hours, and once again I ignored the magnitude of what I was doing.

Three abortions were scheduled before me. I watched from my hospital bed as the women were wheeled out one by one and wheeled back in. When I was finally taken in, I remember being surprised that rock music was piped into the operating room.

"You have music playing," I said to the anesthesiologist. I didn't know until then that surgeries are done with musical accompaniment.

"You don't like it? We can change it," he said.

"Oh no, I didn't mean . . ." But then everything faded to black and I woke up back in the room where I'd started.

The recovery from this surgery is quick which, in my case, might have been unfortunate because it helped me to pass it off lightly. But it changed my life and it ruined something that was important to me. On a romantic level, Bernie's and my relationship didn't recover; the friendship endured and still does because it was rooted in love, but the romantic part suffered irreversible damage. We split up a few months later and I ended up renting a house right down the hill from him.

It was a tiny house that had more windows than walls and was embedded in a hillside. The only heat was from two wood stoves, the floors sloped a little, and the huge stone fireplace was so deep it was hard to keep a fire going in it. But for all its funkiness, I loved this house, and I liked that it was close to Bernie because we had at least held onto a love for each other; we still spent time together and were occasionally still lovers.

At that point, he was my only lover, and when I was late for my period about four or five months after my sterilization, my first reaction was panic. We've split up and now I might be pregnant with his child?

I was back working at The Great American Food and Beverage Company because I was now paying rent again, and I asked every girl I knew at the restaurant what it felt like to be pregnant. In that era of casual sex, almost everyone I knew had at one time been pregnant. I'm still one of the only women I know who never has been pregnant, and who has never had an abortion.

As time went by, I was getting more frightened and one girl at the restaurant suggested that it was my panic that could be delaying my period. But what if the surgery hadn't worked? I thought. Finally, I couldn't stand it anymore; I went to my doctor and had a blood test.

I called him the next day from a pay phone in Santa Monica. I had my new puppy, Freebo, in my car. I was on my way back to Topanga, and I was expecting all my fears to be allayed by the results of the blood test, which had to be negative. I was sure of it.

Instead, the doctor said, "I need you to come in so I can explain to you what has to be done. The test was positive."

I pushed open the door of the phone booth because I suddenly felt like there was no air. "What? How could that be? I had surgery . . . I got sterilized."

"Well, nothing is one hundred percent. It has happened that women have gotten pregnant after sterilization. And it's probably a tubal pregnancy, which means you'll have to have surgery right away or it could rupture and that could be fatal."

I drove to his office in Hollywood with Freebo scampering around the backseat, and my eyes so blurry with tears that I have no idea how I made it there in one piece.

I remember sobbing in his office. He took another blood test, tossing it off as "just routine," and sent me away on the edge of hysteria.

Something took over when I got back in my car; I didn't think about where I was going, I didn't debate it with myself. I didn't even really acknowledge my destination until I was halfway there. I went to the one person who I knew would respond to the crisis I was in—I went to my mother.

I wasn't even sure my parents were in town; we had barely spoken in the few years Bernie and I had been together. But I screeched up the driveway, took Freebo out of the car, and rang the bell. My father answered and I didn't know what to say to him. Freebo trotted into the house and promptly peed on the floor.

"I need to talk to Mom," I said.

"Oh. Well, she's in the bedroom lying down." He was picking up Freebo, going to look for a towel. A dog peeing on the floor was much easier to deal with than a daughter he hadn't seen in months barging in with tears running down her face. He was happy to be left in charge of the puppy.

My mother was lying on the bed and sat up quickly when I walked in, not as surprised as my father was to see me, because nothing ever surprises her as much as it does him.

"A few months ago, I got sterilized," I said, sitting down on the edge of the bed. I was too distraught to be anything but blunt.

"Oh, Patti," she said under her breath.

"And now I think I'm pregnant. My blood test came back positive—he did another one—but if I am, then

I'll have to have surgery . . ." It was a rapid-fire mono-
logue, a repetition of my doctor's dire predictions.

My mother did what she always does in a crisis: She
rose to the occasion, became calm, took charge. She
called my doctor and spoke to him herself, hearing the
same somber prognosis. Then she called my father in
and told him. When she told him that the doctor would
do an ultrasound to determine if it was in fact a tubal
pregnancy, and which tube it was in, my father did what
he usually does in a crisis: He made a joke.

"Like tapping a watermelon to see if it's ripe," he
said.

I had no money for medical care of this kind. I had
no health insurance; I barely had enough money for
rent. My mother said she felt Bernie should assume half
the cost, and then she made an offer she has never made
before or since: She offered to help with the other half.
She said she'd loan me money, or give me money; I'm
not even sure now what the exact words were, it came
as such a surprise.

I had nightmares that night—of long hospital corridors, stark white surgery lights, and harsh voices accusing me, asking me how I could have done this to myself.

The next day when I phoned my doctor, his tone was
completely different.

"You know, the strangest thing happened," he said
cheerfully. "Two women came in the other day for
pregnancy tests—you and a forty-two-year-old woman
who really shouldn't be having any more children.
When I examined you I didn't think you were pregnant—I suspected she was. But then when the blood
tests came back, well, what happened was, the lab
mixed up the tests. But now I have to call this woman
back and tell her."

"So I'm not pregnant," I said in a dull voice. I felt
like I'd been on a roller-coaster ride nonstop for two
days and someone had just thrown me off, smiled, and
said, "End of ride. Have a nice day."

"No, you're not. So if your period doesn't start soon, let me know and I can give you something."

I was at a friend's house at the beach when I made this call and I sat staring out at the ocean, trying to come to terms with the forty-eight hours that had just passed. The doctor suspected what had happened—a mix-up at the lab—yet he let me leave his office hysterically crying and get back into my car; he'd talked to me about ruptured tubes and possible death and then said good-bye, call me tomorrow, have them validate your parking ticket at the front.

I called Bernie; I called my mother, relaying the news in a stunned, monotone voice. "I'll have to talk to you later," I said to each of them.

I don't believe in accidents, or coincidences. So what I think happened with this odd unfolding of circumstances was that I was destined to run to my parents, wedge myself into a family where no one is ever very secure about their place, or their longevity. Only a crisis could have sent me to their front door, so I was sent a crisis to accomplish just that. For the next three years, we had the longest truce in our battle-scarred history.

It was then 1977, and I think part of what contributed to this truce was that no elections loomed on the horizon. Nineteen eighty seemed like a long time away. My parents were in a sort of interlude; the name Reagan wasn't in the news that much. This wasn't the whole reason for our easiness with each other for the following three years, but it helped.

I tried to see Dennis a few days after all this had happened. I drove over to Brother Studios, but as I slowed down to park, I saw Dennis and Karen standing by his car arguing. I stepped on the gas and drove on.

I would never see Dennis again. Our lives would swerve and almost intersect—people we both knew would come back into my life and tell me that he wasn't doing well. Too much drinking, too many drugs. I didn't try to see him. My last memory of him would be

of the night I left his house, of him making me promise
to think carefully about what I was about to do. I didn't
keep that promise—I never thought about it the way he
wanted me to, and there are still days, even now, eight
years after his death, that I want to tell him I'm sorry
and that he was right all along.

CHAPTER 21

. . . .

FOR THE FEW years prior to my father's 1980 candidacy, I pushed everything to the limit. I gave no thought to having a relationship with one man; I was more interested in having sex with whatever man attracted me. Actually, what I told myself was that I didn't want a relationship. I felt like I'd ruined my relationship with Bernie, so I fell into a familiar pattern: brief encounters with men who were destined to leave because they weren't really there in the first place. And when they left, they became like my father and I felt perfectly at home.

There was loneliness underneath this, but I hid it even from myself. If men could treat sex casually, so could I; if they could keep emotion out of it, that wasn't a problem for me. I could detach myself from emotions, too. One guy I went out with a few times suggested that he and I and his best friend try a ménage à trois, and without hesitating I said yes. It wasn't as exciting as I thought it would be; I found it more distracting than anything else. But it helped to cement the attitude I was cultivating, that the heart doesn't have to play a role in sex.

The other thing I pushed into the danger zone was drugs. I began doing coke, but since I couldn't afford it, that meant getting it from people who could, and who had some in their pocket. There were times I ended up in the parking lot outside the restaurant doing coke with a stranger. Or in a motor home behind the Roxy,

or crammed into a bathroom with a few other people,
doing lines with someone I didn't know. It wasn't that
I was blind to the risk, it was that I was getting *off* on
the risk. I drove back to Topanga one night from Hollywood with way too much coke and tequila in my body,
and I knew I was gambling with death on the winding
mountain road. I can handle it, I told myself.

I was tempting myself to become an addict again, the
very thing I swore I wouldn't do. I became friends with
a coke dealer who lived in the canyon, and I often paid
for coke with an exchange system we'd worked out: my
grass for his coke.

I was growing marijuana at my house in an area
where a chicken coop had stood for ten years. The
ground in this spot was rich, black soil, and my plants
grew to almost eight feet. I'd discovered gardening
when I lived with Bernie, and I had focused my talent
for this on my marijuana plants. No more tomatoes and
squash and sweet peas—those were crops you gave
away to your friends. I was growing a crop you *sold* to
your friends, and I was starting to make enough money
that I could quit working in restaurants. I was also still
getting royalty checks from my song the Eagles did, so
between the two I could make ends meet. My days were
spent tending my plants and working on songs and
poems.

My mother wanted to see my house, and I didn't
know how to say no because we were getting along
better . . . but I had these plants. I finally said yes in the
fall, right after I'd harvested them. I had hung my
plants upside down in my pantry so all the juice would
run into the leaves and make the grass more potent. My
whole house smelled like grass.

On the day my mother was to visit, I carried the
plants, one by one, over to my next-door neighbor's
and asked if they could plant-sit for a few hours because
my mother was coming over. Then I opened all the
windows, burned incense, and hoped she had a cold.

I said I'd meet her down the hill at the health-food

store because I knew she'd never find my house. I walked down and waited for a gray Lincoln Continental to pull up, which was not a common sight in Topanga in those days. I loitered in the parking lot, talking to a guy who sold wheat grass juice for a living and a girl who grew herbs and delivered babies on the side, and I ignored their shocked faces when my mother pulled up behind a rainbow-painted van and honked.

By conservative standards, my house was very funky; by Topanga standards, it was perfectly normal. There were no curtains on any of the windows because there were no houses around—I looked out on hillsides. But even if there had been neighboring houses, if you walked around the canyon enough, you saw almost everyone naked at one time or another. So curtains were something I never thought of, and I liked the moon sailing across my face at night and the sun waking me up. I still had my books on shelves of bricks and boards, my stereo sat on a large wooden crate that I'd found in an alley, and my couch was an old second-hand one which had a few holes in the upholstery. Freebo loved it. The wood floor was unvarnished.

A long flight of wooden steps led down to my house. "What do you do when it rains?" my mother asked, following me down the steps.

"What do you mean?"

"It's so far from your car to the house."

"Well, I usually get wet."

I showed her around my house, which took all of five seconds. She glanced at the wooden crate supporting my stereo and suggested I paint it orange. I didn't know why I would possibly want something orange in my living room, but I let it go.

There was something calm about my mother during this period, this interim time between elections. I saw it, understood it, but didn't comment upon it. There wasn't anything for her to be driven about, at least nothing immediate. I knew that my father's political future was still on her mind, but with no election dangling in front of them, there was a chance to be more relaxed.

I think, also, she was more at ease with me because I had come to her in a crisis, and that always made her soften. She never mentioned my pregnancy scare again, although she would allude to my sterilization sometimes, usually in the context of it being information I shouldn't share with any man.

My mother frowned a bit when I showed her my shower, with the glass French doors on one wall that looked right out to the garden.

"Someone could walk right down the stairs and see you taking a shower," she said.

"Yeah, that's true."

When I showed her the pantry, which was a separate room off the kitchen, she glanced at the ceiling and asked, "What are all those hooks doing there?"

"Oh—uh—I think it was the previous tenants. I just haven't gotten around to taking them down."

I made us some herb tea and we sat down at the kitchen table, an old second-hand one that a girl in the canyon had sold to me for twenty dollars. I'd put a lace tablecloth on it to disguise its condition. All the chairs creaked. The table was in a corner of windows, all open right then because I was trying to air out the house.

I don't remember what we were talking about, but in the middle of the conversation, a bee flew in and buzzed past my mother's head.

"Oh my God! A bee just flew in here," she said, swatting at it. "You don't have any screens on your windows."

"Uh, no—I don't. I don't really mind bees flying in and out. Besides, screens aren't really something I want to spend money on."

"Well, Christmas is coming up. What if your father and I bought you screens as your present?"

I envisioned large, aluminum-edged screens sitting under their Christmas tree with red ribbons wrapped around them.

"Gee, I think I'd rather have something else."

"Well, what about curtains?"

I don't know quite how it happened, although it probably had to do with the giddiness of feeling that, at least for a while, we were a family, but my mother's visit led to my parents and Ron coming over one night for dinner. It was 1977, my father was doing his weekly radio show, Ron had already become interested in ballet, and we all seemed a little easier with each other.

I'm not a very good cook—I don't even like to cook. I underbaked the potatoes, overbroiled the fish, and didn't have any dessert because I don't usually eat dessert and I didn't think of it. But everyone was polite about my shortcomings.

It was early November and what was left of my marijuana crop was in plastic Baggies, hidden under my bed, waiting to be sold.

When we moved into the living room after dinner, my father started talking about helicopters flying over the canyons, looking for marijuana plants and people to bust.

"This is the time of year when these plants are harvested," he said, settling into an oak rocker that had cost me about ten dollars at a garage sale. "Thank God I harvested mine early," I thought. " . . . But does he know? Is that why he's saying this?" I will never know the answer, but I suspect he was trying to warn me. It wouldn't look good if his daughter were busted.

"I have information because of my years as governor," he was continuing, "and Topanga is one area they're going to be concentrating on because a lot of people break the law around here and grow drugs. I don't know if any of your friends . . ." His sentence trailed off, and I abruptly changed the subject.

But after they left that night, I called several other growers I knew and passed along the information that had been leaked to me—that narcotics agents would soon be circling over Topanga in helicopters.

"Your father told you this?" one of them said. "Sort

of like a double agent kind of thing? I mean, he's giving us tips about when the narcs are coming?"

"Something like that, I guess. I'm not really sure what his reasons were . . ."

"Well, do you think he'd know exactly when the helicopters are coming? Maybe he has the schedule or something."

My father was very popular in Topanga for the next few weeks. People were camouflaging their marijuana plants because they'd gotten tipped off by the former governor of California that Topanga was a big target area for busts that year. I didn't hear about anyone getting caught.

Playing on the edge of danger is one thing—you can do it for a long time with no consequences; it's when you fall off that you have to take stock.

I wasn't being very discerning about the men I had sex with. I wasn't picking up strangers in bars, but I wasn't being as careful as common sense would dictate. It was probably only a matter of time before I met a man who put me in a situation I didn't want to be in. Now it's called "date rape"; in 1978 it wasn't called anything.

Running out of money again made me consider trying to get some acting work. Someone suggested I try to do commercials, which necessitated having an agent. I went to see a commercial agent, who said, "Well, I'm not sure, but I'll send you out and we'll see what happens." He had an assistant who was young and attractive, and asked me out.

I agreed to meet him at his apartment in Hollywood, and when I got there, as we were deciding where to go for dinner, the flirtation that we'd both been indulging in for a week elevated to kissing, and that kept up in the car, and even in the restaurant. I knew, though, that I didn't want to make love with him. He was attractive, but I wasn't that attracted to him, I guess . . . Whatever the reason, I just didn't want to.

I made that clear when we got back to his apartment after dinner. I probably should have just left him at the curb, gotten into my car, and headed home. But we had been kissing for most of the evening. I thought he was a nice guy and I didn't want to hurt his feelings—I thought I'd just finesse my way out of anything further and then make a graceful exit. The kissing frenzy, at least his end of it, started up again when we walked into his apartment, and he wasn't taking my "no" as a "no." He wouldn't stop.

"Come on, you've wanted this as much as I have," he said, moving me over to the couch.

"No, really, I don't."

I don't think the fear began in a single instant; I think it rose up gradually. I got really frightened when I realized I was being moved underneath him, he was on top of me, and I couldn't push him off. I kept saying no, but his mouth kept smothering the words and his hands were unzipping his pants, pushing up my skirt, and pulling down my underpants. Suddenly, all the strength in my body was gone. Just like that. My arms couldn't push against him anymore, my muscles went limp. It was over quickly, and then he got up like nothing unusual had happened.

"Want something to drink?" he said, pulling his pants up and smoothing his hair back from his forehead. There was something about that last gesture that made me sick—it was so casual, so unassuming.

I shook my head no. I still didn't have enough strength to speak. The word rape didn't enter my mind, because rape was what happened to women in dark alleys or deserted streets at the hands of men they didn't know who put weapons to their throats. Rape wasn't what men who had just bought you dinner did to you.

My hands were shaking as I put my clothes back in place. I didn't know what to call it and didn't have the courage to get angry. I was confused about my own actions. Had I asked for it?

It seemed like a long time before I could stand up and

find my voice to say good-bye, but I know it was only minutes because he was still in the kitchen getting something to drink. I walked out of his apartment and ran to my car, frightened that he would come out after me and try to stop me or talk to me. It all seemed like a bad dream.

On the long drive through Hollywood and along the Coast Highway, I felt like I was miles away from my body. At one point, when I was on the Pacific Coast Highway, I smelled him on me—his cologne, his semen—and I quickly opened the window and let ocean air fill the car.

I didn't fall apart until I walked into my house, took off my clothes, and stood under a hot shower. Then the tears wouldn't stop. I felt what most girls feel when this happens under the circumstances of a date: I felt like it was my fault. I caused it, I encouraged it, I never should have kissed him like that. It was probably the tongue-action that he interpreted as permission-for-intercourse. I felt guilty and ashamed; I told no one.

But that experience made me much more careful. It wasn't as though I had been throwing myself at men, but I hadn't discouraged advances, and I was definitely not reluctant to flirt. After that night, I began keeping to myself more, trying to sober up about life and my actions. I looked at my indulgence with coke, and at the fact I was no stranger to addiction. By doing coke, I was tempting fate. I hadn't been doing it in great quantities, but I felt its impact on my life. I quit coke the same way I had quit diet pills—cold turkey. It never occurred to me to go into rehab, which could have been part stubbornness and part arrogance—I never doubted that I could do it alone. The miracle was, I succeeded. With coke, the only strange thing that happened when I quit was that, once in a while, I'd get this taste in the back of my throat as though I'd just done some. Suddenly it would be there, that bitter taste that I knew so well.

On Christmas Day of that year, 1978, the wheels of a presidential campaign were grinding into motion. I

walked into my parents' bedroom to tell my mother
something. She was in there talking to my grandfather
and I heard her mention Jeane Dixon, the famous as-
trologer. She was starting to repeat whatever Jeane
Dixon had told her, but when she saw me she stopped
mid-sentence and said, "Yes, Patti?" in a tone that
pushed me out of the room.

"Nothing," I said quickly, and left. I don't know
what Jeane Dixon's prediction was, but I've always
suspected it was that my father would become president
in 1980. I could have told them that

In November 1979, I flew to New York to be present for
my father's announcement that he would run for president in 1980. I've thought about that trip a lot over the
years because it was so out of character for me. I disagreed with my father's politics across the board. I did
not want him to be president, for every reason imaginable, and I knew that this image of family unity (all four
children in New York for the announcement) would
fracture sooner rather than later.

The only way I can explain my willingness to make
that trip is that I had never stopped wanting a family.
I had settled for things—moments—that allowed me to
pretend, even though I knew it was an illusion. The only
way I could earn points in the Reagan family at that
time was to be present on the ascendant journey of my
father's political career.

From the outset, I realized how much tumult there
was in a political campaign. On more than one occasion, Mike Deaver has been at the center of the turmoil,
which has never surprised me because I always viewed
him as a sort of surrogate son to my parents. He fell
right into the dramas, the loyalties that could make
hairpin turns and become betrayals, the exits and
reconciliations that keep my parents on the roller-
coaster ride that's come to feel like home. In November
of 1979, tensions between John Sears, my father's campaign manager, and Mike Deaver resulted in Deaver

refusing to attend the announcement. Shortly after
that, he resigned from the campaign. He returned, as I
knew he would, so I didn't pay too much attention to
this drama. It was so familiar.

In New York, I stayed with Cynthia Wick in her
apartment. The Wicks had been family friends for
years, and Ron and I had gone to school with their kids.
In 1985, Cynthia would write me a scathing letter about
my first novel, which she hadn't read, and it would be
our last communication. But in 1979, we were still
friends.

The night of the announcement, we sat at the front
table in the ballroom of the Hilton Hotel—my mother,
Ron, Maureen, Michael, and I—four siblings who were
awkward and tentative in each other's presence. What
I remember most about that night is looking up at my
father while he was speaking and being unable to clap
at strategic points—like his mention of the continued
use of nuclear energy, more funding for defense, less
funding for abortions. Everyone around me was clapping, and I sat there with my hands in my lap, thinking,
"I can't applaud this. It's wrong—he's wrong. I'm not
that much of a liar."

I stayed in New York for four days. I didn't really
know anyone there, but there was one person I could
talk to honestly. Paul Simon had been introduced to me
by a songwriter friend of mine, Libby Titus. Paul was
in the midst of shooting his film *One Trick Pony,* but he
managed to have dinner with me a couple of times, and
I think those dinners saved my sanity, which I was
starting to feel was on shaky ground right then.

"It's like every political disagreement I have ever had
with my parents around the dinner table is now going
to be played out in front of the whole country," I told
him. "I don't know any way around that. I can't just sit
back and pretend I'm happy about this. I think he's
wrong on everything—I think some of his politics are
dangerous."

"Well, you're allowed to speak your mind, too," Paul said. "There's no gag order on you."

There weren't any easy answers for what I was going through, and he didn't try to offer any. He listened, which was exactly what I needed right then, because everyone else around me was applauding my father's candidacy. I'll always be grateful to Paul for his humor, his wisdom, and his willingness to listen. He helped ground me at a point in time when everything seemed to be spinning out of control.

That Christmas was the first time I met Doria Palmieri, who has now been Ron's wife for eleven years. Their relationship was still fairly new at that point; they had met at Stanley Holden's Dance Center, in Los Angeles, where Ron was working to pay for his classes. Doria was also working behind the desk. My mother had complained to me over the phone that Doria was too old for Ron (she's seven years older) but I'd tuned out her complaints.

Ron and I rarely talked, but just before the Christmas holidays and the Wicks' annual Christmas Eve party, he called.

"I might not come to the party," he said.

"Why not?"

"Mom said Doria couldn't come. She said the Wicks don't have enough plates."

"*Plates?*" I said. "They're multimillionaires and they don't have enough *plates*? Couldn't she come up with something better than that?"

"Yeah, like maybe the truth," Ron said.

"Well, let's not get overly ambitious here."

"So I said if she can't come, then I'm not coming, and then they'll have an extra plate."

Ron and Doria both came, and there were enough plates. I went over to Doria as soon as I walked in; I can't stand seeing people subjected to the arctic winds of my mother's disapproval. Anyone in that situation has my immediate support.

"You're very brave," I told her at one point in the evening.

"Oh, not really," she demurred. "I care about Ron and I want to be with him."

"Give yourself credit, Doria. You're very brave. It's not going to be made easy for you, you know."

"I know," she said.

She told me how surprised she was, after she and Ron started going out, when she saw how he lived. His apartment was tiny and sparsely furnished, and she said that he routinely put water on his cereal because he couldn't afford milk.

"You should probably brace yourself for more surprises, Doria. I'm sure there will be some."

My life in Topanga ended because of torrential rains that winter; the creek turned into a raging river and one boy was swept away and died. The two-lane mountain road leading into the canyon crumbled and left only one access—through the San Fernando Valley. This meant that to get to Santa Monica, you had to drive for at least forty minutes as opposed to fifteen. I hung on until the summer, but the canyon was so isolated, and it was going to take a year to rebuild the road. I had to leave the canyon more frequently then because I was trying to get some acting work, which meant readings and auditions. I was always on the road. I was also running out of money, because I wasn't getting much work, and my landlords had raised my rent.

If my attendance at my father's announcement was strange, the next short period of my life was completely bizarre. I put all of my things in storage and moved into my parents' Pacific Palisades home while I looked for an apartment in Santa Monica. My parents agreed readily to this—I suppose it didn't fall into the category of supporting me. I had nothing with me but a few clothes, my guitar, and my dog, Freebo. My parents weren't there very often because they were both out on the campaign trail, but they were around sometimes,

and we didn't fight or argue. We were cautious, awkward, and so polite with each other that a perceptive
person would have looked at us and said, "Something
is about to blow here."

Something was, but I drifted through that summer,
wandering through the house, retracing steps that were
familiar. I looked in my father's closet to see if the gun
he kept was still there; it wasn't, but I found it in the
drawer of his bedside table. I checked my mother's
medicine cabinet for pills and found a bottle of Dalmane. I tried to convince myself that it was encouraging
that there was only one type of tranquilizer there, but
I wasn't encouraged. The bottle was large.

Even though I had the house to myself most of the
time, I hid whatever I wrote, just because that's the
effect that house with all its memories had on me. I tried
to not look at the spot by the window where my mother
used to hit me. I always locked the bathroom door
behind me even though she was miles away in another
state. It was like a collision of past and present, adult
and child.

I knew the harmony I was enjoying with my parents
when they were around was an illusion, and that it
would end, but I was content for it to last as long as
possible. In that spirit, I went to the Republican Convention in Detroit.

When I got to the hotel, I walked into a family crisis.
This time it involved Ron. Doria had come with him,
and when the two of them arrived in my parents' hotel
suite, my mother's expression turned glacial. The argument arose over Ron wanting Doria to stand on stage
with all of us when my father was announced as the
nominee. She wouldn't hear of it; Doria wasn't part of
the family as far as my mother was concerned, and the
look she was giving Doria suggested that she didn't
even think she was part of the human race. Ron said
that he wouldn't go onstage if Doria couldn't be with
him, and then the two of them walked out of the suite.

"What are you trying to do—lose your son?" I asked

her. I was a little stunned, because Ron was her favorite child and she was treating him with the coldness she had usually reserved for me.

They finally cut a deal. If Ron would go onstage without Doria, my mother would be nicer to Doria in the future.

Ron and I were scheduled for a number of interviews, one with Walter Cronkite, one with Barbara Walters, and others which I can't remember because I was in a perpetual state of terror the whole time. I couldn't pretend to be supportive of my father's politics, yet I didn't have the courage to say how I really felt. My deepest fears had to do with the victory I knew was imminent. I was frightened for the effect that my father's politics would have on the country and the world.

Ron, Doria, and I were walking through the lobby of the hotel during the convention and a woman came up to us, shook our hands, and said, "Oh, you must be so proud."

"Yes, I am," Ron said.

The woman looked at me because it was my cue to speak, and I just stood there, speechless, the same collision of emotions stealing my voice. I'm supposed to be proud. I *am* proud of his achievement at this stage of his life. But how can I be proud of an ideology that scares the hell out of me?

"Can't you just say yes and let it go?" Ron said later.

"That's just it—I can't. I'd feel like a liar. It's not that I don't have any pride, it's that I have a lot of other feelings, too, all of them negative."

"So just lie. It would have made that woman feel better," Ron answered.

"This is why I'm not a good Reagan," I thought. "I just can't rationalize dishonesty."

Ron and I were on our way to be interviewed by Barbara Walters when the television screens that were all over the hotel showed my mother taking a wrong step as she went to her seat and disappearing from the camera. The commentator said she was all right, just bruised, and I remember turning away from the television screen and shutting my eyes for a second. The thought that went through my mind was the bottle of Dalmane that I knew was somewhere in her hotel room. I don't know if that was responsible for her falling—I'll never know—but I considered it.

When my father was formally announced as the candidate, we got on stage (without Doria) and smiled as we always do when the cameras are on us. We waved to the crowd and hid a lifetime of dissension.

On the flight back to California, I thought a lot about the conflict I always felt every time someone discussed the pride I must feel in my father. I decided that what I'm proud of is being part of a family that made its mark in the world. My parents didn't choose to live small, insular lives; their sights were set high and they worked to achieve the goals that were important to them. I can't be proud of an ideology that I disagree with so deeply, and that's where the conflict comes in. But I admire the motivation and the passion that turned my parents toward politics. Too many people don't think beyond finding their toothbrush in the morning and figuring out where to have dinner in the evening. That's not a complaint I could ever have about my family.

When I got back to California after the convention, I finally found an apartment in Santa Monica that I could afford. I was still getting some royalty checks from my song on the Eagles album, and a friend of mine cosigned a two-thousand-dollar bank loan for me. I had no credit, so I needed a cosigner, and it wasn't something I would have asked of my parents.

With enough money to last me for a short while, I moved into a tiny, one-bedroom bungalow, painted it myself, plugged in my amber lights, put my worn Indian rug on the floor, and breathed a sigh of relief that I had my own home again.

CHAPTER 22

· · · · · · · · · · · · · · ·

As THE 1980 election drew near, I felt like I had turned dishonesty into an art form. I lied about the depth of my political disagreements with my father, passing them off as issues we discussed rationally and respectfully. In fact, I was avoiding political discussions with him because we were so far apart. Mike Wallace interviewed me for a "60 Minutes" segment about my father, and I deliberately gave the impression that we were just a normal family in which differing philosophies and opinions were tolerated, and yes, we'd had our problems, but what family doesn't. We get along fine, all four children; there's the age difference, but we're still close.

In another interview, I was asked if I was registered to vote. I said yes, as an Independent, although this was untrue. I wasn't registered at all, but I quickly ran out and registered to cover up my lie.

I also lied about drugs. I was asked about marijuana and I said, "Sure, I used to smoke pot but I don't anymore. It makes you forget things—like where you live." The truth was, grass was the only drug I hadn't given up because it eased the fears that were gnawing at me.

Another thing I kept quiet about was my horror at how the hostage situation was being discussed inside the Reagan camp. Since my contact with my father was limited, most of this was filtered through my mother. The phrase "October Surprise" kept cropping up and was soon campaign rhetoric. The more I listened, the more I realized that they were actually dreading the thought that the hostages might be released—if it happened at a time they thought would be inconvenient for their election plans.

"It would be just like Carter to get those hostages out right before the election so he could win," I heard my mother say on the phone one day. I'd gone up to the house and she was obviously talking to someone who was agreeing with her, judging by the "Yes, I knows" that she was injecting into the conversation.

"Well, it would make him a hero," she said, her voice tightening with disapproval. "He might easily win then."

I waved good-bye before she hung up and left the house; I felt sick. She was only voicing rhetoric that must have been going on for months. These are human beings, I thought, taken hostage, tortured, imprisoned. And they're being discussed like pawns in some game. But I said nothing.

I also lied about wanting an acting career. What I wanted was acting work because I needed money, but it wasn't my passion. Writing was, and always had been, but part of me was still that young girl, hiding poetry from her mother. Writers are dangerous was the message that had gotten through to me from my mother's judgmentalism. Eventually they get to the truth, and that's not something we want in this family.

The year before, my mother had asked Aaron Spelling to give me a small part in one of his shows so that I could get my Screen Actors Guild card. Getting a SAG card is one of the Catch 22's of the movie industry. You can't get it unless you have work, but people don't want to give you work unless you have it. So either someone has to do you a favor, or they have to be so knocked out by you that they can't imagine anyone else in the role. The latter was not going to happen to me, so I took the favor. I did a bit part on "Love Boat," paid for my SAG card, and ended up with a few hundred dollars in my pocket, which was a fortune to me then.

Just before the election, Jay Bernstein, who had managed Farrah Fawcett and Suzanne Somers, took an interest in me. Suddenly, I was being marketed, groomed, sold, promoted. He sent me to a Beverly Hills hairdresser, advised me on clothes, and approached the William Morris Agency about representing me. He took me to Ma Maison for lunch and told me I had to get out more—to premieres and functions and to be seen by the Hollywood Elite. I didn't care about any of this. Just give me a cabin somewhere and a typewriter. But he was also talking about money, which I desperately needed, so I smiled and went along with it. From song royalties and odd jobs, I had about three thousand dollars left to my name. I was paying $350 a month in rent; I had no credit cards, my used Toyota had seventy thousand miles on it, and Jay was suggesting I buy clothes at Giorgio's.

"What, are you kidding?" I said to him. "I've been buying tennis shoes at Woolworth's for the last five years."

I was discreetly involved at this time in anti-nuclear activities because I was so disturbed by my father's rhetoric regarding the Soviet Union. I was appalled by his quotes about "godless monsters" and the "evil empire," and his emphasis on more military buildup. I had started to do extensive research through various organizations on the nuclear situation. I was spending time with people from the Alliance for Survival, the antinuclear group that was the most visible at that time and which was, I thought, doing some of the best work on the issue. I was keeping quiet about this, but I knew I wouldn't remain silent for long. I was being given visibility because of my father's candidacy, and the only thing that made sense to me was trying to do something significant with it. Standing shoulder to shoulder with people who were trying to rid the world of a nuclear threat seemed not only significant, but a clearly constructive use of fame. I couldn't do anything about the visibility that was thrust on me, but I could do something *with* it.

A few days before the election, I drove down to the beach at sunset and walked along the shore. Freebo raced past me, chasing seagulls. I tried to imagine what it would feel like to have armed Secret Service agents following me, right on my heels. Can I live like that? "Oh God," I thought, "isn't there an island I can escape to, to wait out the next four years?"

But then I thought about all my idealistic plans to introduce a liberal, anti-nuclear ideology into a rabidly conservative, pro-nuclear White House. I was sure I could do it—after all, I was part of the family; I'd have the unlisted phone number. I could bring my friends over for dinner. One fantasy was to introduce my father to Daniel Ellsberg over hors d'oeuvres.

I took a long look at the beach that evening because I knew it might be the last time I could walk like that, alone with my dog. It just wouldn't be the same with a band of heavily armed men behind me, getting sand in their walkie-talkies.

The day of the election, I went up to my parents' house in Pacific Palisades. My mother was getting her hair done and she said, "I'm so nervous, I have a headache and my stomach is upset."

I wish now I'd asked her what she was nervous about—if it was because their dream was finally going to be realized.

She had to know he would win—how could she not? Everyone knew. I left their house and went to vote. I took the card into the booth, stood in there for a few minutes, put it in the envelope, and dropped it in the slot. There wasn't a single hole punched in it. I couldn't vote for my father, I thought he was wrong on everything. But I couldn't vote against him because that would have taken more courage than I had right then.

So I did nothing, which is probably about as cowardly as you can get. In a subsequent interview, I was asked if I voted for him. "Yes," I lied.

That night, I borrowed a black halter dress from my girlfriend, got in my Toyota, and started driving to the home of my parents' friends, Earle and Marion Jorgensen, who were having a dinner party for them. From there, everyone was to go to the Century Plaza. I had turned the television off when I was getting dressed—I wanted to delay the inevitable as long as I could. By the end of the evening, my father would be president; I had visions of Secret Service agents staking out my apartment, waiting for me to return.

I was driving along Sunset Boulevard when I thought, "This is ridiculous. I should turn on the radio and see what's happening." President Carter had conceded defeat a couple of hours earlier; my father was already the newly elected president.

I pulled off Sunset onto a side street and parked in front of a huge mansion, well lighted and marked with Security Patrol signs. In the dark space of my car, I took a joint out of my purse. I had rolled it earlier just in case I had trouble getting through the night. I lit it because I was already having trouble and the night had just started. President, First Family—I rolled the words around in my head, trying to absorb the reality they now represented.

When I walked into the Jorgensens' house, the mood was euphoric. I went over to my father, waited for him to notice me, because he was talking to Alfred Bloomingdale, and then kissed him on the cheek. "Congratulations," I said, but the word felt foreign to me. I was very clear on what I was *supposed* to be feeling; but there were too many other feelings that got in the way.

Ron was, by that time, living in New York with Doria, but they had flown back for election night. Later, at the Century Plaza, when it was clear that once again Doria was not going to walk onstage with us, I asked Ron if they were ever going to get married.

"I don't know what the point of marriage is. It's just a piece of paper," he said.

"The point is, for you, that she'll keep getting punished for the two of you living together out of wedlock. That piece of paper might buy peace of mind."

Just before we were to walk onstage, my mother looked me up and down and said, "You look very svelte in that dress, madam." There was something icy and critical in her tone.

"It's starting already," I thought, "backtracking to our old battlegrounds."

"What does *that* mean?" I asked. I wasn't asking what the word itself meant—I knew that. I was asking what *she* meant. What was she really trying to say to me? Her look was saying more than her words.

But she took the question literally and gave me Webster's definition of the word svelte. The reason this exchange stays in my mind is that it was a hint that we were about to make a return journey. Harmony is a short game in our family—a couple of innings at the most. I took her comment, and the look her eyes gave me while she was saying it, as a warning buzzer.

The Secret Service didn't show up right away; I had about two weeks of freedom, but it didn't feel like freedom because I was waiting for them, which was starting to feel like waiting in the dentist's chair. One day, I asked my mother, in as casual a voice as I could, when they were coming. The next day I got a call from the head of the Western Division of the Secret Service that they had to come talk to me about protection.

Three agents came to my apartment, all in suits, which always makes me nervous. Too many men in suits, and I think I'm being audited. What they wanted to know, right off, was: What was my daily schedule?

"I don't really have a set schedule," I said. "I mean, it varies from day to day. I work out every day—in the mornings usually."

"Where do you do that?" one of them asked.

"Jane Fonda's Workout."

"Uh-huh. We'll need the address. Now, do you drive your own car?"

"Of course I do," I said. "Did you think I ride around in limos or something?"

"We'd prefer it if you let us drive you everywhere. We can do our job better that way."

"You want me to stop driving?" My parents did that; in fact, they're still driven around. I don't know at this point if they even remember how to drive. "What if I say no?"

He gave me an exasperated look. "Then we'll just have to follow you in another car. But we'd prefer it . . ."

"You'll have to follow me."

"We're going to be with you twenty-four hours a day, three hundred and sixty-five days of the year for the next four years," he said. "So we'll have to get used to each other. We don't want to invade your privacy, but you'll have to let us know where you're going and when. Sometimes we'll have to send an advance man ahead to check out a location. So as much notice as you can give us, we'd appreciate it."

I didn't do well with this situation. On one of the occasions when I drove too fast and lost the agents who were following me, the head of my Secret Service detail said, "We all understand how difficult this is for you, being followed twenty-four hours a day, but what you don't seem to understand is that if something happened, any one of these men would die for you. So you might think it's funny, taking off and losing them, but think about what their job is, and what they might have to sacrifice."

He was right, and I had no answer—except to feel badly about trying to make fools of them. But it never got easier having a small contingent of men monitoring my every move.

The only part of my life that made sense right then was my own political growth. I was spending more and more time with people from the Alliance for Survival, and the interviews I was giving were becoming more revealing about my true beliefs.

The fear that I had felt at the Republican Convention had become a permanent state of mind for me. I couldn't find any issue which made me feel any closer to my father's politics.

I drove up to my parents' Santa Barbara ranch one weekend and found my father throwing magazines and colored newsprint into the fireplace, something which is not environmentally responsible because of the dyes used.

"You shouldn't be burning colored paper like that," I told my father. "The dyes are very harmful when they're burned."

"What's the difference?" he said. "It just goes up in the air."

The only people I felt I was in accord with right then were those who shared my priorities—specifically, people in the anti-nuclear movement. Everyone else around me was concentrating on things which seemed irrelevant.

Jay Bernstein was trying to "make me over." He took me to Ma Maison for lunch one day and afterward, in the parking lot, he said in a low voice, "Patti, do you know that you have two hangnails on your right hand? Can't you get a manicure?"

"So what if I have hangnails?"

"And not only that," he continued, "but when you had tea, you left the tea bag in the cup instead of taking it out and winding it around your spoon." He was completely serious—this was important stuff to him.

"You have to be fucking kidding me," I said, and got into my Toyota with the "One Nuclear Bomb Can Ruin Your Whole Day" bumper sticker, waved good-bye, and drove off.

The problem was, though, that I needed to make a living. I couldn't just spend my days working on the anti-nuclear issue. So I had to go along with some of

Jay's ideas, such as being "seen" in the evenings. It seemed to work, because I got a $100,000 contract with NBC, which came at the right time: I was just about out of money. I began taking acting classes again, so I could earn my salary.

When I called my accountant, who for years had just filed the short forms for me, and told him I was getting $100,000 and wasn't that great, he said, "Actually, you're not."

"I'm not?"

"No. You have a manager and an agent. That's twenty-five percent right off the top, and then there will be taxes."

"Taxes?" I'd always gotten money back at tax time because of restaurant work. "I forgot about that," I told him.

My only extravagance with my fortune was to buy a new Toyota.

Ron and Doria were having money problems, too. Ron was dancing with the Joffrey Ballet, but he was barely making ends meet, and Doria was working as an editor at *Interview* magazine. In one of our phone conversations, they told me they couldn't get credit cards because they didn't make enough money and had no credit.

In another conversation, Ron told me they were going to get married. I remember the date of his call because it was the anniversary of John Kennedy's assassination—November 22.

"But don't tell anyone," he said.

Two days later, Ron and Doria were married in a New York courthouse with a friend and a Secret Service agent as witnesses. The press found out before my parents did and called them before Ron did.

Then my mother called me. "Did you know about this?"

"Uh . . . yes. As a matter of fact, I did."

"And you didn't tell us?" she asked.

"No, I didn't. I didn't think it was my place," I answered.

"Can you see how embarrassing this is? We have to try to explain to the press why our son got married without letting us know."

I had nothing to contribute to this conversation. I just listened and waited for it to end. On the surface, it seems strange that Ron, who always enjoyed a better relationship with our parents than I did, would conceal his marriage plans. But I look at it as further evidence that closeness is not part of our family, not on any deep level.

One night, when I was having dinner at Morton's (another must-be-seen-at place), I noticed Tim Hutton across the restaurant. We had met briefly in New York months before at Andy Warhol's studio; we were each being photographed for *Interview* magazine, Tim because of the film *Ordinary People,* and me because my father was running for president. We'd only spoken for a few minutes that day, but he'd made an impression on me, so I went over and reintroduced myself.

For the next hour or so we kept stealing glances at each other across the restaurant, and when I got up to leave I did something I've never done before or since. I wrote my phone number on a piece of paper, folded it up, went over to Tim, slipped it in his hand, said, "Call me, okay?" and left.

A few days later, he did. Tim and I had something in common right then, which was being newly famous, a bad ingredient for a new relationship. It didn't matter that he was younger than I. We were *both* young in this game of paparazzi, gossip columnists, and no privacy. The *Enquirer* found out about us and was going to do a story, but somehow Jay got them to kill it. I'll never know what really happened, but often in these situations, one story is swapped for another.

If we went into Westwood Village for dinner, we walked into the restaurant separately. Tim would go in first, I'd wait a few seconds and then walk in. It sounds ridiculous, and probably was, but if you add the Secret Service to the equation, it becomes obvious how conspicuous we were. My agents had traded in their dark suits for more casual clothes, trying to blend in with my life-style, but there's something glaring about two men with walkie-talkies striding purposefully down the sidewalk behind their "protectee." They tend to turn heads, and then passersby focus their attention on whoever is being followed; if it's two famous people, traffic starts to slow down.

I don't know if Tim and I could have had a lengthy relationship, or if we were well suited to each other at all; we never got a chance to find out. I don't know how any relationship can grow in that kind of circus atmosphere. It eventually just got to be too much.

While we were seeing each other, I took him up to my parents' house one evening. He had just been cast in *Taps*, which was going to start shooting soon. My parents were in the den, watching television, and we sat down for a few minutes. My mother asked Tim what he was going to be doing next and he started talking about *Taps*.

"This isn't an anti-military movie at all, though," he said, directing himself mostly to my father. "It's a very balanced picture of the military and doesn't bash them or make it seem like it's wrong to enlist." He went on like that for a few minutes, and my mouth must have been hanging open. Suddenly he'd turned into a spokesman for recruitment. I knew Tim's politics—they weren't conservative—yet William F. Buckley would have been proud of this speech.

"Well, I'm glad to hear that," my father said, beaming. "There's just been too much of that over the years, particularly since the Vietnam War—this thing of making the military into the villain—it's just propaganda. When I was in pictures, the army movies we made showed what heroes these men are . . ." His speech went on for longer than a few minutes.

When we left and got back in Tim's car, I said, "Do you mind telling me what that was all about? You don't believe all that stuff you were saying. What the hell came over you?"

"I didn't want to antagonize your parents."

"Fine, but don't you think you went a little overboard? You sounded like you were auditioning for the Young Republicans."

"But, look, it made them feel good hearing that. It's not my place to go up there and criticize them politically," Tim said.

We argued about this for a while, but I understood what had happened. It's so much easier to tell my parents what you know they want to hear, and they have that effect on almost everyone. My father is so genial that you don't want to ruffle him, and my mother is intimidating, so you definitely don't want to ruffle her. The result is that strange things come out of people's mouths.

Things kept escalating, and my father hadn't even been inaugurated yet. At least to me they were escalating, because I'd forgotten how to stand my ground and say no.

Jay called me one morning and said, "I want you to have more exposure. I'm going to release a story that you were offered a million dollars to write a book."

"I was?"

"No, you weren't. But I'm going to say you were. And you turned it down."

"I did? Oh—well, okay."

My mother asked me to do an interview defending her because she'd started to get some bad press. "Oh—well, okay." The reporter sold it to the *Star*. I called Ron in New York and said, "I can't believe I was tricked into doing an interview for the *Star*."

"Why didn't you say no to the interview in the first place?" he said. "I did."

"You did? No has been a difficult word for me lately."

But right about then I was given time to slow down
and look at what I was doing. I usually get sick only
when things in my life are causing havoc with my emotions. The rest of the time, I amble through flu seasons
wondering why everyone around me is coughing so
much. That December, I got a fairly bad case of bronchitis and was honest enough to tell a reporter, much
later, that I thought emotional stress had been the
cause. Over the years, this has been repeated as everything from a nervous breakdown, to a collapse, to an
undisclosed ailment. It was bronchitis—nothing else.

But it hit me in the middle of the night. Suddenly I
didn't feel like I could breathe, and I called the Secret
Service on the special phone and said "I'm having trouble breathing" to the agent who answered. There was a
small stampede to my door, they put me in the back of
their station wagon and drove me to the emergency
room of Santa Monica Hospital. Their car was
equipped with a siren, and I don't actually remember if
they used it, but they should have because they were
seriously over the speed limit.

The doctor made me inhale some sort of mist, pro-
nounced me ill with nothing more than bronchitis—
hardly fatal—and said I could go.

"You should call your parents," said the agent who
had been posted in the examining room.

"Why? It's two o'clock in the morning," I said.

"They may have heard you were taken to the emergency room. It went out over the radio. Their agents
might have woken them up to tell them. They might be
worried."

My father's voice answered with some unintelligible
sound like "Huh?"—clearly indicating that no one had
woken him up prior to my call. He'd been sound asleep
for hours.

"Hi, Dad," I said, my voice hoarse and whispery.

"Who's this?"

"Patti. I just wanted to tell you that I had to be taken

to the emergency room, but I'm fine. Just bronchitis. I'm going home now." I felt like a complete idiot.

"You sound funny," he mumbled.

"My voice is hoarse—the bronchitis. I'm going home now."

"Oh, okay. Good night." And then he hung up.

For the next two days, I lay in bed, contemplating this new life that was mine whether I wanted it or not. I have to do something constructive with this, I lectured myself, and that kept leading me back to politics, and issues, and my fantasy that I could make inroads into the conservatism of the newly elected administration. It would turn out to be a pipe dream, but it got me out of bed and gave me a reason to endure all the other craziness around me.

I was still light-headed from being sick on December 8, when John Lennon was gunned down outside the Dakota. My mother happened to call me the next day, for some reason that she never even got to, because the somber tone of my voice sent her in another direction.

"What's the matter with you?" she said. "You sound like someone just died."

"Someone did," I answered tersely. "John Lennon. I'm sure you heard about it."

"Oh—yes."

Flashes of déjà vu crashed into me. John Kennedy, Robert Kennedy, Martin Luther King. My grief was always colliding with my mother's casual air.

"You only care about the deaths of people who agree with you politically," I said, and then before she could respond, I added, "I'm a little upset right now. I don't want to talk about this any further." Now I realize I was probably too harsh with her, but when I'm in pain, I'm not always careful about the things I say.

We never did talk about it. But at that moment, we were back on our home turf, pitted against each other. We'd had a long truce, but it was over.

CHAPTER 23

· · · · · · · · · · · · · · ·

I STOPPED SEEING Tim before the inauguration in January. I don't think we even talked about it—we just parted ways. It was clear to both of us that it wasn't working out.

Jay Bernstein and I also parted ways, but not as amicably. He had told me that he should escort me to the inauguration; actually, it was more like a declaration. It was during my "I forgot how to say no" period, so of course I'd said yes. Then he wanted to know about limos and accommodations, and a lot of other things, and my mother started harassing me from the other end, saying, "We can't make arrangements for your manager." Finally, I threw up my hands and said enough. I told Jay this was really not going to work out, injecting himself into the inauguration. He blew up, yelled at me, called me names, and turned me over to Larry Thompson, his partner at that time. Larry then became my manager.

January 20, 1981: My father was being sworn in as the fortieth president of the United States. The snow, piled against curbs, was melting to slush. Maureen came with her fiancé, Dennis Revell. Michael and Colleen brought their son, Cameron, the sole Reagan grandchild at that point. Michael and Maureen had been the only offspring to campaign for my father, so they were euphoric about Inauguration Week. Ron and Doria, by then legally married, could finally appear together onstage.

As we were waiting to walk onto the platform, something happened which became more significant to me as time went on. Someone (I think it was Ed Meese, but I could be confused about that because several men run together in my mind and become faceless) came up to my father and said, "The hostages have just lifted off." My father closed his eyes and said, "Thank God," almost under his breath. Then he said to my mother, "They've just left Iran."

Moments later, we were seated on the platform, and my father was standing solemnly, his hand on his mother's worn, Scotch-taped Bible, swearing to uphold the office of President of the United States. I looked past him to the sea of people down below—the tens of thousands who had come to see Ronald Reagan sworn in as the fortieth president—and I tried to think of the event in those terms—that this was my father up there. But I couldn't. Because all my life, he has been a figure on the television screen, or a figure onstage giving a speech, or a photograph in the newspaper. He comes home as that same person. I know the public man, the same one the rest of the country has seen. It's not a question of reconciling two halves of the same individual, the public person and the private. It's the fact that, to me at least, there is only the public figure.

Naively, I expected my father to begin his inaugural address with the announcement that the hostages had just left Iran. It was only then, when he didn't, that the significance of what I'd witnessed hit me. Of course he couldn't announce that. He wasn't supposed to know about it yet. He wasn't yet president when he got the news. He wasn't supposed to have had anything to do with it. In my view, what was whispered to him was an indication that he'd been involved before he was in office.

He announced the release at the luncheon following the swearing-in. He said it as though he'd just gotten the news. At the end of the luncheon, I heard my mother say to someone, "Well, you know why this happened.

They were afraid of Ronnie. They knew he'd take action and not be meek like Carter." Aside from some bad luck with helicopters, I don't think Carter was meek, but more important, I don't think the hostages' release had anything to do with fear of any kind. It had to do with a deal, struck before the deal-maker was in office.

People who haven't been to the White House all have the same question: What's it like? Those who have been there never forget it and are eager to talk about it.

It's smaller than one would think, and feels even smaller inside. There is indeed an aura of history there. I felt a strong sense of reverence. Wars have begun and ended inside those walls; history has been molded, changed, written.

People walk by briskly, everyone with a job, a reason for being inside. No one takes their presence there lightly. They have "Clearance" badges that say they've been checked out and allowed to enter. It's like a secret society—not everyone gets in.

It's a world apart. I used to walk in and suddenly not be sure what year it was. Fashion trends come and go outside the White House; inside, the women dress conservatively, in two-piece suits, low heels, hems below the knee, and subdued colors. Men wear black or dark blue suits—the ones who don't wear uniforms.

The second-floor living quarters reinforced my feeling that I had crossed a border into a tiny, sequestered country. From most of the windows on the second floor, I could look down and see the black iron fence that surrounds the White House. People were always standing outside it, staring in. But they almost didn't seem real because the thick white walls and windows that didn't open made me forget that there was a world outside. If I wanted to make a phone call, I just picked up the receiver—the operator made the call for me. There is a story that when Eisenhower left office, he realized he'd forgotten how to dial a phone.

Time slows down there. I visited the White House only four or five times in eight years, but every visit had that effect on me. It was like being a kid again, staring at the clock and swearing it must have stopped. The hours crawl, the day lingers.

The first time I went to the White House was the evening after my father's inauguration. I walked around the second floor, looked out of the windows, down to the grounds and the black fence. And I felt the isolation of this house. I started to understand how presidents lose touch with the people, with what's going on in the neighborhoods and the cities. The White House is in the middle of downtown, but downtown is just a view from the windows. It's not real. You can't hear it or smell it, or feel its energy. The walls are too thick and the fence is too high. All you can hear are soft, deliberate footsteps of people doing their jobs, and all you can smell are the fresh narcissus that seem to be in every room. It's easy to lose touch—too easy.

During that Inauguration Week, Mitch Snyder, the homeless activist, had set up a "tent city" across the street from the White House, trying to draw attention to what has become America's shame—people living and dying on the streets. I said something to my father; I tried to put it in front of him. Look, it's winter, it's cold, they're trying to tell you something.

"Mitch Snyder is just grandstanding," my father answered. "There are shelters—places they can go."

That evening, walking around the White House for the first time, I was struck by the realization that this was a perfect house for my father—removed, up on a hill, protected by fences and guards. Isolated. He has mentioned to me sometimes a recurrent dream he used to have of a large white mansion that he walked into, knowing he belonged there. He belonged in the White House—they were made for each other.

It was a perfect house for my mother, too, because it's a confined environment and her influence could easily be felt everywhere. And because the entire community of the White House orbited around my father, which is the way she thinks the universe should be arranged.

I was never comfortable in this environment. I felt claustrophobic and was bothered by the sense of isolation. I would end up returning to the White House sooner than I'd anticipated, when my father was shot. And I would go back for two Christmases, one non-holiday visit, and the second inauguration. Political differences, family fractures, and a general discomfort with the world-apart feeling of the White House all combined to make me an infrequent visitor.

On the first day of my father's presidency, I flew back to California. But before I left, I went into the Oval Office to say good-bye. It would be the only time in eight years that I would enter that office. It feels like no other room in the White House. It's not muted, with dark paintings on walls, like some of the rooms. It's bright and open—the sky shines through on three sides—and my first thought was of all the photographs I'd seen of the Oval Office; Johnson with his head in his hands, the weight of the Vietnam War beating him down, John Kennedy with John-John playing under the desk. And the table behind the desk where every president puts photographs. Maybe the room has never changed except for the photographs. Standing there, you can believe it hasn't. You can imagine Roosevelt or Eisenhower staring out at the trees, pacing on the rug with the presidential seal. I don't know if my father had these thoughts—I didn't ask. We stood on the rug, at the edges of the presidential seal, and said good-bye. He hugged me, kissed my cheek, and turned back toward the desk, grabbed a handful of jelly beans and sat down.

I found out, shortly after the inauguration, just how inconvenient the Secret Service can be. I had hosted a segment of the television show "Midnight Special" and following that, the show was going to have me do some more segments. The idea was to have me interview actors or musicians—whoever interested me.

I asked Kris Kristofferson if I could interview him. He was in New York, we had a few phone conversations, and he agreed to do the interview. But by the time I got on a plane for New York to do the segment the future of the show itself was in doubt because of poor ratings. I got together with him anyway, at his hotel, and I didn't come down that night. I would never have named Kris as my companion that night had Kitty Kelley not told this story in her biography of my mother.

My night in the hotel with Kris was the first time something like that had happened since the Secret Service had been assigned to me, but I was living my life the way I had been living it for a long time. I was twenty-eight, I was used to doing what I wanted, and I was not accustomed to announcing whom I was going to sleep with.

I came down the next morning and found three Secret Service agents glaring at me. They had coffee and donuts from some take-out place, their car had ice on the windshield, and they looked as though they wanted to open fire on me.

"What's the problem?" I said.

"These guys have been out here all night because they didn't know when you'd be coming down," the head of my detail said to me in a parental, admonishing tone.

"They have a radio, they could have called for someone to replace them," I said. "And logic would suggest that if I didn't come down after two in the morning, I probably wouldn't be coming down until sometime after sunrise."

"We can't operate like this. We have a job to do." He was not going to let up.

"So when exactly should I have informed them that I was spending the night? I mean, I was with someone— I'm trying to have a life. I suppose I could have just gotten dressed, run down to the street, said, 'Hey, guys,

I'm spending the night,' gone back up, and picked up where I left off. Sounds pretty romantic to me—it's amazing I didn't think of it." I wasn't going to let up, either.

He just stared at me, unable to think of a comeback; finally, his face started to relax.

"Tell you what," I said. "On the occasions when I know my plans ahead of time, I'll let you know. The times I don't you'll have to wing it. I can't always predict what will happen in my life."

That eased tensions for the moment, but this episode was not over. When I returned from New York, I called my mother and her voice when she answered was so chilly I thought the New York winter had followed me back to California. In a way, it had.

"Is something wrong?" I asked patiently.

"I realize you have a long history of promiscuity," she said, "but your father is president now and I think you could manage to be considerate of that fact. Shacking up with men in hotels . . ." She cut off her own sentence with some sound that indicated disgust at the whole concept.

"And how did we find out about this?"

"Things get around. You're a public person now; I would think you'd be concerned about behaving with a little more decency," my mother said.

"I think we can leave the moralizing out of this. I asked how you found out."

"I told you—things get around."

I went outside to the Secret Service command post, which they'd set up in the garage.

"You guys send reports back to Washington?" I asked.

"We send the logs back, yeah," one of them said.

"Uh-huh. And how detailed are these logs?"

"Time, location, length of stay."

"And who reads them?" I persisted.

"They just go in a file."

"Well, I think they might be going through the White

House living quarters before they're filed in some archive. And I don't appreciate having my sex life logged, filed, and passed on to my mother. I'm well above the age of consent and I don't need my mother on the phone telling me what a slut I am." I really wasn't angry at them; they probably didn't know my mother had a long history of snooping. But I think they were a little more vague in the logs they sent back to Washington after that.

Since I was back on familiar, rocky ground with my mother, I decided there was no reason to be tentative with her. I had been avoiding telling her something that I knew would anger her, but she was already angry, so it seemed like an appropriate time. I'd been curtailing some of my anti-nuclear activity prior to the election, including pulling out of the 1980 Survival Sunday, a large anti-nuclear event at the Hollywood Bowl. But now that my father was in office and I couldn't be accused of trying to ruin his chances, I was scheduling things, including participation in the 1981 Survival Sunday that June.

I prefaced the conversation with "You're not going to be happy about this." Which turned out to be an understatement.

"Well, I certainly am not happy with it," my mother said after I told her my plans. "And your father won't be either. How can you do this to him?"

That question again—someday I'll think of an answer for it.

"I'm standing up for what I believe in," I answered. "Just because my beliefs are in disagreement with yours doesn't mean I have to forfeit that right."

"You're just being used. The only reason they care about you is because of your father. Embarrassing him is what matters to them, not you."

"Thank you," I said, trying not to sound angry, but my hands were shaking and sweat was running down my sides. "I realize you might see familial connections as my only worth, and that there are others who might agree, but I'm going to proceed as if I do have something of value to contribute because I think I do."

"Well, you're just being used," my mother repeated.

"I think you've already made that point, so we might be at an impasse in this conversation."

End of discussion. I'm not sure who hung up first—I think it was my mother.

Denial takes different forms and one of mine has always been my smart mouth. What I wasn't willing to acknowledge at that point was how deeply my mother's comment about my worthlessness wounded me. I'd heard it before; I'd grown up hearing it—that I was only important because my father was governor and then president. I had let this choreograph my life in many ways, tried to prove, even to myself, that I had worth as an individual. But I had never admitted my true feelings about this struggle. If it had been anyone else other than my mother, I'd have said, "How can you justify trying to make another person feel worthless?" But I could never be that direct with her.

There was a part of me that could imagine my parents supporting my commitment to an issue—not embracing it, or endorsing it, but supporting the effort. This might have been, in part, naivete, but I think, more than that, it was a projection of how I felt about them. We all tend to project our own attitudes onto others. And no matter how strongly I disagreed with my parents' ideology, I respected their ambition and their commitment. So it seemed reasonable to me that they could respect mine. Because I probably learned it from them.

"Didn't you raise me to speak up for what I believe in?" I asked my father on the phone. "Haven't I grown up seeing you do that?"

"You're just being used," he answered, parroting my mother.

I had asked for another disappointment and had gotten exactly that. An angry part of me thought, "Well then, I'm not going to respect their efforts, either." But I did respect them, and still do. The disagreements stand apart, with more troubling feelings attached to them.

CHAPTER 24

. . . .

TOWARD THE END of March, I went to the Chateau Marmont to read for Martin Scorsese, for the role in *The King of Comedy* which ended up going to Shelley Hack. Robert De Niro, who was the star, was there, too. I was so excited that I had met both Scorsese and De Niro, it almost didn't matter that I didn't get the part.

Two days later, the three of us found our lives connected because of a film they once made, *Taxi Driver,* and bullets from John Hinckley's gun.

On the morning of March 30, I was in the office of a therapist I had recently started seeing. He was an older man who is no longer alive, but what I'll always remember most about him is his arm around my shoulder when I got the news, as though he were holding me together. His office was in the back of his house and my session was half over when a Secret Service agent knocked on the door, pushed it open, and said, "Patti, I'm sorry to interrupt, but there's been a shooting in Washington."

From that moment on, the day shifted into slow motion. The Secret Service wouldn't let me drive my car home. "We can't take any chances right now," they said. It would stay in my therapist's driveway for three days.

I knew no more than the rest of the country. I was on the same roller-coaster ride as everyone else. Jim Brady's dead . . . no, he's not. The president has not been shot . . . this just in, the president has been wounded. He walked into the hospital . . . collapsed . . . is now in surgery. I kept the television on, made coffee, tried to do normal, mundane things. Friends stayed with me. I tried to call the hospital, but couldn't get through. Reporters had staked out the apartment, but I wouldn't go out and talk to them. I waited for the Secret Service to tell me when I could fly to Washington; they wouldn't let me take a commercial flight because of security concerns.

By evening, they had arranged for an army transport plane to take me, Michael, Colleen, Maureen, and Dennis back to Washington. The sun was going down when we boarded. Even when we first saw each other, there was no real contact or connection. People reach out to each other at times like this only if they know how, and we didn't. I thought about that as I took a seat on the plane. None of us had called each other, none of us had gotten through to my mother, nor had she called any of us. Ron was on his way to Washington from Nebraska, where he'd been on tour with the Joffrey Ballet. No one had spoken to him. "What kind of family is this?" I wondered. "Even a bullet can't bring us together."

The inside of the transport plane was ridiculously loud; if someone had said the engine was in the seat right behind me, I'd have believed them. They'd given us earplugs and lunch boxes. Or dinners, since it was almost night and we were flying east.

I was sitting alone. In another part of the plane, Michael sat with Colleen, and in still another part, Maureen was with Dennis. I considered the labels "half-brother" and "half-sister" that have always been part of our family. They stand between us like measuring sticks, and what they measure is distance.

I'd grown up thinking I had only one real brother. On this night, he was in another part of the sky, and I was looking through the darkness and the noise that churned between three people who'd had the word "half" to protect them from each other.

We had lives we didn't share and memories we each tried to run away from in our own ways. But on this night there was a single thread connecting us. Our father lay in a Washington, D.C., hospital, leaking blood from a bullet wound. Leaking life, maybe—we didn't know. We still knew no more than the television news had told us. No one had called from the hospital or the White House.

There was something else uniting us. Each of us knew, in some part of our hearts that, although our presence was expected there, it wasn't really important. Ronald and Nancy Reagan are two halves of a circle; together, they are complete, and their children float outside.

I got up and walked down the aisle, past Secret Service agents who were scattered around the plane. As I sat down next to Michael, I thought "my brother"—forcing myself to remove the word "half" from my thinking. I tried to look at him as someone I knew.

I started crying, and he put his arms around me, pulling me against his shoulder.

"He'll be all right," Michael said, assuming that I was crying about our father's condition.

I said nothing. "That's not why I'm crying," I thought. "I'm crying because if he dies, I won't know who it is who has died. He's my father, but he's as much a stranger to me as you are."

I don't remember sleep that night, only dreams—bad ones, my mother's face crumbling. And the time I spent with her the next morning seems, in my memory, both short and long. Probably not that much time elapsed while I was sitting on the edge of her bed, but a lot happened.

It was midmorning when we went to the hospital—my mother, Ron, Doria, and I. Michael and Maureen have written in their books that they were excluded, told to come later. I don't know if that was the case—it's possible—but some of that morning is still blurry to me.

There were crowds of people and a swarm of reporters outside the hospital. But there wasn't a lot of noise as there usually is when a crowd has gathered. Inside, the hospital seemed filled with Secret Service agents.

When someone has stared back at their own death, they must change inside. When I walked into my father's hospital room, I saw a serene, peaceful look in his eyes, as though he had a secret he couldn't share because it was too personal, too exquisite. His skin was pale, almost translucent, and that made him look serene, too. I couldn't stop staring at him. Ron and Doria had arrived early enough the night before to have been present for some of the more frightening moments, when he was fighting for breath, when he was slipping. I think my father made some joke about his suit being ruined, but I was only half-listening. I was too mesmerized by his appearance, by the way he just seemed to float there, pale and calm.

Weeks later, when he was released from the hospital and I flew back to Washington, I asked him if he had thought he was going to die.

"Oh no," he said, tossing it off.

I knew he was lying, but I didn't blame him.

He told me something else in that conversation. My parents and I were having dinner in the second-floor dining room.

"I prayed for that young man when I was lying there," my father said.

"For Hinckley?" I asked incredulously.

"Yes. He's disturbed. I prayed that God would forgive him. And that he would ask for God's forgiveness."

No one has ever amazed me as much as my father did at that moment.

"I don't know that I could ever have that much forgiveness," I said to him. "To pray for someone who shot you? I don't know how one does that."

In the aftermath of the assassination attempt, there was a coming together of sorts in my family. My mother and I talked often on the phone; I had more contact with Ron. But old habits hung on—Michael and Maureen were not brought into the fold, as they have always wished to be. I noticed this, but it's something I've always been helpless to change. They are reminders to my mother of my father's first marriage, before she entered his life, and she can't bear to think about it.

I noticed also that as my father mended, we splintered again. It's all we really know how to do; it's just that crises make us huddle together.

"I would hope that all this would make you rethink your political activities," my mother said in one phone conversation. My father was feeling better, stronger, taking away the reason for us to pull together.

"My views are still the same," I told her. "So is my commitment."

"Your father's hearing has gotten worse since the shooting. It's a reaction to the trauma."

"I understand. But you're talking about two unconnected things."

But to my mother, they were connected, because everything is connected in some way to my father.

My parents came back to California during my father's recovery period and went to their ranch in Santa Barbara. My father couldn't ride yet, and he complained about that, but just being there seemed to be good for him. I drove up on a Saturday, spent the day there, and when I was saying good-bye to my mother, I hugged her and realized for the first time how tiny she is. This woman whose presence has been so enormous in my life, who has seemed to tower over me, was almost lost between my arms. That one moment will always be etched in my memory—with the sun at my back and my arms around her small shape. It told me that my perceptions were starting to change.

CHAPTER 25

· · · · · · · · · · · · · · · ·

A FEW WEEKS later, I was cast in a made-for-television movie about male strippers that starred Gregory Harrison, Dinah Manoff, and Marc Singer, but when my mother said, "Oh, wonderful—a TV movie. What's it about?" I answered, "Um, it's . . . it's about a struggling actor." Which wasn't a lie, but it was more of a subplot in *For Ladies Only*.

We shot in New York for about a month, and even though Ron and Doria lived there, I saw very little of them. It's difficult to connect lives that have never been connected. I learned about another aspect of life with the Secret Service, though. When they go to another state, they have to hook up with the agents from that area. It's a "hey, this is my turf" philosophy. So I had twice as many agents around me and the New York guys had the last word. On the occasions when I did see Ron and Doria, I learned there were times when they had returned to their apartment to find evidence that agents had been inside. Ron said he didn't think he could endure it much longer; he was already thinking of getting rid of Secret Service protection.

"We can do that?" I asked. We were sitting in their Greenwich Village apartment and I remember glancing at the walls, wondering if the place was bugged.

"Children of presidents aren't required to have Secret Service," Ron said. "It's optional. They just don't like to tell you that."

It would be a couple of years, but we would both end up taking advantage of that fact.

While I was in New York, I had a chance to see Martin Scorsese and Robert De Niro again, and I found out that both of their lives had turned chaotic following the assassination attempt on my father. Because of Hinckley's fascination with the movie *Taxi Driver,* they had hired bodyguards and were being pummeled with questions they never thought they'd have to answer when they made the film. An assassination attempt is an odd link to have between people and it still seems curious to me that we met just days before the shooting.

I also met Dan Aykroyd and John Belushi at a party, and a few nights later went with them to a small bar in Tribeca that they were planning to buy. John left after staying only a short while, and Dan and his girlfriend suggested going back to their apartment. Dan had a car that was a vintage something—a Cadillac, maybe, I'm not sure.

"A boat car," I commented when we went outside and saw it taking up a third of the block.

We piled into the car, but before I could close the door, a Secret Service agent jumped right in the backseat beside me.

"Oh God," I moaned.

"Sorry," the agent said.

"Oh, that's all right," Dan said. "Hey, where do you guys get those sunglasses, anyway? Do you have them specially made or what? I mean, they're so dark, no one can see your eyes. They're probably government-issued, right?" He was loving the whole thing.

Publicity for the June 14 Survival Sunday, the antinuclear event at the Hollywood Bowl, was going to start soon, and I knew that I should probably mention again to my parents that I was going to be participating. Bruce Springsteen, Jackson Browne, and Bonnie Raitt were a few of the entertainers scheduled for the event, and the speakers included Ron Kovic, Mike Farrell, and Robert Kennedy, Jr.—but I knew my parents wouldn't be impressed with the lineup.

I called my mother one afternoon when the weather in New York was hot and windless. I had the hotel-room windows open and the noise of traffic filled the room; somehow it was comforting to hear the outside world. It made talking with my mother seem less claustrophobic.

"Well, I just assumed you wouldn't do something like this after your father was shot," my mother said, after I reminded her of the upcoming event.

"One thing has nothing to do with the other."

"It most certainly does, young lady," she said. "You're going to wound him more than the bullet did."

"That is not fair," I told her. But then everything is fair in war, and we were at war again.

"I don't have anything else to say to you. I'm sure your father will have something to say, but I hate to put him through this."

It should be noted that my father was making a rather remarkable recovery, but that my mother's recovery from the trauma of the shooting was much slower. I wasn't oblivious to this at the time, but I felt, and still feel, that that reality stood apart from my commitment to speak out on an issue I believed in.

There wasn't much time between my return from New York and Survival Sunday, but it seemed like a lifetime.

My mother wasn't speaking to me, but my father called and said, "This is very foolish, what you're doing. No one is going to like you."

"No one is going to *like* me?"

"No. People don't like children who go against their parents."

"I'd just like to make this one point, if I may," I said. "My purpose here is not to go against you as my father. What everyone in this movement is going against is a nuclear situation that could destroy this planet. No one is suggesting that the situation began with your administration. But it's time we turned this around. It's a larger issue than just one person's administration, although I don't agree with your viewpoints."

"What you and these anti-nuclear nuts are supporting is unilateral disarmament," my father said.

"I have never heard a single person support the idea of unilateral disarmament. What is being supported here is dialogue with the Soviet Union, as opposed to name-calling," I told him.

"What is being supported is Communism."

This is sort of like the "how can you do this to your father" question—I never know how to respond when my father invokes Communism in the course of a political discussion.

"Didn't you raise me to tell the truth and have integrity?" I asked, trying to avoid the subject of Communism.

"We tried to, yes."

"Well, that's what I'm doing."

"Patti, we've always encouraged you to express your opinions . . ."

"You have?"

". . . but you don't have to do it publicly."

"Uh-huh. So I should think for myself, but keep it to myself?"

"Yes."

Then Bill Hayes, a Hollywood agent who was an old friend of my parents', called me. The only way he could have gotten my phone number was from my parents; it was an unlisted number and we didn't have any other mutual acquaintances.

"If you want this acting career at all," he said, "you won't do this."

"Could you be a little more specific?"

"Producers won't hire actors and actresses who are political. You're not going to get work."

"Vanessa Redgrave gets work," I argued. "And Ed Asner and Jane Fonda and Mike Farrell."

"Well, you're just starting out, and you'll finish yourself off before you've even started."

I thought about his dire prediction and started calculating how long I could hold out on the money I had. I wasn't tempted to change my plans, but I did want another opinion, so I called Jackson Browne.

"Jackson, do you think I'll have no career because of speaking out on the anti-nuclear issue?"

"If there's no planet left, none of us will have any careers anyway," was Jackson's response.

"Good point. Thanks."

I didn't have any more job offers at that moment, but it might have just been coincidence.

A. C. Lyles called me also, from his office at Paramount, and said, "This is very risky, what you're doing. If you want to be an actress, why are you being so controversial? You should be thinking of your career."

"Why is trying to save the earth controversial?" I asked. "And besides, if there's no earth left, none of us will have careers anyway."

Goldie Arthur, whom I used to call "Aunt" when I was younger, even though she wasn't, wrote me a letter which said, in part, "Your mother was so happy the day you were born. But if she'd known you would turn around and do something like this to them she certainly wouldn't have been as happy. You should be ashamed of yourself."

During those weeks, I played Bruce Springsteen albums at ear-splitting volume because they gave me courage. I read voraciously about nuclear weapons and nuclear power plants, and I wrote a three-page letter to my father explaining that I was taking actions I felt to be right because of deeply held convictions, and opinions based on research, not on any vindictive wish to embarrass anyone. He never answered it.

Just prior to the event, the Alliance for Survival held a press conference at the Los Angeles Press Club. I sat with Mike Farrell and a couple of people from the Alliance for Survival behind microphones to discuss the event and the issues at hand. I was asked a lot of questions about how much I'd discussed this with my father and I sidestepped them and kept returning to the issue. One of my father's predictions, other than the one about people not liking me, was that the press would crucify me. The fact is, I was never misquoted or assailed in the press through any of this, though it's possible I missed something. There were plenty of people trying to crucify me, but I wouldn't include the media in that group.

Survival Sunday happened on a day when the temperature was in the triple digits and smog choked the sky. But despite that, it was a magical day. The energy in the Hollywood Bowl was the energy of the Sixties; we were going to change the world and have a good time doing it.

Downstairs in the dressing rooms, Ron Kovic was showing Bruce Springsteen how developed his arms were from pushing his chair miles every day. Bonnie Raitt was sharing her cooler full of juice, water, and champagne with everyone. Jackson said to me, "Glad you're here."

"I wasn't backing down," I told him. "I just needed some words of wisdom, so I called you."

It took a few minutes to gather my nerve, but I went over to Bruce and said, "I had a couple of rough moments the last few weeks over doing this, and your music pulled me through every time."

He stood up and hugged me and I'll always treasure that hug because it spoke volumes. A friend of mine who was an activist in the Sixties once told me that one of the great things about a movement is the bond that's created by a common purpose, that sometimes nothing needs to be said—everyone knows why they're there. That's what Bruce's hug meant to me.

I discovered Ron Kovic that day, and would rediscover him at other anti-nuclear events. He put everything in perspective for me. I stood in the wings and watched him wheel himself onstage, raise his fist and his voice, and raise the passion and commitment of everyone in the audience. I thought, "Whatever price I have to pay for speaking out, it's nothing compared to the price he pays every day of his life."

Mike Farrell introduced me by saying, "It's always difficult to disagree with one's parents, but when one's parents are in the White House, it's even more difficult." I spoke for a few minutes about the need for re-thinking our dependence on nuclear energy, and the need for bilateral disarmament.

There was coverage of the event on the evening news, and on the front page of the *L.A. Times* the next morning; I wasn't surprised that I didn't hear from my parents for a while.

It was during this time that I started trying to put together a plan I'd had for a while, which was to have ongoing discussions between my father and people in his administration, and key people in the anti-nuclear movement. In my idealism, I never doubted that I could pull it off. After talking it over with a few people, I decided that Helen Caldicott, the Australian pediatrician who had made the anti-nuclear issue her cause, would be the best person to launch my program. It would be over a year before this meeting would take place, but the seeds were planted then.

If it hadn't been for the August 1981 air-controllers' strike, I might not have met Peter Strauss. I was supposed to be in Canada doing a guest appearance on a talk show there, but I wasn't sure who was controlling the air, so I cancelled the trip. Instead of being in Vancouver, I was at a small dinner party in Los Angeles, where I met Peter. I think I fell in love with him right away. I suspect that all of us secretly wish for someone to come along and say, without hesitation, "This is what my life is about and I'd like you in it." And in a sense, that's what happened. I hadn't dared to think that anyone would want me in his life with everything that was included in mine right then, all of which gave

new meaning to the term "baggage." Who wants to be
followed around twenty-four hours a day by armed
men in station wagons? I certainly didn't, and I felt
guilty about imposing it on anyone else. But Peter
didn't seem to mind. During the months that we were
together, he was far more polite than I was about telling
them where we were going. I was always driving too
fast, cutting through alleys, and trying to lose them. In
retrospect, I realize that they were only doing their job
and I should have appreciated what they were doing for
me. But I didn't.

It's dangerous to start out any relationship with a lie,
but it's a certain recipe for destruction in a romantic
relationship. I told the same lie to Peter that I had told
to every man I'd been with since splitting up with Bernie. When I was asked about birth control, I would say
I had an IUD. With Peter, I rationalized my dishonesty
by telling myself that he wanted children someday, so
he would have difficulty accepting what I'd done. The
longer you tell a lie, the harder it is to turn around and
tell the truth; it becomes like quicksand, and I was
sinking fast and deep into my lies.

In part this was because of a question my mother
repeated every time I started seeing someone. "Does he
know about you?" she would say, her tone suggesting
that if whoever it was did know, he'd drop me as if I
were damaged goods. I'd started to see myself that way,
too.

Shortly after Peter and I became involved with each
other, he went to New York to rehearse for a play called
Einstein and the Polar Bear, and I went also to be with
him. I had read for the part of the female lead and had
been offered the understudy's role, but I'd turned it
down because I wasn't sure what effect working together would have on this new relationship.

During those weeks in New York, I didn't have that
much to do while Peter was rehearsing, and now I see
what a gift that was. I got to know the city, I worked on
my writing, and the free time finally allowed me to think

about what I had done five years earlier when I'd chosen to get sterilized. More accurately, I began to think
about *why* I'd done it. For the first time, I admitted to
myself that I'd been trying to ensure in absolute terms
that I would never continue an abusive cycle with a
child of my own. All of the other reasons that had
attended my decision paled beside that one.

I remember one day standing in front of the window
display of a maternity shop on Madison Avenue with
tears running down my face. "I made a mistake," I
thought. "I could be a good mother—I wouldn't hurt
my child."

I think now that if I'd been honest with Peter and
explained what I was finally admitting to myself, he'd
have understood. But the pattern of dishonesty was too
strong.

Shortly before my birthday in October, my mother
called me in New York, and I don't know what precipitated it, but she asked again, "Does Peter know about
you yet?"

"No," I said. And then, in a rush of guilt, I added,
"I'm thinking of looking into getting it reversed."

"The hospital where your uncle works does a lot of
those surgeries."

My uncle on my mother's side is a neurosurgeon in
Pennsylvania.

"How do you know that?" I asked her.

"He told me." I should have known that my sterilization had been discussed among family members.

This led to my most elaborate lie yet. I told Peter I
was going to fly to Washington and stay at the White
House for a few days—just a little, innocuous family
visit.

"But you don't *like* it at the White House," he said,
giving me a puzzled look. And he knew enough about
my family to know that family visits were never innocuous.

I don't remember what excuse I invented to make this

seem plausible, but I can't imagine it was very convincing.

My birthday present from my parents was a plane trip from Washington to Pennsylvania where I visited my uncle in his office and he told me that many reversals of tubal ligations were being done with a relatively good success rate. At one point, I was fighting back tears and I said, "I wish I hadn't done that. I really regret it."

My uncle is fairly rigid and not given to displays of compassion, but he said, very matter-of-factly, "You can't blame yourself for doing something you thought was right at the time. You've changed your mind—that doesn't make you wrong. It does no good to beat yourself up over it."

Then he took me down to meet with a doctor who actually did this kind of surgery. I got as much information as I could that day, and left feeling slightly encouraged that maybe I could be put back together again.

"It's major surgery," I explained to my mother when I returned to the White House. "If I do this, I'll have to come clean with Peter and tell him."

"No, you won't," she said. "You could just tell him something else is wrong. There are other reasons women have surgery."

"You want me to go through an operation and not tell him why?"

"I think it would be better," she answered.

I knew at that point I was too confused and too mired in lies and guilt to be wheeled in for any kind of surgery. My uncle had said to call him and let him know if I'd made any decision. When I called the next day, I learned from him that, while I was in the air on my way back to Washington, my mother was on the phone with him. And she had gotten angry at him for his efforts to assuage my guilt; according to her, he shouldn't have told me not to beat myself up over a choice I had made when I thought it was right. He said it as though he were asking me to explain her anger.

"I'm too confused about all of this right now," I told him. "I can't make any decisions."

For Ladies Only aired that month; Peter and I watched a tape of it before it ran on television, and I don't think he was too thrilled at the sight of half-nude men gyrating onstage, a fact which I foolishly mentioned to my mother. A few days later, the White House issued a statement that *I* wasn't happy with the movie. There was no way I could compete with press statements from the White House; all I could do was call the producer and explain that I hadn't really said that.

Gregory Harrison and I had done an interview for *Playgirl* magazine to promote the movie (which was, it seems to me, an appropriate magazine in which to promote a movie about male strippers). That issue came out just before the movie aired, and it brought a call from my mother.

"I am shocked that you would do an interview in here. Do you know what's in this magazine?" she said.

"A lot of naked men with erections?"

"You watch your language, young lady."

"You asked me a question."

"I burned it in the fireplace," she continued. "I couldn't have this lying around for your father to see. Can you imagine what he would think if he saw me with a magazine like this?"

Peter and I didn't make it to the New Year, and I put some of the blame on my secrecy and the lies that had been piling up. I did finally tell him that, at twenty-four, I'd had a tubal ligation, but I didn't go further than that basic fact. Learning to tell the truth happens in stages, and I was at Stage One; I was still getting accustomed to the idea of telling myself the truth. I don't think I'd even discussed with Peter the long war my mother and I had been engaged in since I was a child. It would have explained a lot, but he was deprived of that explanation. In a sense, I led him toward the very reaction I had feared.

Peter has children now, and I wish him every happiness. Even though it didn't seem like it at the time, I was learning to tell the truth about myself and my life, and he was part of that journey.

In the summer of 1982, the anti-nuclear event that had previously been held at the Hollywood Bowl was moved to the Rose Bowl. Over three hundred thousand people showed up, and the event lasted from noon until after ten at night. Stevie Wonder, Crosby, Stills and Nash, Jackson Browne, Stevie Nicks, and Bob Dylan, who joined Joan Baez onstage, were some of the performers. At the press conference a few days before the event, Stevie Wonder, Graham Nash, and I answered reporters' questions, many of them directed to Stevie about whether or not Paul McCartney would show up since he and Stevie had just recorded a song together. (He didn't, but Stevie kept them guessing.)

After the conference, with reporters standing around scribbling on notepads, Graham said to me, "You know, you have a great ass for a president's daughter."

"I had a great ass before I was a president's daughter, Graham."

The exchange ended up in *Rolling Stone* magazine. It was indicative of just how angry my parents were at my continued political activities that I didn't hear from my mother about this news item. Usually, she would use something like that as an excuse to lecture me. When I had informed them that I was going to be speaking again that year, they said I had told them I wasn't going to do any more events. I had never said anything remotely like that, but there was no sense arguing about it. I had grown up accepting that my parents had an ability to invent a reality that suited them, and somewhere along the line I'd grown tired of fighting it. So, during most of the summer of 1982, my phone was unusually quiet because my mother wasn't speaking to me, having convinced herself that I had gone back on a pledge to curtail my anti-nuclear activities.

I got more warnings about destroying my career, and

there is a possibility that there was some truth in that. Except for a role in Blake Edwards's film, *The Curse of the Pink Panther,* I was not getting work, which could have been due to a lot of things. I noticed that I wasn't being allowed to read for parts that other women my age were all reading for. I don't really blame Holly-wood, particularly, since I wasn't approaching this with great passion. I just think that people often don't know what to do with controversy, and along with me came controversy. One producer was brutally honest about it. He told my agent, "I don't want to waste my time having her read. I'm not going to hire her. She's the president's daughter, she's political, and I don't want the Secret Service on the set." I actually admired his honesty.

I have often wondered if my mother made some dis-creet calls, telling people not to hire me or let me audi-tion. I will never know the truth.

In August, someone from my mother's office called me and said that my grandfather was hospitalized in Phoe-nix, and that he didn't have much time left. The mes-sage from my mother was that I could fly out there if I wished, or someone could just let me know when the services were going to be.

Refusing to let my mother push me away with that kind of message, I got on the next plane for Phoenix. During the plane ride, I thought about the last few times I'd seen my grandfather, and the feeling I'd had that he was preparing for his own death. I hadn't told my mother about my visits with him, and I don't know if he did. Several times, I flew to Phoenix for the day and spent a few hours getting to know my grandfather in a new way. As he approached the end of his life, he softened, became more gentle and philosophical.

The last time I had seen him he said, "I want you to make me a promise. I want you to promise me that, when I go, you won't let anyone sell this house and move your grandmother out. I want her to stay in this house. Promise me that."

"But how can I prevent that from happening?"

He was asking me to go against my mother, if she chose to sell the house. I knew it and he knew it. But his eyes were pinning me down.

"All right," I said finally. "I promise."

That was the last day I saw my grandfather conscious and aware. And the last words he said to me as I left his house were, "Remember your promise to me."

I never forgot my promise. But I would end up breaking it.

When I got to the hospital in Phoenix, my grandfather was lying motionless in the bed, his breathing loud and labored. His eyes were closed and his skin was colorless. My mother was sitting beside the bed, holding his hand. It was a ritual she would keep up during this vigil—she didn't want his hand to go unheld.

"His kidneys have failed," she said when I walked in. "It's just a matter of time."

We sat there the entire day, often in silence because we had little to say to each other. Sometimes, my grandfather would mumble words, as a person having a dream might. As I watched him, I thought that he was having a dialogue with his own death, because he would say, "No—not yet," or "I'm not ready." The more I watched this, the more I thought that if I saw him actually die—saw the moment when the light left him—I might be less afraid of death.

At one point, my mother had to leave the room, and she put his hand in mine—a transfer so smooth that there wasn't an instant when the air touched his hand. It was moved from flesh to flesh. He began talking again, shaking his head and saying, "No."

"It's okay," I whispered. "Just let go."

I could see him struggling, and I wanted him to be free, but as I whispered that to him, I had the thought that if he went right then, with only me as a witness, my mother would never forgive me.

Toward evening, the doctor came in and was predicting "Not much time left." He then added, "He's not in any pain, he's not suffering." We listened and didn't say anything, because what is there to say about that? Suddenly my mother let go of my grandfather's hand and touched the doctor's arm.

"Listen," she said, "I forgot my pills at home and I haven't been getting any sleep. I'll be okay for another night, I guess, but then I'll really need something."

I looked down at my grandfather, his hand naked on the bedclothes, and as I reached for his hand I understood the desperation that had turned my mother's attention away from him. In fact, when I looked at her, I thought I was looking in a mirror. I had been clean for years—I wasn't even smoking grass anymore. But it all came back to me. There is this fear that you won't get the drug you need, and it drives everything else away. But you can't show the fear, you can't act desperate— that's not the technique that will get results. She was good at this; I had been, too. I knew everything that was going through her mind right then. There's a moment after you make your pitch when you wonder if the doctor is going to give you what you want, or give you a hard time.

"What are you taking?" the doctor asked.

"Dalmane."

My mind was so plugged into hers that I actually breathed a sigh of relief—just as I knew she did. Logic and conscience would suggest that I should have been disturbed about the doctor's failure to question her. But I knew the game too well. And I knew that if he said no, she'd have gotten the prescription somewhere else, from some other doctor.

Later that evening, Ron and Doria arrived and while they were in the room, my mother was called away for a phone call from my father. When she came back, she said she hadn't told him how close my grandfather was to death.

"Why?" I asked.

"Well, he's having such a hard time with Congress over the budget."

"I'm sure he can deal with two things at once," Ron said, but my mother didn't seem to hear.

Ron, Doria, and I slept at the Biltmore Hotel that night because staying at my grandparents' house might have alarmed my grandmother. She was already in poor health, and her thoughts faded in and out; she hadn't been told that my grandfather was dying. That night, Ron mentioned that their house might be sold; our grandmother might be moved to an apartment.

"Mom told you that?" I said.

"She mentioned it, yeah."

I knew I had in front of me one of the biggest challenges of my life—a promise I'd made versus my fear of my mother, a fear that always turned back time, made me young and weak. I didn't say anything to Ron, or to anyone. But I knew that night I couldn't stay and watch my grandfather die. Whatever courage I'd thought I had, I couldn't find it.

The next morning, before my mother had arrived at the hospital, I went in to see my grandfather one last time.

"I'm sorry," I whispered to him. He looked peaceful and calm; he wasn't talking or struggling, and I knew it wouldn't be long. "I just can't stay," I told him, hating myself for my cowardice. "I'm sorry."

Before my plane landed in Los Angeles, he was gone.

I was back in Phoenix a few days later for his funeral, and for the gathering of family and friends at my grandparents' house following the service. It would be the last time I'd ever see the house.

That night, my parents, Ron, Doria, and I were in the living room after everyone left. The nurse was putting my grandmother to bed, and when she came out, my mother and I went in to say good night to her.

"Do you think he's dancing tonight?" my grandmother asked, her eyes focused on some distant spot.

"I'm sure he is," my mother said.

That began my tears and I was still crying when I walked back out to the living room.

"Why are you crying?" my father asked.

I almost reminded him that we'd buried my grandfather that day—I always seemed to be reminding him of things—but this was one time I didn't. I just let the question go.

For some reason, my father decided that right then would be a good time to have a discussion about what was wrong with this family. This led to Ron explaining, in very eloquent terms, how difficult it was to have something as enormous as the presidency injected into our lives. Even a healthy family, Ron pointed out, would have trouble living with that, and we had always been—well, somewhat less than healthy. My father then began talking about how victimized my mother had been, how she's been blamed for everything and had to shoulder all the burdens herself.

"She sat there while your grandfather was dying," he said, "all alone. No one was there with her."

"That's not true," Ron reminded him. "Patti was there."

"Oh, well—yes—but I couldn't be there because I was in Washington," my father said, waving his hand through the air as though to dismiss me.

I couldn't help it—I laughed. Probably because if I hadn't, I'd have broken in two.

Not long after the service, my mother put my grandparents' house up for sale and found an apartment for my grandmother. She explained that it was easier for her to get around in a smaller place, and easier for the nurses, since she had round-the-clock care. I said nothing. I didn't even attempt to honor the promise I'd made to my grandfather. Each time I thought I'd gathered the courage, I felt the old fear of my mother.

I thought about the last words I'd said to my grandfather before he died. I thought I was saying "I'm sorry" because I didn't have the courage to watch him die. But now I think I might also have been apologizing in advance for the promise I knew I wouldn't be able to keep. I'm sure that my mother honestly felt that my grandmother would be better off in an apartment, and I'm also sure that relaying my grandfather's wish wouldn't have altered her plans. But he had asked me to try; he'd expected me to convey his wishes, and he'd entrusted me with that responsibility. What he was really asking me to do was to stand up to my mother, just once in my life. He didn't put it in those exact words—he didn't need to. I didn't even have the courage to try to keep my promise, and I still find myself saying I'm sorry to him sometimes.

CHAPTER 26

· · · · · · · · · · · · · · ·

ABOUT A YEAR ago, while he was researching *President Reagan: Role of a Lifetime,* Lou Cannon asked me, "How in the world did you get your father to agree to meet with Helen Caldicott?"

I said, "I told him that President Carter had surrounded himself with people of divergent viewpoints. He listened to all of them and then formed an opinion. By contrast, my father surrounded himself with people who all agreed with him. There is an undeniable logic to the way Carter did it, so by meeting with Helen, he would be showing people how open-minded he could be."

Lou smiled and gave me a long look, sizing me up. "You're no dummy," he said. "Mentioning Carter always got to your father."

"I know, but it was kind of sneaky, don't you think?"

"It worked, didn't it?" Lou said.

It worked, the meeting was scheduled, but it turned out to be a devastating experience, both for Helen and for me. I had intended it to be the first of many such meetings. In my mind, I was already imagining taking Daniel Ellsberg, Dick Gregory, and Jesse Jackson for intimate chats in the Oval Office, uniting the two sides on a critical issue. It's both sad and funny to me now that I could have been so naive.

I got to the White House the night before our scheduled meeting and was told that I was sleeping in Lincoln's bedroom. On my pillow there was a note from my father, telling me that he and my mother had gone to the Kennedy Center, that the meeting was to take place not in the Oval Office, but in the downstairs library, and that he didn't want either me or Helen to talk about it publicly.

I saw my father briefly the following morning and he said, "You got my note, didn't you? My request that this be kept confidential?"

"I can't promise that," I told him. "I'll pass along your wish to Helen, but I can't make any guarantees." I was afraid he might cancel the whole thing, but I wasn't going to make a promise that might not be kept.

Helen and I met for lunch and then went back to her hotel room. Helen is very spiritually oriented, and we sat down and prayed that this meeting would lead to a change in policy, and a change in the course of the world. It was a prayer-not-answered.

It was early December, the sky was pale and wintry, and the White House was starting to look like Christmas. There were ornaments, and decorations filled corners and hallways.

My father was waiting for us in the downstairs library. Helen began talking about how decades of nuclear proliferation had left us on a precarious ledge; she pointed out that, between the United States and the Soviet Union, we could destroy the world several times over. "We're into overkill," she said. "The madness of that cannot be ignored any longer." Helen is one of the most compelling speakers I've ever heard. I've watched her bring audiences to tears, and I've been one of those weeping. I kept glancing at my father, looking for signs that she was evoking some feelings in him, but the expression on his face was all too familiar. He wasn't listening. He was waiting for her to finish speaking so that he could say what was already on his mind.

When she paused, he launched an attack on the antinuclear movement which surprised me, and I thought I was beyond surprise when it came to my father's political judgments. He said that all of us were dupes of the

KGB, that the entire anti-nuclear movement was a creation and a mission of the Communist party, designed to weaken the United States so that it could be taken over by the Soviet Union.

"Did you get that from *Reader's Digest*?" Helen asked.

"No," my father answered. "I got it from my intelligence sources." (Helen later found an article in the *Reader's Digest* with the same message.)

He went on to say that the Soviet Union had never honored any treaty, so expecting them to start dismantling their nuclear weapons would be naive and fruitless. Helen pointed out that we have the intelligence capacity to verify what's going on in this area, and that obviously any bilateral agreement between the two superpowers would have to include provisions for verification.

"They don't honor treaties," my father answered. "We know this from the past. These people are godless monsters, treaties mean nothing to them."

"That philosophy can destroy the world, can't you see that?" Helen asked.

Before he could answer, I handed him a copy of a 1982 Defense Department report that is available to the public. It concluded that we basically had parity with the Soviets in the area of military strength. My father glanced at it and said, "That's a forgery."

"You didn't even look at it," I said.

"I don't need to. It's a forgery."

The entire meeting lasted a little over an hour and as the minutes ticked by, we got further and further away from any kind of communication. When Helen and I stood up to leave, my father didn't extend his hand. I saw Helen's start to move, but she must have felt that her handshake would be unreturned; the meeting ended with that kind of distance.

"I'm really frightened now," Helen said when we stepped outside into the cold winter day.

"I know—I am too."

I shared her fear about what the remaining years of

my father's administration would bring. But there was more than that going on inside me. I dreaded the thought of having dinner with my parents that night. I now realized that my father and I could never find any thread of communication between our widely divergent political views. As I left Helen and walked back inside, I decided that I wouldn't discuss politics with my father ever again. It was too painful, not because I couldn't change his mind, but because I couldn't get him to listen.

I sat at the dinner table that night, drinking too much wine, trying to drown out the sound of my father telling me that I was being taken advantage of, that the people I'd chosen to believe were puppets of Communism. "We've all been taken in by people in our life," he said. "These people, like your friend Dr. Caldicott, are trying to destroy this country. This is exactly what the Soviet Union wants—to undermine us, to destroy us from within."

I sat in Lincoln's bedroom that night, my head swimming with wine, and I tried to think of someone I could call and confide in. But there wasn't anyone who could really identify with this situation. Who could I call who would be able to say, "Yeah, I remember when my father was president and I tried to expose him to another viewpoint . . ."

I felt like I'd let down an entire movement. I thought I could be the link to the White House, but obviously this had been a fantasy. I had also thought my father might understand that I was doing what I'd been raised to do—speak up for my beliefs. Throughout his political career, he'd often held fast to unpopular beliefs. And no matter how strongly I opposed those beliefs, I admired his tenacity. That night, I let go of the hope that someday he would admire mine.

Not long after that, my mother chose to make the anti-drug issue her campaign. I always felt that it was a subconscious cry for help.

It's not insignificant that Michael Deaver, now a

recovering alcoholic, helped craft the crusade. The whole thing was a road map of denial.

I've heard my mother berated for using a slogan to combat a drug crisis which destroys the lives of both adults and children. " 'Just Say No'? That's like a Band-Aid over a bullet wound," was one comment I heard. That's true. I can't defend telling inner-city kids whose lives are full of no's (no education, no jobs, no way out) to "Just Say No" to drugs. Often, drugs are not only an escape from lives they hate, but a way to bring in some money, too.

What *I* heard behind the slogan was the soft voice of a victim and the louder voice of denial. Of course my mother chose that issue—I knew why.

I have read about her visits to drug rehabilitation centers, where she listened to stories of prostitution and crime, all as ways to support drug habits. Teenagers told her about getting high on household products— paint thinner and cooking spray. But to my knowledge, she never addressed the vast numbers of people who became addicted to prescription drugs that they got, perfectly legally, from doctors.

More than a few wives of political figures have had substance-abuse problems; Betty Ford and Kitty Dukakis are the most visible. What is it about the world of politics, particularly for women, that it is so rigid and suffocating and thankless that it sends some of them rushing to doctors for something to make them feel okay? I see my mother as a victim of two worlds— medicine and politics.

The difference between my mother and both Betty Ford and Kitty Dukakis is that they were taking combinations of drugs along with alcohol. That's more obvious and is not as easy to hide or rationalize. My mother doesn't drink, she doesn't mix types of drugs. But she is still a woman who has trouble coping without the help of drugs. I've been there, too, and I have nothing but sympathy for her.

CHAPTER 27

. . . .

I MET MY future husband in the summer of 1983, but I hadn't the slightest idea that he would become my husband, or that we would become involved at all. Paul Grilley was my Yoga teacher and I thought he was nice, funny, and attractive, but I didn't think about him too much more than that. I was seeing someone else, and I generally think about only one person at a time.

My life was slipping in ways that made me nervous. The man I was seeing liked life in the fast lane—late-night parties, coke—and I found myself in the passenger seat. I really didn't want to get back into drugs. After years of being clean, I was starting to take a little coke again. And I was drinking too much wine, not getting enough sleep, staying out too late, and feeling jaded and strung out.

Paul was from Montana and was one of four sons. His father was a building contractor—a very different world from mine. He was also interested in spiritual studies, and I found this very appealing. I began to feel attracted to Paul, and he reciprocated.

We'd been seeing each other only a few weeks when I had to go to Michigan to do the play *Vanities,* which had been a hit off Broadway. But we talked on the phone often and I felt the security of being in a relationship with someone I trusted, who wasn't into all-night parties and drugs. *Vanities* was the first work I'd gotten in a long time, and it came just as I was almost out of money, which has been a pattern in my life. Just when

I'm wondering how I'll pay my bills, something comes through.

But patterns are never completely dependable. I got enough money from the play to keep me going for a while, but I needed work. I read for parts when I could, but there were a number of times when I couldn't get into an audition even though the part was for a woman my age.

The money I got from my NBC contract was almost gone. Between commissions and taxes, and draining my savings account for living expenses, money was something that always seemed to be slipping away.

The only thing that looked like a firm work offer was an idea for an American Express commercial. This would focus on me-as-the-president's-daughter, and I just couldn't do it, no matter how poor I was. Besides, I couldn't imagine how they would make it seem plausible. Put me in front of the White House and have me say, "You don't know me—and they don't either"?

By fall, Paul and I were living together in my tiny, one-bedroom apartment. Neither of us had much money, and I was starting to lose faith that my usual pattern of last-minute work would bail me out.

"Why don't you just ask your father for some money?" a friend said.

"You don't understand," I told this man whose father had always been very generous with him. "That's not something we do."

"Have you ever tried?" he asked.

"Well . . . no."

"Then maybe you'll be surprised."

The more I thought about it, the more I was able to convince myself that my friend's idea was a very good one, and I'd probably been wrong all my life. Maybe I *could* turn to my parents in financial hard times—I'd just never given it a chance.

I knew Ron was having money problems also, and he had given my parents an original Andy Warhol print as collateral against a loan. He had gotten to know Andy

in New York, and the print had been a gift. I had
nothing of value to offer, so I just called my father,
explained that I was almost out of money, and, nervously, I asked for a couple of thousand dollars. I said
I'd repay him when I got some work. And when he said
yes, I was surprised and thrilled. But then I made a
mistake. I had been so tentative about this request that
the money I'd asked for wasn't enough to buy me very
much time. So I called my father again and asked to
borrow five thousand more, again saying I would repay
it as soon as I got some work. He said he would have
someone call me later.

That night, his lawyer called me and said he was
drawing up a contract which stated that I was borrowing this money and that I would make monthly pay-
ments to my father. "He's not going to charge you
interest," he said. "So what can you pay back every
month?" I said twenty-five dollars, and one of the first
checks I wrote on the first of every month for years
afterward was to Ronald Reagan for twenty-five dollars.

Paul was out of town that Thanksgiving, so I drove
up to my parents' Santa Barbara ranch by myself. It
was raining and on the drive up the coast I kept wishing
the road would wash away and I'd have to turn back.
Just days before, my mother had given a newspaper
interview in which she said that Michael was estranged
from the family and had never really been close to the
Reagans. Michael had returned the volley with some
disparaging remark, also transmitted through the press.
I did not want to hear about this battle, did not want to
be used as an audience for my mother's grievances
against Michael, but that was always how these things
were played out. I had another reason to dread this
Thanksgiving visit, but I didn't know that yet.

I was to stay overnight in the guest house, and I knew
something was up when my mother kept pushing my
father toward the door of the ranch house, asking him
to show me the guest house. "Show me the guest

house?" I thought. I knew where it was, I'd been there before—something was going on here.

Once in the guest house, my father stood awkwardly by the chairs in the sitting room, his fingers laced together, waiting for a signal. Which he got in a matter of seconds from my mother.

"Oh, yes . . . well . . . why don't we all sit down," he said.

Years were peeling off me. I was thirty-one years old, but suddenly I felt like I was twelve. I took my seat dutifully, trying to avoid my mother's eyes, trying to still the fear that was rising up in me.

"Now, Patti, what are you doing with your life?" my father asked. "You just don't seem to be making anything of yourself."

"I—uh—well, I've been trying to get acting work," I said.

That actually was only half the truth. I had already decided that I wanted to write novels. A year before he died, my friend, the novelist Thomas Thompson, said to me, "If you want to write, write. Screw everything else." And I had always wanted to write something longer than poems and songs, something I could nurture for a year or more.

"Well, you're obviously not doing very well," my mother said. "So maybe you should have something to fall back on."

"Such as?" I asked.

"You could work in a department store, something like that. Saks maybe, or Magnin's." My mother's eyes were punishing me, but there was a hint of amusement in them, too, which scared me.

I knew where this was coming from; I had asked my father for money. I had done the forbidden, and I was going to have to pay for it.

"It's fine to want to be an actress," my father said. "But if you're not getting work, then maybe you should give up and do something else."

"So do you have any ideas about a job?" my mother asked.

"Actually, I was thinking of writing a book," I said, meeting her eyes, trying to grow up quickly and hold my ground.

Her eyebrows arched. "Oh? And what would you write about?"

"I haven't decided yet." I stared back at her; I knew I'd hit a nerve.

"Well," she said, standing up and directing herself to my father. "Why don't *you* continue this conversation with Patti, honey." And she left—vanished into the rain.

My father and I sat there uncomfortably. It was like the day at my boarding school when my mother had stormed off to sit in the car. We didn't know what to say to each other when she wasn't around to stir things up, to plan the strategy.

Finally, my father said, "You know, Patti, you shouldn't go into auditions dressed like that, in jeans."

"I don't. Why did you think that I did?"

"I don't know. I just assumed."

I don't think I said more than a few words through the entire Thanksgiving dinner. Maureen and Dennis were there, my aunt and uncle, and I let all of them talk, tuning them out when they began discussing Michael. But the next morning I was alone again with my parents at the breakfast table and my mother said, "I just don't deserve being criticized like this by Michael in the press."

"Didn't you start it?" I asked. I'm always for the underdog, even if I don't want to get involved.

"The family made an agreement," my mother said. "Well, I mean, we discussed it with Ron and Maureen. And we all decided that whoever gave the next interview would admit that Michael was estranged from the family. And it just so happened that I was the first one to do an interview."

This had been brewing for weeks. My parents were

convinced that Michael was a kleptomaniac and had stolen some small item from a store. One of his Secret Service agents had reported something he thought he saw. (It turned out that he hadn't seen everything—he hadn't seen Michael pay for the item.) And my mother, by giving this interview, had baited Michael, knowing he would answer her in the press. He did, saying my mother pushed him out of the family. It was a news item for more than a week, moving aside headlines about the famine in Ethiopia, and providing my family with more high drama.

I took Paul back to the White House for Christmas, and Paul's sense of humor worked miracles. My mother didn't adopt that attitude she often does with people who are from a different level of society. She asked Paul about his family, about his father's construction business, and didn't blink an eye when Paul said they'd lived in a motor home when he was younger, and that his cradle as a baby was a drawer.

I, however, did blink on Christmas morning when Paul opened his gift from my parents, and it was Soap-On-A-Rope. Ron and I glanced in shock at each other, but Paul said, "Oh good, I can wash up for Christmas dinner."

We were already living together by that time, but this didn't cause the same consternation that living with Bernie had. I think by that time, my parents were tired of fighting me on this.

Paul went with me to Paris, where I had gotten a job doing some modeling and promotion for Courrèges. We were in a jewelry store where I was trying on a ring that was not too expensive. I put it on my left hand because I already had a ring on my right. A photographer who was doing some pictures for Courrèges took one of Paul and me, sold it to *Newsweek*, and said that we were engaged. We came home to a lot of phone messages congratulating us.

We looked at each other and said, "Well, what do we want to do?" We were jet-lagged. It seemed like a lot of trouble to put out an announcement that we weren't engaged, and we were already living together. So that was it. We decided not to argue with *Newsweek*.

We also decided that, if we were going to do this, we might as well make both sets of parents happy and have a traditional wedding. I let my mother plan the whole thing. She suggested the garden of the Bel-Air Hotel, which was fine with me and was a lovely place to have the wedding. Everything clsc—the menu, much of the guest list, the time of the wedding—I left to her. I know all this sounds strange, but I was feeling happy about getting married and didn't care about the details.

I didn't meet Paul's family until the day before the wedding. Paul's family is very genuine and down-to-earth; I don't think my parents spent a great deal of time socializing with them at the wedding. But I didn't notice any tension, either, so I was grateful for that. It was an interesting array of people who assembled to see us get married. Friends of my parents mingled with friends of mine from the anti-nuclear movement.

There were some conspicuous absences, too. The Secret Service agents who had been following me for three years were gone. A few months before, I had "signed off"—exercising the constitutional privilege of which Ron had informed me. He had given them up first, after coming back to his apartment and finding that agents had been inside. My action hadn't been precipitated by anything like that; I just couldn't live that way anymore.

When I told the Secret Service to get out of my life, they tried to scare the hell out of me. They came to see me, wrote me letters, and spun frightening tales about kidnapers and terrorists.

"Yes, but you're talking about possibilities," I said. Eventually, they stopped the warnings and I enjoyed my newfound freedom.

Paul and I went on a honeymoon to Canada, where he had a friend who owned an exercise studio. Paul taught some classes there. We walked around Vancou-

ver, went out to one of the islands for a few days, and
had a peaceful, relaxed week.

The first phone call I received when we returned
home was from the office of my father's lawyer.

"Uh—your mother asked me to call," his secretary
stammered, clearly uncomfortable with her assignment.
"Apparently you forgot to send us your twenty-five-
dollar payment last month."

"Oh. Well, I got married. I had a few other things on
my mind."

"Yes. I know. Congratulations. It's just that your
mother called, and . . ."

"I'll send the check today," I told her, not wanting to
draw out her discomfort anymore.

In July 1985, my father was diagnosed with cancer of
the colon. He wasn't supposed to know about it, and
neither was anyone else, apparently. My mother confided it to Ron, and Ron told me. No one told my father
until after he awakened from surgery. Prior to that, my
mother told him that the doctors had just "found a little
something," not defining what the "little something"
was.

I called my mother and said, "Don't you think you
should tell him the truth about his situation?"

"I'm doing what I think is best," she said angrily. I
could hear tears pushing at her voice, so I didn't argue.

"Ron wanted to fly out here," she added. "But I
don't want to alarm your father."

The doctors resected about eleven inches of his colon
and during his recovery, only my mother was at his side.
A year later, I was asked in the course of an interview
why I hadn't rushed to my father's bedside. I gave no
answer, because the truth was simple, but hard to tell.
My parents' world has two people in it; anyone else at
my father's bedside would have been extra baggage.

CHAPTER 28

. . . .

MY FIRST NOVEL, *Home Front,* came out in 1986. It irrevocably damaged my relations with my family. *Home Front* was on the bestseller list for about a month. It brought some moving letters from readers and some nasty comments from reviewers.

But it enabled me to finally do what I wanted with my life, and make a living at it. I no longer needed a theatrical agent because I no longer needed to find acting work to pay my bills, although there would be times in the following years when the bills would pile up. I just wrote faster in those times, never doubting that this was what I was meant to do with my life.

I had the basic idea for the novel, wrote an outline, and had a literary agent shop it around. I can't even remember what the outline was like, but I know the story changed dramatically as I got deeper into it. I chose to collaborate on this novel because it was my first, and I had been writing poetry and lyrics for so long I needed to think in a different format—a longer format. My literary agent suggested Maureen Strange Foster, a writer who had two novels to her credit and was particularly good at writing dialogue. From our first meeting, I knew it would be a good creative marriage, and it was. We were the same age, had similar literary tastes, and approached work with a sense of humor, which made working together a great experience.

Writing fiction is, in some ways, a what-if game. You

271

take an idea, or circumstance, and you say, "Now, what if this one aspect were different?" Or "What if this character were older, or younger, or in love, or fighting in a war?" Games like that.

The framework I started with in *Home Front* was based on my life, and it was the only purely autobiographical element in the novel. A girl with strong liberal views grows up in a house where politics isn't just the dinner-table conversation, it's the family business.

The what-if game I played was: What if I'd been older in the Sixties, in college, a nationally known anti-war protester while my father was governor? What if my friend Tony who had gone to Vietnam in high school had been my lover? What if he had come back suffering from post-traumatic stress, and I'd found him living alone in the woods? The biggest what-if question of all was: What if my family had been able to talk about our differences, argue about them, fight about them even, rather than turn silent and accusatory? What if my brother and I had spent time together, hung out, had fun, shared things? What would it have felt like to have been part of a family like this? The family that evolved from these questions was one I envied and missed when the book was finished, because it's a reality I know only in fiction.

For the year that it took to write *Home Front,* I lived with this fictional family, the Canfields. I learned from them how other families work things out, because for all their differences, they had a bond between them that I'd never known. I also got to experience, vicariously, the Sixties I'd never known, since I was in high school during the height of the anti-war movement. I sought out Vietnam vets because I was doing research for my novel; some of them have remained in my life because they're some of the most incredible human beings I've ever met.

The harshest criticism of *Home Front* was leveled at the character of the mother, Harriet Canfield. Ironically, she was one of the characters I liked best. She was funny, endearing in her confusion over the Sixties revolution exploding throughout the country and within her own home, and quirky in some of her dialogue. I was accused of writing a caricature of Nancy Reagan. But I knew she was nothing like my mother. Maybe they're both fashion-conscious, but Harriet Canfield would never hit her child. She didn't have that kind of anger or insecurity.

The night before I started my book tour, Ron called me. He and Doria were living in Los Angeles by this time, and his agent had express-mailed a copy of *Home Front* to him from New York.

He said, "I thumbed through it and you really trashed our folks. I certainly don't think you should expect kudos from anyone."

"You thumbed through it? This is a pretty harsh reaction for a book you haven't read, isn't it?"

"I recognized some things," he argued.

Ron's reaction hurt me more than anyone else's because I have tried never to judge him, and I wish he had read the book before judging me. He, better than anyone, would know the differences between the Canfields and the Reagans, and if he had read the story, I don't think he would have found any unkind motivation in it.

My parents' comments ranged from curt to confusing. My father said, "I hope she makes a lot of money." My mother said, "It's a novel piece of fiction." Maureen called the novel "disgusting." Another family conflict was being played out in the media, much the same way that Michael's conflict with my parents had been publicized.

As a writer, I would be flattered if my first full-length work of fiction had been powerful enough to warrant a full-scale controversy. But I don't think *Home Front* had that kind of power. It was an adequate first novel— tentative, as first novels often are. Like most writers, I would much rather that people paid attention to the novels I wrote later.

The climax came when my appearances on two talk

shows were cancelled at the last minute. Merv Griffin
was first. Two hours before I was supposed to walk on
stage and sit down beside him, Judy Hillsinger, who was
handling the West Coast publicity for the book, got a
call that I was off. The message was that Merv had read
the book and couldn't bring himself to promote it. But
I knew better—not only because Merv Griffin is a friend
of my mother's, but because for most of my life, I've
known what my mother would do before she did it. My
first question to Judy was, "Do you think Joan Rivers
will cancel me too?" (Joan Rivers was, at that time,
hosting for Johnny Carson.) But I already knew the
answer to that, too.

It happened the same way. A couple of hours before
I was to tape the show, Judy got the same call: Joan had
read the book and just couldn't bring herself to promote it.

It was now a news story. Phil Donahue admitted
publicly that he'd been pressured to take me off his
show, which didn't deter him from putting me on. He
didn't specify exactly who pressured him; he didn't need
to. Reporters staked out the front of my house; I
climbed over the back fence to avoid them. They chased
down Joan Rivers, who said, "No comment." They
chased down my parents. My mother said nothing. My
father said, "Nancy had nothing to do with it." More
than anything, I felt badly for my mother because the
whole thing was so ridiculous and unnecessary.

One of my biggest disagreements with my father's administration was—and still is—the support of the Con-
tras. My anger over this was the seed of my second
novel, *Deadfall*. The Iran-Contra scandal had not
erupted when I began the novel, but when it did, it
became research material for me.

I started writing *Deadfall* while I was still promoting
Home Front. Later, I wrote in a hospital bed, and during several seemingly interminable months of recovery.

•   •   •

It's difficult to summarize how finally, at age thirty-four, I knew that I would never continue the legacy of my own childhood, that I could, in fact, be a nurturing, generous mother. It had to do with therapy, with self-analysis, with relentlessly peeling away layers in my life and scrutinizing them. It was all of that and probably more.

Having my Fallopian tubes put back together again meant major surgery. It scared the hell out of me. But it was a small fear compared to what I'd been living with. All my life I'd been terrified that, if I had a child of my own, I would become my mother; I would see my own childhood repeated. History would be duplicated and I would be powerless to stop it. That terror had led me to a county hospital and a surgeon willing to do a tubal ligation on a twenty-four-year-old girl. The decision I was making ten years later would mark an end to the fear that I had felt since I was a child.

"I won't know for sure if I can do it until I get in there," the doctor told me. "It will depend on how much of the tubes were destroyed."

"I don't want a general anesthetic," I said. "I want to be awake. I'll do it with an epidural block." I figured if they could do cesarian sections with epidurals, they could do this surgery. I'd be numb from the waist down, but I'd be conscious.

"It's going to be a long operation," he cautioned. "At least four hours."

I explained to him that the risks of a general anesthetic weren't acceptable to me, but there was another reason for my vehemence about this, which I didn't tell him. This was the most important thing I had ever done in my life. I was closing a chapter, moving on, opening myself to new possibilities. I was healing a very old wound and I wanted to be awake for every minute of it.

The surgery took six hours, and I was awake for most of it, watching the doctor's face above his mask, looking for signs. I finally dozed off for a couple of hours. When I woke up, the doctor leaned over me and said,

"You have one healthy tube. I'm going to do the other one now."

"How long have I been here?" I asked.

"Almost four hours."

The last thing the doctor said to me, after two more hours had passed, and I was sewn up, was, "You should be able to get pregnant."

For months I felt fragile and weak. My stomach muscles had been pulled apart and clamped for six hours. I had no strength in the center of my body. I walked slowly and carefully, which is not how I usually walk, and I started to get that feeling that most people get when they're recovering—the maybe-this-will-never-end feeling. But it does end; the body heals, and even forgets. The emotions are a different story.

I had the surgery done in June 1986; by September, I'd finally started to feel strong again. But then, one night, I woke up gasping, with a sense that the breath in my body had been cut off, that if I hadn't woken up I'd have died. I was trembling and cold, and my heart was racing. Paul tried to comfort me, but I don't think anyone could have comforted me right then. It was a feeling of terror that was so deep, I didn't want to go back to sleep. I lay in the dark, shivering, wondering what was happening to me.

This began to happen every night and then during the day. I would be in a store and suddenly my breath would get shallow, my heart would start to race, and I would feel light-headed. I knew it wasn't physical, even though all the symptoms seemed physical. I went to acupuncturists, to my analyst, to spiritual healers. But it was a friend who finally helped me find the cause.

"You haven't forgiven yourself," she said, and the simplicity of her words stunned me.

"What do you mean?" I asked her.

"You went through major surgery to have your tubes put back together, but you haven't dealt with the twenty-four-year-old who had them cut and cauterized in the first place."

I started crying, and as soon as I did, I understood how badly I had needed to cry—for that twenty-four-year-old, and for the child who didn't understand why her mother wouldn't love her. But also for someone else—for the mother who couldn't stop her hand from striking her child, whose rage ate up her love. That was the mother I'd always feared I would become. But there was more to all this than just discovering I wouldn't become that woman; somewhere, buried inside me, was forgiveness for my mother, who had probably not wanted to become that, either.

Tears became my remedy. As soon as the panic would come over me at night, waking me up with a feeling that I was suffocating, I'd let myself cry. Almost immediately, my heart would slow down and something in my chest would seem to open up so that I could breathe again.

Gradually, it stopped happening, but before it was completely a thing of the past, I happened to see a segment of "Larry King Live" that dealt with panic attacks. The symptoms being described were the ones I'd experienced. I had the sense of relief that most people have when they discover that there's a name for what they have, and that others share their experience. I listened to a discussion about support groups and medication, and I realized that I'd treated myself with tears. It was probably fortunate that I didn't know the name of my ailment until I was almost all better.

In October, the Iran-Contra affair began with a plane being shot down in Nicaragua. Eugene Hasenfus, the only survivor, started talking and my father's administration was at the center of a storm. I watched this with a strange sense of detachment—strange mostly because it was all so familiar. What I saw was the dishonesty, attempted cover-ups, and a search for scapegoats. I felt this was the story of my family being played out on a different stage, with different players. But the script was basically the same.

It seems a curious juxtaposition that during this time, I was trying to get pregnant. Paul and I didn't have a child, which I now think was for the best. But it was important that I regained the possibility of being a mother and that I was no longer frightened of my own history being repeated.

In the fall of 1987, during the height of the Iran-Contra controversy, the news came over the radio that my mother had breast cancer. Before I could gather the courage to call her, it was reported that she'd had a mastectomy.

I hadn't spoken to anyone in my family for over a year, since *Home Front* was published. I probably would have called my mother without someone urging me to, but it helped that someone did. My mother's brother, my uncle Richard, called and said, "It would mean a lot if you phoned your mother. This is a terrible thing to go through."

"I was going to," I said, adding to myself, "as soon as I got the nerve."

Her voice was soft and vulnerable over the phone. I told her I was sorry about the cancer and the surgery, and I was trying to think of something positive to say, which isn't easy when you're on the subject of breast cancer.

"If you decide to have reconstruction," I said, "I know several good plastic surgeons in Los Angeles."

Her pause told me I had made a mistake. "I don't want to have more surgery," she said.

"Oh, well, I just thought—if you decided down the line . . ." I let my sentence trail off.

When I read my mother's autobiography a few years later, I learned that she felt I was being abrupt and insensitive by suggesting reconstruction, which was not how I'd intended it. But at that point, with so many battles behind us, there was probably nothing I could have said that would have been right. I am sorry, however, if I caused her more pain.

Shortly after this, I walked into the house one afternoon and Paul's face told me something had happened.

"What?" I asked.

"Your grandmother died. Someone from your
mother's office called. Here's her name and number."

My first reaction was relief for my grandmother. She
had been trapped in a body that was no longer functioning, and her mind had been sabotaging her for
years. She didn't know who people were, and she
couldn't remember things. I hadn't seen her since the
night of my grandfather's funeral, because I didn't want
to remember her like that. The last words I'd heard her
say were, "Do you think he's dancing tonight?" And
I'm glad that is my last memory.

But then I realized something else. Funerals are family reunions, and I was more removed from my family
than I had ever been.

"I can't do it," I told my husband. "I can't go there
and be with everyone from my family, after all the
criticism over my novel. It would feel like walking into
a lion's den."

"You can only do what you're ready to do," Paul
said.

Faced with a situation like that now, I would go. I'd
be scared, but I'd go. But I'm a different person now
than I was in 1987. I just wasn't brave enough then. So
I did what I had been raised to do in a difficult situation.
I lied.

I called my mother's secretary, who had left the message for me, and I said that I was scheduled to be out
of the country, that it was a work-related trip, and that
it couldn't be cancelled or postponed. And I asked her
to please give my mother my condolences.

I probably should have called my mother personally.
I probably should have sent flowers, or a card. I probably should have gone to the funeral. But fear is powerful, and at that point, my fear was not only of my
mother, but of the entire family.

Elaine Crispin, my mother's press secretary, released

a statement that my failure to attend my grandmother's funeral was "another crack in an already broken heart." My mother gave interviews later in which she called me selfish and callous. My sin, in my opinion, was lack of courage. My grandfather had asked me to have the courage to stand up to my mother and relay his wish that my grandmother stay in their house. I backed down and said nothing. In a sense, my grandmother's death, coming as it did, asked me to be brave about facing my family, despite all the bad feeling on both sides. Again, I couldn't do it.

CHAPTER 29

. . . .

WHEN MY FATHER'S eight years as president were over, and George Bush had been inaugurated, the contrasting images between the outgoing and incoming presidents were startling. George Bush had family over his shoulders, under his feet, wrapped around his knees, and on his lap; they almost didn't fit in a single photograph. And there was the image of my parents, two people walking toward the plane, leaving the position they'd worked so long to attain. This evoked sadness in some who saw it, a sense of loneliness. But I couldn't feel sadness for my parents, because their world is complete. They have each other.

My parents had been in California for a couple of months when my father called and asked me to come up to their house for a "meeting."

We hadn't spoken for about three years at that point, which is not unusual for my family; we're veterans of stalwart silences. I said okay to the invitation because I thought to say no would just be delaying the inevitable. But when I hung up, I panicked. Paul wasn't home, and by the time he got there I was pacing the floor, chewing my nails, and checking out plane flights to Canada.

"I'm terrified," I told him, which was not something I needed to point out.

"Maybe it's time you dealt with that. I'll go with you. You're an adult, Patti—they can't do anything to you."

On Sunday afternoon, Paul and I and our dog Sadie piled into my Volvo and headed for Bel Air. I've frequently employed the safety-in-numbers theory when dealing with my parents; that's how Sadie ended up going. On the way down Sunset Boulevard, we passed two hitchhikers.

"We could pick them up and take them along, too," I said to Paul.

"A little nervous, Patti?"

"Yeah—I feel like time has reversed gears on me. Have braces suddenly appeared on my teeth? Is my face breaking out?"

"No, but you're biting your nails."

"Thanks for noticing."

A Secret Service agent answered the gate, let us pass, and my father answered the front door.

"Oh, you got a new dog," he said.

Actually, Sadie had sat by his feet at Thanksgiving dinner four years earlier and begged, but I didn't remind him.

"Her name's Sadie," I said.

My mother appeared, tensions increased, and we were taken on a tour of the house—Sadie on a tight leash because I was so afraid her tail would knock over a priceless Ming Dynasty something-or-other.

"This was Mother's table," my mother said, pointing to a small end table in the living room.

In the dining room, she continued the refrain: "And this china was Mother's."

In the bedroom: "This stool used to be in Mother's room, and of course you remember the afghan."

This was not an ordinary Sunday afternoon house tour; it was turning into a tour of everything my grandmother had ever owned. It was the do-you-feel-bad-enough-yet game, because if you don't, there's another chair here, and then this photograph, and this jewelry box, and this lace doily, and this silverware.

Then we were shown the backyard, which has luxurious flowers, a lush lawn, and a sweeping view of the city. At this point, my mother was called in for a phone call and my father sort of drifted after her, toward the house, leaving us alone, except, of course, for the Secret Service. We all seemed to be waiting for something.

"That wasn't very subtle—all that stuff about your grandmother," Paul said.

"Subtlety isn't really a family trait," I reminded him.

We were, after a minute or two, called into the den and directed to an apparently preordained seating arrangement. Sadie sat on the floor at my father's feet, which he didn't seem to mind.

"Patti, what went wrong?" my father asked.

"Well, uh, that's sort of a big question. You know, we've never exactly been a close family . . ." I was going for subtlety.

"That's just not true. Why, I remember when we picked you up from nursery school one day when you were about three, and you ran right past me and into your mother's arms."

The conversation sort of went on like this, with him pulling out examples of what might have passed as closeness to the most casual observer, and me trying to point out that perhaps there were other things going on under the surface. What I didn't attempt to say, but should now because it's important, is that I think a child will often run to a parent who has withheld love. Children's expectations are utterly pure, and they run to that parent, no matter what has greeted them in the past, with an expectation that this time, they will be running into love.

"It was at a specific point," my father said, "when you just wouldn't speak to your mother, when you turned away from her."

I glanced over at my mother, small and frail in a chair that seemed to swallow her. In one of those split-second, freeze-frame kind of things, our eyes met. We both knew why I'd turned away from her; we both remembered what went on when we were alone in the car, or alone in the house. Neither of us said anything, and our eyes didn't meet again for the remainder of the afternoon.

"I know in the Sixties, your generation just thought parents were always wrong," my father continued.

"You know, the Bush children were all sent away to boarding school, too," my mother interjected, apropos of nothing at all.

My parents often speak in code. They don't start sentences with "I was considering . . ." or "It's possible that the reason was . . ." or "Do you think it might be . . ." Instead, they throw out a comment that seems to make no sense, such as the boarding school comment. I knew their code by then, so I knew what was going on. Between them, they had decided that boarding school was at least partially responsible for our battered family. If Patti had stayed at home, the discussion probably went, she wouldn't have fallen prey to bad influences, politically incorrect people, etc.

At this point, my father got up, left the room, and returned with a scrapbook. "Look at this," he said, opening it to a photograph of me, diapered and barely a year old, crawling across the floor to my mother. "We were a very close family."

"But, Dad, I was a baby. I couldn't talk yet. Don't you think that might not be a good example?" I couldn't finish my sentence because I was caught by his eyes, by that bewildered, sincere look that has always made me feel guilty for things I haven't even thought of yet.

I left their house with the scrapbook and one bronze baby shoe. My mother had sent the other one years before; she has a habit of doling these things out. I also came away relatively unscathed. I did not throw the truth at them as if our meeting were some sort of encounter group session. I was never too sure that encounter groups were such a good idea anyway. Sometimes I think the most considerate thing you can do for another person is keep your hands off their illusions.

•   •   •

The night of the San Francisco earthquake, in October of 1989, Paul and I were watching news coverage of the quake; every hour, we'd been trying to get through to friends in San Francisco, but the lines were down. In the middle of this, someone knocked on the door, and I opened it to find a Secret Service agent standing there with a gift-wrapped package.

"A birthday present from Mrs. Reagan," he said, handing me the gift.

It was a copy of her book, *My Turn*, inscribed "To Patti and Paul, from Mom."

I did exactly what you'd expect me to do. I looked up my name in the index and read what she'd written about me. The whole thing seemed almost surreal, because I was reading about what a difficult baby I was—that I'd cried a lot, and spit up—and at that exact moment I thought I might be pregnant. I was a few days late with my period and I'd been trying so diligently to get pregnant; I'd spent those few days praying, chanting mantras, crossing my fingers, and whatever else I could think of. A baby crying and spitting up was exactly what I *wanted* in my life, so it was strange reading complaints about this, and then of course there was San Francisco crumbling and falling on the television screen. All this took on a sort of dream-like quality.

What I thought about most was the fact that my mother had sent the book to me as a birthday present. Once again, I was trying to interpret her message, but I couldn't really figure it out.

When my mother abruptly withdrew her commitment to help Phoenix House with their plans for a new drug rehabilitation center, she invited, and got, a barrage of criticism. She had allied herself with Dr. Mitch Rosenthal, the director of Phoenix House, and had helped to raise over three million dollars before she pulled out. She had someone else call Dr. Rosenthal with the news. The stated reasons had to do with opposition from residents of Lake View Terrace, the proposed site of the

center, and the threats that my parents' Bel Air house
would be picketed.

What she did, in terms of public opinion, was turn a
weapon on herself and fire. It was the ultimate act of
self-sabotage, prompting people to view her previous
efforts as insincere and shallow.

My first reaction, when I heard about her withdrawal
from the Phoenix House project, was anger. But soon I
felt only heartache, not only for Mitch Rosenthal, who
has devoted his life to helping kids kick drugs, not only
for those kids who would have benefitted from my
mother's assistance, but for my mother. In a part of her
soul, I think she knew why she chose the anti-drug
issue, and why it frightened her so much. By the time
the new Phoenix House project arose, she was just too
scared inside, and she wanted to run away from everything.

I'd been worried about my mother ever since I first
heard about her pledge to help Phoenix House. The
more elevated her anti-drug campaign got, the more
nervous I became. I knew how close she was getting to
herself, and I knew she was denying it every step of the
way. I saw it in her eyes—wide, determined, focused on
some distant spot—and in her fixed smile.

Sometime after the Phoenix House crisis, my mother
participated in a ludicrous, staged "drug raid" with
Darryl Gates. A police motor home was outside the
target house, and, of course, television cameras. There
was also a Secret Service detail parked on the corner.
How the people in the house still managed to get
caught, I have no idea. After the drug bust, my mother
stood in front of the cameras and commented on the
dirty rooms and the lack of furniture. For the next
week, comedians had a field day.

I may have been the only person in America watching
her on television who thought, "Of course she's going
to focus on no furniture and dirty floors. She's not
ready to dig deeper than that—she won't let herself."

Through everything, I have wished for sympathy for

my mother, understanding rather than accusations of fraud. But that wasn't possible without people knowing the truth. There is an odd contradiction in being a public figure, which is that a public persona is a great hiding place for our private selves. My mother's abandonment of Phoenix House and the gimmick of her "drug raid" provoked unkindness and looked disturbingly like insincerity. But behind all that was the confusion, pain, and denial that everyone who has taken drugs of one kind or another knows and learns to hide.

I learned more about love when Paul and I decided to divorce in 1990 than I had at any other point in my life. I learned that if friendship is at the core of a relationship, there really isn't any divorce, there's just a change in the form of that relationship.

Paul had interests I didn't share—the history and language of India, Yoga, the study of other ancient cultures and religions. And my political and environmental activism wasn't something he shared with me— not because he didn't care, but because he's just not as much of an activist as I am. That is also fine—he contributes to the world in ways that are no less valid. However, I think that, over time, having few common interests or passions erodes a relationship. You end up without a lot to talk about. We were drifting further apart, and it's possible that we were always better at being friends than we were at being husband and wife.

When we let each other go, it was really an act of love, because we knew that it wasn't healthy to hold someone in a situation that was no longer positive and nourishing. We helped each other through the divorce and emerged good friends. That was why I didn't hesitate to go to his wedding. There were people who thought I was very strange for doing that, but it was perfectly normal for me. I would like him to be happy, and I wanted to be there on that happy occasion.

Paul and I released each other from a marriage that

was no longer a healthy, growing environment for us. We never abandoned each other.

I've thought about this in relation to my parents. In some measure, I have virtually removed myself from their lives because my presence confronts them with things they don't want to see. In a sense, I am helping them hold on to their illusions. But I have to be honest about the fact that there is more than that keeping me away from them. I think that the end point of forgiving anyone should be telling that person your feelings. But that's not risk-free. The person could answer you with blame, or accusations, or just reject that forgiveness entirely. I'm not sure at this point that I have the strength to see both my parents. I feel like being in their presence right now would be like trying to cure a fear of heights by skydiving. I'm up in the plane, I'm at the door, and I have a chute on my back, but I'm just not ready to make that jump yet.

Somehow, it is easier for me to deal with my father. I went to see him last year to tell him I was writing an autobiography. I knew he had already heard about it, but I felt that the responsible thing to do was tell him in person. Yet I hadn't let go of all my childishness; I still held some of the same needs.

"I know you've heard I'm writing an autobiography," I said to him in his Century City high-rise office. "I wanted you to hear from me that it's not about blame or accusations. It's about telling the truth and learning how to put things in a different perspective."

I could feel my mother's presence in the office—in the stiff, too-perfect decor, in the assemblage of art objects. And, as always, I could feel her presence between me and my father.

"Well now, Patti," he began, and I knew he hadn't listened to what I'd said. "How can you say this family is dysfunctional? I've read where you've said that. We're not dysfunctional. We were a close, loving family. I've looked at the scrapbooks, the pictures." This was a familiar refrain by now and I had my same answer.

"Dad, a picture freezes a moment in time, it doesn't reflect a lifetime."

"But suddenly you just changed. One day, your mother came back from picking you up at school and burst into tears because you had turned away from her in the car and wouldn't speak. You moved as far away from her as you could."

"She hit me in the car," I said quietly.

"No, she didn't."

"What about the lies, Dad? What about my birth story—hanging on to ribs? Even the premature part. Why did you cling to that until I was in my twenties? Don't you see the damage of such lies?"

"Well now, Patti, you were premature."

"Oh, please—can we stop with this? Are you telling me Mom wasn't pregnant when you got married?"

"Well, if the studio hadn't made us change the wedding date, you wouldn't have been premature."

I had no response to that; we sat for a few seconds, staring at each other.

"Were you there the day I was born?" I asked, because Kitty Kelley had written in her biography of my mother that he wasn't.

"Yes. I was there the whole time."

"Okay. I just wanted to hear it from you. It was important for me to know."

"Your mother was in so much pain, the pain wouldn't stop. And then they just whisked her away and did an operation."

"A C-section," I offered.

"And the doctor told her you were hanging on to her ribs. That's what he said. We didn't lie."

I used to watch people around my father—cabinet members, political associates, even journalists. I'd see them puzzled by his distance. I'd see them baffled by statements that didn't seem to make sense; I'd watch them hold back, try to convince themselves that maybe they just heard it wrong. My father is so sincere, so disarming, that you want to believe and trust him.

I walked out of his office, fighting back tears, thinking, "He's the same as he's always been." I had come there, in part, hoping that *he* would be different toward me, that *he* would have changed. And even as I was driving back to Santa Monica, grumbling about this, feeling hurt and abandoned again, I didn't yet see the fallacy of that kind of thinking. I didn't see that *I* was the one who had to change my expectations and my way of looking at the situation. I started then to understand that I had to revisit my childhood, not to reinforce my pain, but to get past it, to finally let it to.

Until I accepted my father the way he was, I would never be able to grow up and get on with my life. My father did the best he could at parenting, given the fact that he came from an alcoholic home and didn't have a fair idea of how a normal family functioned. What finally dawned on me was that I had to stop fantasizing and accept reality. And one aspect of my father's reality was that he was emotionally remote.

I had fantasized about my mother, too: If only she were different . . . If only she hadn't hit me, if only she had been more loving. But no woman wants to hit her child. No woman has a baby and thinks, "Oh good, now I have someone to fight with." It's easy to lose patience with a child—any mother knows this—the line between striking your child and not is sometimes a shaky one. But in the Fifties, that wasn't discussed. Now, a woman who comes close to that line, or crosses it, has information and help available to her. Then, she really didn't have anything, except feelings she couldn't control.

Children look at their parents only as parents; they don't consider that those two individuals have lives outside of parenting, that they were also once children and may, in some ways, still be. Adults look at their parents as people with histories and complexities and, often, mysteries that will never be fully unraveled.

Hours after I had left my father's office, I decided to go down to the bluffs in Santa Monica that look down on the ocean. The sun was setting and, in one of those incongruous California oddities, the smoggy day had produced a beautiful sunset. A little man in baggy pants and a straw hat was tossing bread crumbs in the air for the pigeons. The birds were circling above him, hundreds of them, catching the bread crumbs in the air. I stood watching him. When he noticed me, he said, "I don't want them to feel they have to come down to the ground. They're birds—they belong in the air."

I walked away thinking that my parents belong in the world they've designed for themselves, a world of just the two of them. It may look like a lonely existence to outsiders, and it may sadden their children. But forgiving your parents means growing out of childhood, and letting them be people, too.

EPILOGUE
....

TWO BOOKS SOLIDIFIED my decision to write this story. One was my own—my third novel, *A House of Secrets,* which allowed me to explore, through a fictional character, what it would feel like to tell the truth about one's life. The other was Kitty Kelley's book on my mother. I read the book, recognized many of the stories, and came away thinking, "This is never going to end unless someone tells the whole story. The misperceptions and the judgments will just keep piling up."

The most difficult part of deciding to tell this story was reeducating myself to tell the truth and being confident of the worth of that. Anyone from a dysfunctional home has grown up with the same lesson: If you tell the truth, you will be punished. I grew up with a code of secrecy, in some measure because we were such a public family. Yet the very fact that so much is known about our lives means that it would make no sense to me not to share the understandings that I've now come to.

For years, I've told myself that I was nothing like my parents. But that isn't true for *anyone.* Our parents imprint us; even in our efforts to separate ourselves from them, we show those imprints.

My father has a solitariness about him. There was a moment once at a cocktail party, shortly before he was elected president in 1980, when I looked over at him standing in the middle of a crowd, alone. People were around him, but no one was talking to him. Little pockets of conversation were all around him, but for a brief few minutes, he wasn't included in any of them. It was one of those cocktail party moments that usually goes unnoticed. Except I noticed, and I remembered it. I think of that image now when I notice the solitary parts of my own life. I move through long stretches of time alone, thinking, "I should change this—get out more, meet more people." I usually don't; I just wait for things to change around me.

I know my father will never accept the sense of political and social commitment that drives me, that compels me to speak out. My politics are completely opposite from his, but I inherited his sense of commitment.

My mother and I have shared the same realities of pill taking and denial. And enmity. I've fought her with tactics she taught me. In my determination to be different from her, I have actually moved a little closer to her—not in personality traits, but in understanding. It might have been the effect of stepping back, getting a broader view—but compassion has finally become part of my language rather than a word that sounded foreign.

I might not be completely clear yet about all the reasons for my separation from my brothers and my sister. I think a lot of it has to do with the fact that we weren't raised to be close to each other. But it's also that I view my family these days as standing together, linked by a fragile peace treaty—peace in my family is always a fragile thing. If I go toward one family member at this time, I'm going toward everyone, and that brings up issues of courage.

There are different reasons keeping me from my mother and from my father. With my father, I don't know what to do about the request he makes for me to tell him we are not a dysfunctional family. With my mother, there is still some fear there. There is still a young girl afraid of her mother. I don't have all the answers to this parent-child drama; I just have more than I did before.

147

I live these days in the house that Paul and I once shared. Huge trees shade the property, and birds wake me up, clamoring for the food I give them daily. Recently, someone drifted into my life romantically, almost magically. I knew very quickly that I loved him; there were moments with him when I felt like I was going to cry, not out of sadness, but just because the emotion was so overwhelming. Because of circumstances in his life, he drifted out of mine as suddenly as he had appeared. I found myself saying, "That's okay—whatever you need to do." This was not how I would have responded before. It confirmed for me that coming to some resolution about my family situation had influenced all the other relationships in my life.

When I was very young, my father used to take me outside at night and tell me about the constellations—Orion, striding across the heavens with his sword, and the winged horse Pegasus. He would point to the Big and Little Dippers. And then he would show me the North Star and tell me how sailors located it in the skies when they were lost at sea to help them navigate their way home.

When I cut myself adrift from my parents, I could look back at them with more clarity, more perspective, and more forgiveness. And then it felt like I was on my way home.